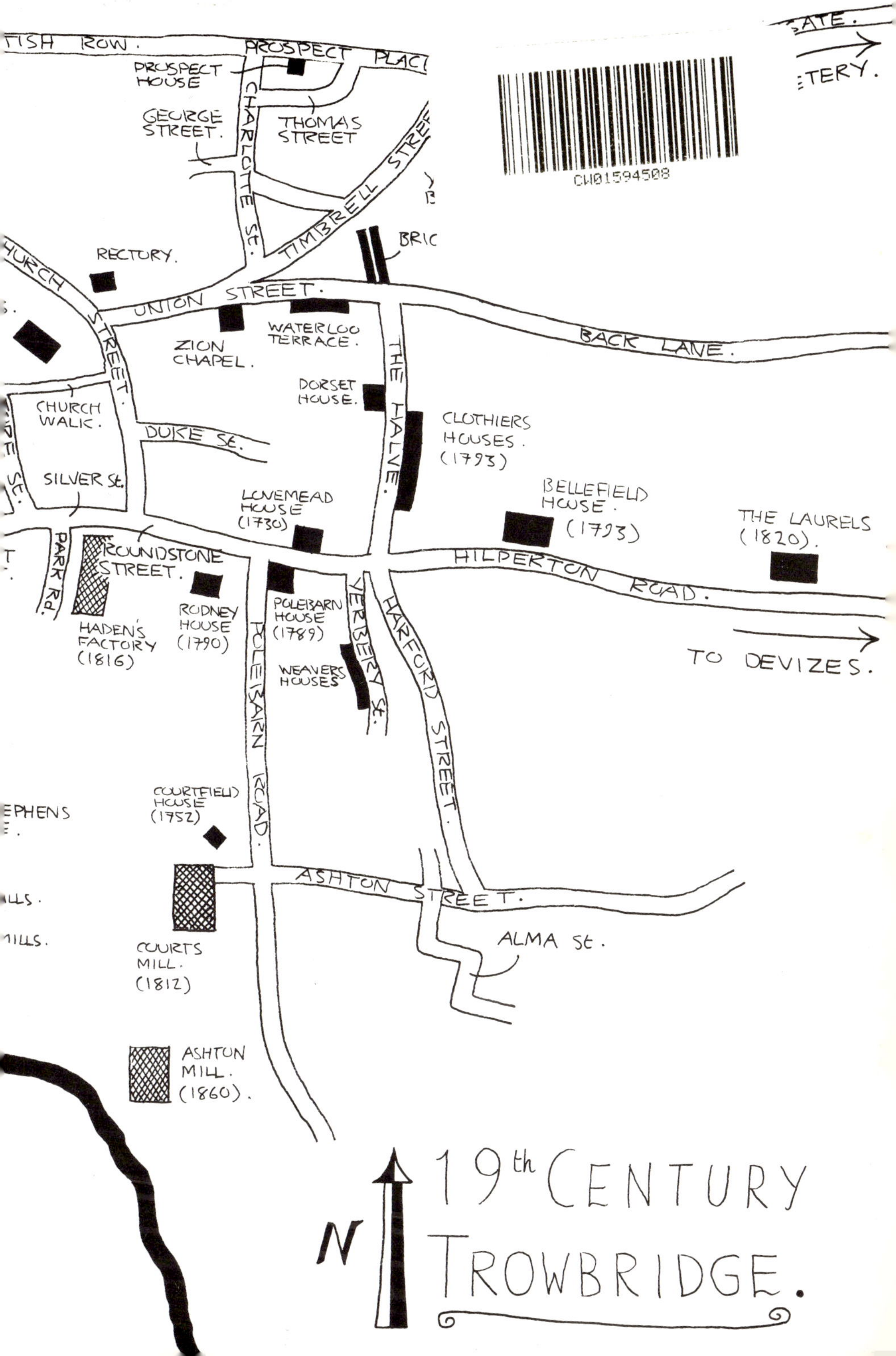

PROSPECT PLACE
PROSPECT HOUSE
GEORGE STREET.
THOMAS STREET
CHARLOTTE St.
TIMBRELL STREET
RECTORY.
UNION STREET.
WATERLOO TERRACE.
ZION CHAPEL.
BACK LANE.
CHURCH STREET.
CHURCH WALK.
DORSET HOUSE.
THE HALVE.
DUKE St.
CLOTHIERS HOUSES. (1793)
SILVER St.
LOVEMEAD HOUSE (1730)
BELLEFIELD HOUSE. (1793)
THE LAURELS (1820).
ROUNDSTONE STREET.
PARK Rd.
HILPERTON ROAD.
RODNEY HOUSE (1790)
POLEBARN HOUSE (1789)
HADEN'S FACTORY (1816)
TO DEVIZES.
WEAVERS HOUSES
YERBURY St.
HANFORD STREET.
POLEBARN ROAD.
COURTFIELD HOUSE (1752)
ASHTON STREET.
ALMA St.
COURTS MILL. (1812)
ASHTON MILL. (1860).
N
19th CENTURY TROWBRIDGE.

John Warburton

Servant of a Covenant God

Oil Painting of John Warburton by T.G. Brooks about 1830.

JOHN WARBURTON

SERVANT

OF A

COVENANT GOD

J. R. Broome

Gospel Standard Trust Publications,
12b Roundwood Lane, Harpenden, Herts. AL5 3DD

1996

ISBN 1 897837 05 4

Published by:
Gospel Standard Trust Publications,
12(b) Roundwood Lane,
Harpenden,
Hertfordshire,
AL5 3DD

Cover Picture: Ladydown Mill Pool, Trowbridge, where Warburton baptised between 1818 and 1823

Origination and Reprographics by
Avonset, Midsomer Norton, Bath BA3 2JT

Printed and bound in Great Britain by
The Cromwell Press,
Broughton Gifford,
Wilts, SN12 8PH

Contents

Acknowledgements

Having read Warburton's *Mercies* before I first came to Trowbridge for interview in May 1959, for a teaching post at the Trowbridge Boys High School, I managed on that day, between a morning interview with the Headmaster, and an afternoon interview with the Governors, to walk across the town and visit Warburton's grave, working on the assumption that it *might* be the only opportunity I might ever have of seeing it. Little could I then know that, I should spend the next thirty-six years in Trowbridge and have the time and opportunity to study his life in depth.

The greatest single asset I have had in my research has been the presence in Trowbridge of the Wilts County Archivist Department, the Wilts County Library, Local Studies Department, and Zion Chapel itself, with its complete set of Church Records. Constant help and advice has been forthcoming from Ken Rogers, former Wilts County Archivist, and from the Head of the Local Studies Department, Michael Marshman, a former pupil of mine at the High School; also from Andrew Jones of Zion Chapel, who has himself closely researched the Zion Records. I am greatly indebted to the Zion Church for constant access to their Records. Colin Edmunds, another former pupil, has helped me with research in the Evangelical Library in London, and Stephen Pickles has done research at Regents College Baptist Library at Oxford, into the lives of Richard Davis, William Eacott and Nathaniel Rawlings, supplying some information from the research work of Karen Smith Ph.D. Jonathan Burgess has provided the excellent maps and diagrams, and the drawing of Zion Chapel.

I am indebted also to Ben Snell, Librarian of the Gospel Standard Library at Brighton, for the loan of various records, to John Howarth for the loan of the Hope Chapel Rochdale Church Books, and to Clifford C. Ashton for pictures of Hope Chapel; also to Peter Hill of Rochdale for 19th century maps of the Stand area. Else Faasse of the Netherlands has provided various early family photographs. Mr Rummings of Trowle Common, Trowbridge has provided a picture of the old cottage [long since demolished] in which Warburton lived. Paul Ramsbottom has provided me with information on Coaching, and B.A. Ramsbottom and M. Pickles have provided information regarding Warburton's Sermons. Finally I am grateful to the present generation of the Warburton family, who have researched their family history and shared it with me, especially to Dr Hugh Benham and his wife, whose connection is via John Warburton Junior of Southill.

Illustrations

PREFACE

Who that knows anything of the wondrous doings and dealings of the Lord in providence and grace can say that miracles have ceased? It is true that the croaking raven no longer brings bread and flesh morning and evening to an Elijah by the Brook Cherith; nor does the palsied leave his bed, or the dead come out of his grave, as in the days when Jesus walked here below; but wonders as great though less visible to the eye of sense, are daily and hourly wrought by the same Jesus now sitting at the right hand of God.

The life and death of John Warburton proclaim this truth as with trumpet tongue to those who have ears to hear and write it up. He was indeed a special instance of those miracles of providence and grace which testify to the power and presence, the mercy and love of a covenant Jehovah. When faith is in living exercise and can roll out and read the long and it may be intricate scroll of by-gone years, sweet is it to see the providence of God in well nigh every line. However long may be the chain, it is all linked together from beginning to end, nor can one link be severed without breaking asunder the connection of the whole.

Why born of such and such parents; why so in earliest infancy brought up; why so circumstanced in childhood; why so situated in this or that locality; why exposed at this or that period to such trial and difficulties; why directed to such a spot as years grew on; why in youth cast into this or that deep trouble and heart breaking sorrow; why these fair prospects blighted, these warm affections withered, these airy castles shattered when least expected and least able to bear the shock; why this sudden and unexpected turn of events, bringing on the hour when grace first visited their souls. All who have any living experience of the path of the christian, have their own, individual life history in which they can at times trace the wonder working hand of God holding the marvellous chain, and winding out link by link all these varied circumstances.

All it is true cannot tell the moving history recorded in *The Mercies of a Covenant God.* They have had neither the deep troubles nor the blessed deliverances of the Lancashire weaver. Their goods have not been marked for rent, nor they and their children trundled off to the workhouse. They have not had the heavy trials in their families, in their churches, or in their own souls, which infinite wisdom had assigned to John Warburton. Still less have they had his great blessings and powerful manifestations of the love and goodness of God in providence and grace. Nor has their tongue, if ministers, been clothed with that rich savour and divine unction which so marked his words in the pulpit and the home.

God designed him for a great work in the church of Christ and therefore eminently qualified him for it. The whole series of anxieties and distresses through which he was called to pass, all connected as they were with the manifestations of God's love and mercy to his soul, mysteriously tended to make him what he eventually was, a minister to the church of Christ, a feeling, experimental man of God to the broken in heart and the contrite in spirit.

But it has been well and wisely said, that though God saves by the foolishness of preaching, He does not send fools to preach. This is eminently true in the instance before us. John Warburton was not a man of learning, or even much education, but he was naturally possessed of a sound, vigorous understanding. What John might have been had his naturally strong and vigorous intellect been cultivated by a sound education in his youth, we shall never know. But most certainly, it would have spoilt him. We might have had Warburton the acute lawyer, or Warburton the learned divine, but we should not have had Warburton the preacher, Warburton the feeling and experimental minister, the tried and exercised man of God. That he might not thus be spoiled, God Himself took charge of his education, by placing him in his youth in the school of Christ. Moses was made his schoolmaster, and first caught hold of him in Bolton church, where instead of charming his ears with the tones of the new organ, he sounded in them such a terrible peal of death, hell and judgment to come, that his pupil dropped down at his feet condemned.

Here he learnt his A B C in experimental religion. Here Moses shook over him for the first time the rod. Here the first lesson set him amidst many sighs and tears, was to learn to spell the first letter of that dreadful sentence, "Cursed is every one, that continueth not in all the things written in the book of the Law to do them." What school or college could have experimentally taught him what he first learned in Bolton church, that he was a sinner under the curse of God's righteous law ? What course of lectures could have made him cry out, "God be merciful to me a sinner ?"

Education is admirable in its way, but no education, classical, theological, moral or religious, could have made, though it might have marred a John Warburton, either as a christian or as a minister or brought him with sighs and groans to the Redeemer's feet. And when peace and pardon first reached his heart, when rich, free, sovereign, and superabounding grace poured salvation into his soul, as he sat in Mr Roby's chapel, he learned more in one moment what the love of God was, whence it came, and whither it lead, what it could do and what bliss and blessedness it could create, than all the lecturers and tutors could have taught him in half a century. When fierce temptations assailed his soul, when hell rose up in arms, and Satan enraged to see so apt a tool, lost to his service and enlisted in God's hurled his fiery darts thick and fast against him, he was still learning better and wiser lessons, than the University could have taught him.

When dark clouds rested upon him in providence, when poverty and want knocked hard at his door, when little work and scanty wages, hard times and an increasing family, plunged him into a sea of embarrassment and distress, he was still learning deep and blessed lessons never learnt at University. When the clouds of darkness broke in showers upon his head, when the Sun of Righteousness gleamed upon his path in providence and grace, when he could set up an Ebenezer here and a Hill Mizar there, what books could have taught him there was such a God in Israel, or have raised up in his heart, such faith, hope and love towards Him ? So with all his long experience, what substitute could be found in human learning for this course of heavenly instruction?

We are not setting up John Warburton, but the grace of God in him. Could he speak out of the cemetery, he would bid us be silent, with that voice which has struck awe into whole congregations, and would admonish us in tones that would make us tremble, to ascribe the glory first and last to God. By the grace of God alone, he was what he was. Grace began, grace carried on and grace completed the whole work, from first to last upon his soul. Great, especially in his early days were his afflictions, and proportionately great were his consolations. But the Lord was with him in all his troubles and sorrows, temporal and spiritual and brought him triumphant through them all. His debts which had lain so heavy a burden upon him for so many years, he was enabled honourably and fully to discharge mainly through the blessing of the Lord resting on his little work, *The Mercies of a Covenant God.*

Thus his very providential trials, proved providential blessings, and his debts were paid by his experience of their burden. Yet many were his mercies, if many his miseries. He was blessed with a large measure of health and strength for many years; was favoured with an affectionate wife and family, some of whom he had the happiness of seeing called by grace; was much loved and esteemed by the church of Christ to which he was made so signal a blessing; was spared to a good old age, without many of its usual infirmities; was sweetly supported upon his bed of affliction by the presence and love of his dear Lord; and after many longings to be gone, yielded up his spirit into His bosom with "Hallelujah" upon his lips.

He was not indeed without his faults and failings, but these much sprang from, and were closely connected,with the warmth of his natural feelings. If at times he was irritable, it arose not from moroseness and sullenness of temper, but from that same warmth and depth of feeling which flowing in another channel, made him so fond of his wife, children and grandchildren, and so opened his heart to sympathise with their afflictions and trials, and take such a lively interest in all their concerns. He was also often considered arbitrary with his church and congregation. But Scripture and experience alike show that in a church as in every other body, there must be order and government. If then the pastor does not exercise his legitimate influence and authority, there are those in every church who will rule the rest if they can, and as the other members will not quietly submit to this, the necessary consequence is strife and confusion.

If John Warburton held the reins with a strong hand, and sometimes sharply lashed the unruly, it was in most cases for the general good of the whole. He viewed himself as the father of the church and congregation, as indeed he was, for the former was chiefly made up of his spiritual children, and the latter was gathered and kept together by his gifts and grace. If then as a father, he fed them, as a father he thought it right to govern them. His post was to lead not to follow, to rule and govern, not to yield and obey. If sometimes he stretched his power beyond the usual limits of a pastor, and used the rod as well as the crook in ruling the church and congregation committed to his charge, it was not to exalt himself, make divisions or introduce error, but for the good of the cause and the glory of God.

He was naturally gifted with much sound good sense, knew the weakness and wickedness of the human heart, and seeing how soon divisions arise in a church, and what havoc they make of its prosperity and peace, he at once with his broad weighty foot, trampled upon the rising flame, which other ministers, of weaker and less determined minds, would let smoulder on, lest in putting it out they should burn their own fingers. He might sometimes when thwarted and opposed speak sharply and look angry, and there was something in his fine portly person, commanding look and loud voice, that struck terror into the timid, and silenced the talkative, but a tenderer heart never beat before the throne of grace and at the footstool of mercy. There indeed he was a little child, a babe, a humble broken-hearted sinner. Much has been said of his temper and obstinacy, especially of late years when painful divisions broke out in his church. But we challenge all his opponents and detractors to name a minister more broken and humble than he was before God. We have known many ministers, many good and gracious servants of God, but we never knew a man more tender in real soul feeling, more broken and simple and childlike, when the hand of God was upon him.

His temper was naturally stubborn and obstinate, but this made the contrast all the greater to what he was by grace. Thousands can testify to what he was in the pulpit. No one who knows what spiritual tenderness, and heavenly blessings are, could hear him pray or preach when the Lord was with him, without feeling there was a peculiar savour and power in his words. This dew and unction, with which he was favoured above any living minister, made him so acceptable to the tried and experienced family of God. It was not his gifts of eloquence, or powers of thought and expression, it was not the beauty of his language or the force of his arguments, for in these external things he did not shine, that drew such crowds to hear him in London and the country, but the peculiar savour and sweetness that dropped from his lips.

He was truly and peculiarly an experimental minister of God's truth. He preached what he knew in his own soul by the power of God, what he had tasted, felt and handled of the Word of Life for himself, what had been wrought in his heart and conscience by the operations and influences of the Holy Ghost. For him it was eminently true, that, "The heart of the wise teacheth his mouth, and addeth learning to his lips." [Prov. 15.23] He was therefore, "A minister of the Spirit, not of the letter," "A workman that needeth not to be ashamed rightly dividing the Word of Truth." He honoured God and God honoured him.

No minister in these last fifty years, except William Huntington and William Gadsby, has been so blessed to the Church of God or had so many seals to his ministry. We seem to see in his last word, "Hallelujah," the dear man's soul passing at once from earth to Heaven, ravished with its opening glory, and swallowed up in its bliss, the moment before he entered eternally into it. Dry must be that eye which drops no tear over such a death, and hard that heart which does not inwardly sigh, "Let my last end be like his."

J.C. Philpot.
Gospel Standard 1857 pp. 190 – 196.

Chapter 1

Introduction

John Warburton, the author of *The Mercies of a Covenant God,* was born at Stand, in the countryside, five miles to the north of Manchester on 28th October 1776. The area now developed with housing, still retains much of its open areas over the Stand and Whitefield Golf Courses. It lies about a mile to the north-west of Junction 17 of the M62 Motorway. Here in the autumn of 1776 John Warburton arrived in this world, one of two boys, in a family which he describes as 'poor.' Little could he or his parents know that he would become a minister of distinction in his own day and an author of renown, and that his autobiography would be repeatedly republished in England, the United States and Holland, as late as the last decade of the twentieth century.

The country into which he had been born was in the throws of great changes, spiritual, social, industrial, and commercial. The eighteenth century had witnessed a spiritual revival since 1735, in the ministry of George Whitefield and his contemporaries. Twenty-five miles to the north-east of Stand at Haworth on the Yorkshire Moors, William Grimshaw had been the means in the Lord's hands of a revival lasting for over twenty years until his death in 1763. At Huddersfield, twenty miles to the east, Henry Venn had preached to thousands with great blessing from 1759 to 1771. George Whitefield had only just died in the United States in 1770, six years before Warburton's birth, after a lifetimes work, which had had remarkable spiritual effects not only in Britain but the United States. In 1776, leading men of the Eighteenth Century Awakening who were still living, included Charles Wesley [died1788], William Cowper [died1800], John Newton [died1807], John Berridge [died1793], Augustus Toplady [died1778], William Romaine [died1795], Daniel Rowland [died1790], and Henry Venn [died1797].

Another significant movement which was in progress at the time of his birth was the Industrial Revolution. In 1774 James Watt had set up his famous partnership with Matthew Boulton and in 1775 had extended the patent on his steam engine for twenty-five years and moved south from Scotland to work with Boulton at the Soho Works at Birmingham. The way was set for industrial development in the north-west with all its social consequences. In the last quarter of the eighteenth century Manchester was to double its population from 50,000 to 100,000, Bolton to the north-west of Stand, from 5,000 to 17,000, and Oldham to the east from 400 to 20,000. Industrial development caused a great migration of labour to the North West and an influx of Irish workers into the area of Liverpool and Manchester.

Inventions in spinning and weaving rapidly increased production. In 1733 Kay's flying shuttle had increased the output of the hand-loom weaver and so increased his demand for yarn. This demand was met by Hargreave's jenny in 1764 which improved spinning machines. In 1769 Arkwright made a spinning machine which could be run by water and so increased the output of yarn. Crompton made further improvements with his mule machine in 1779 so that the production of yarn was increased an hundredfold. In response to this came Cartwright's power loom. These inventions first benefited the cotton industry and then a decade or two later the woollen industry. It was as a woollen weaver in the Whitefield area of Manchester that John Warburton was to make his living for the first twenty years of his working life. So these developments were of considerable significance for him. It would seem probable that his father had been a weaver before him and that there were many weavers working in the Stand area, probably when work in their trade was short, helping in the agricultural community.

King George III had been on the throne for sixteen years at the time of Warburton's birth. He and his Government had attempted to impose direct taxation on the American Colonies with the result that war had broken out and the American

Colonies had declared their Independence on 4th July 1775. When peace was eventually signed between Great Britain and the United States of America on 30th November 1782 Warburton was a lad of six. A new era was beginning to appear in the world, the era of democracy and freedom. The first signs had appeared in America, soon they were to rise in France. In 1789 the French Revolution broke out and by 1793 the French monarch had gone to his death on the guillotine. By this time Warburton was a lad of seventeen. England was being led by an able young man, William Pitt, who had become Prime Minister at the age of twenty-four on 19th December 1783, and was to stay in office until 1801. Four weeks after the execution of their King, Louis XVI, on 1st February 1793 the French declared war on England. That war was to last until the defeat of Napoleon at the battle of Waterloo on 18th June 1815. Warburton was to feel the consequences of it in his home, in the deprivations that came to the nation, especially in the high price of food. By the time it was over he had left Lancashire and was living in Trowbridge in Wiltshire, where he arrived on Friday 31st March 1815.

Here he was to pastor a congregation of Particular Baptists until his death on 2nd April 1857. He would feel the effects of the Corn Laws passed by Parliament in 1815, which kept the price of bread artificially high, and caused serious hardship to the poor. He would hear of the Peterloo Massacre in 1819, back in his old home area of Manchester, when a crowd of between fifty to an hundred thousand people, protesting at the high price of bread and low wages, and demanding political reform, were charged by four troops of the 15th Hussars and eleven were killed and seventy injured. Later such mass protests were to be staged in Trowbridge itself at the time of the Chartist Movement in 1838 and 1839.

While Warburton travelled for most of his life by Stage Coach, he saw the opening of the Railways, and was able to travel on Brunel's line from Paddington to Bristol, which he could reach by Stage Coach after it came to Chippenham in 1840, and later by train when it reached Trowbridge with its broad gauge line in 1848. Then the lad who had been born in the days of Charles Wesley saw the wonders of the first Electric

Telegraph System installed in 1839 by the Great Western Railway on their line between Paddington and West Drayton. Equally he lived to see the Atlantic crossed by the *Great Western* steamship as early as 1838, and no doubt had first hand reports of such voyages from members of his congregation, who emigrated to Canada and the United States.

As the years passed away he witnessed the advent of another Revolution in France in 1848 and the appearance of another Napoleon in the Coup d'Etat of 1851, to be installed as the Emperor Napoleon III in 1852. All this must have sounded ominous to him. Two years later at the close of his days Britain went to War with Russia, as the Crimean War broke out in 1854. A street in Trowbridge was named after the battle of the River Alma [20th September 1854] and Warburton lived to hear of the charge of the Light Brigade [25th October 1854] and their heroism, peace being signed in March 1856, after the great loss of 25,000 lives. No doubt he heard the name of the Hampshire girl, Florence Nightingale, who tended the wounded.

Warburton saw many social changes in the country in the forty-two years he was in Trowbridge. The one that would have affected him most immediately would have been the Marriage Act of 1836 which allowed marriage in Church, Chapel or before a civil registrar. But of greater importance was the 1832 Reform Act. Riots in Bristol and much unrest in the country eventually brought about changes in the voting system. While he himself had surprisingly had his name on the Electoral Register in Trowbridge for the election of 1819, now he saw his home town of Manchester finally enfranchised for the first time and given two Members of Parliament. Equally he saw the practice of slavery abolished in 1833, and the introduction of the Poor Law Amendment Act in 1834, by which the able bodied poor were forced into the workhouse to receive relief, instead of being given relief in their own homes. He himself in his early married life, in 1801, had almost been forced to go with his family to the Poor House. The Repeal of the Corn Laws in 1846 would have been a matter near to his heart, as it was to his great friend, the minister, William Gadsby of Manchester, who had spoken in the Manchester Town Hall to large gatherings of people on this subject. The violence of the Chartist movement [1838-1848] did not appeal to him, and he warned the members of his church to keep away from this rather revolutionary organization. Many considered that, he once a poor weaver, betrayed the poor cloth workers of Trowbridge, by withholding his support from this movement.

Towards the end of his days, in 1851, the Victorians celebrated their achievements in the Great Exhibition, and it is probable that even if he did not see it himself, some of his children did. His son, Gideon had left Trowbridge for London, in 1839 and stayed there all his life until his death in 1879. His son John, had gone to London about the same time, and since 1846 had lived at Southill in Bedfordshire, where he was Pastor of a Particular Baptist Church.

John Warburton's life had spanned an interesting period of English history. The first fifty years of his life had been under Georgian monarchs, the last twenty under the young Queen Victoria. Politically his life covered the period from William Pitt to Lord Palmerston, with such famous names as the Duke of Wellington and Sir Robert Peel. But while we set the background of his life and times we now turn to meet the company of his close friends among the Particular Baptists, and the Independents, with whom he had close association, and who numbered such men as William Huntington, John Vinall, William Gadsby, John Kershaw, John Grace, Joseph Charles Philpot, William Tiptaft, Thomas Godwin and many other ministers among the Gospel Standard Baptist churches throughout the country, of which he is numbered with William Gadsby and John Kershaw as one of the founders. In outlining in a biography for the first time his life and work, it is our aim to reveal the truth behind the assertion that he was a founder of the Gospel Standard Churches.

For long [since 1839] he has been judged solely on account of his autobiography *Mercies of a Covenant God.* His only other writings have consisted of a number of his letters, published in various spiritual magazines, and a group of his sermons, recorded as they were preached. A volume of ten of these sermons was published in 1976 under the title *The Gospel of a Covenant God.* His autobiography is remarkable in its simple, straightforward account of the Lord's dealings with him in his soul. It avoids temporal things about him, and mentions them only in so far as they relate to his spiritual experience. So the *Mercies* are practically entirely devoid of any structure of dates. They were quite unimportant to him. The book bears a close resemblance to John Bunyan's Autobiography, *Grace Abounding.*

It has been our task to provide a structure of date, fact and circumstance to his life, not only in Trowbridge, but also throughout the country, as he travelled widely, spending regularly a month of each year preaching to large congregations in London and then reaching out with his ministry into the counties, often into Lancashire and Yorkshire, or down to Sussex and around his own county of Wiltshire. An equally interesting search has been made into his family, his twelve children and their descendants, some of whom have done research into their own roots. It has been a labour of love to trace the footsteps of this godly servant of Jesus Christ, not without his faults and blemishes, as J.C. Philpot shows in the preface to this biography; yet a man who has a gracious warmth and spiritual affection about him. He was greatly loved by his people [a congregation of a thousand] which worshipped at Zion Chapel, Union Street, Trowbridge, during the forty-two years of his pastorate there [1815-1857], and also by many of his hearers throughout the country in his own day, and since then by that large body of readers of *The Mercies of a Covenant God.* May this study enhance our understanding of him and our love for his memory. "The memory of the just is blessed." [Proverbs 10.7]

Chapter 2

Ruined in the Fall

'I was born at Stand, about five miles from Manchester, in October 1776. My parents being poor, I had but little opportunity of acquiring human learning, though by the tender mercy of God, I obtained a little reading and writing, a blessing for which I have often been thankful.'[1]

These few lines from *The Mercies* contain the principal facts that John Warburton reveals about his early years and his home. Stand lies at the centre of the area surrounded by Radcliffe to the north, Whitefield to the east and Prestwich to the south. Running for a mile from Ringley Road [A667] in the south, northwards to St Pilkington Way [A665] is Stand Lane. Half way up Stand Lane is Chapel Field and the Radcliffe Stand Independent School. Here was the Stand Independent Chapel. When in the National Census return of 1851 Warburton recorded his birth as 28th October 1776, he stated that he was born at Pilkington, which would suggest that his parents' home was possibly toward the north end of Stand Lane.

He tells us that his parents were 'poor.' As he himself was apprenticed as a cloth weaver, it would suggest that his father was in the same trade. No reference is ever made in any of his writings to his father. This is quite a mystery and may mean that his father died early in his life. In *The Mercies* he mentions his brother William and also his mother, to whom he refers with great affection. Records show the Warburton family in the area in the 18th century. William Warburton married Mary Barlow at St Mary Church, Radcliffe on 6th September

---

[1] John Warburton, *The Mercies of a Covenant God*, Reiner Publications, Swengel, PA. 1974, p. 1.

1772, and this has all the appearance of being his parents. There are records of Warburton babies being baptised at the Independent Unitarian Chapel in Stand Lane and parish records show Warburtons in the Prestwich area as early as 1713.

The first early recollection to which Warburton refers in *The Mercies* occurred in 1784, when he was eight. He writes,

> 'My dear mother was, I believe, a vessel prepared unto glory before the mountains were brought forth. This God made manifest when I was about eight years of age, in a manner that has often filled me with surprise. I had frequently been astonished to see my dear mother sighing, groaning and weeping when reading her Bible, but upon one occasion, I distinctly recollect that a neighbouring woman called in and observing my mother in tears, asked what was the matter with her that she was in so much trouble.
>
> My mother as soon as she was able to speak, cried out that her poor soul was lost for ever and ever; at which the woman was astonished and so was I. The woman endeavoured to comfort her by telling her that she had been a good wife, mother and neighbour, and consequently could have nothing to fear; for if such good people as she were lost, woe to thousands besides! My poor mother, however could not drink in such doctrine as this, but exclaimed, 'Oh I am the greatest sinner that ever was upon the earth, and lost I must be for ever. There is no salvation for me! O that I had never been born!'[2]

John Warburton says that this sight of his mother in soul trouble had a profound effect on him, for he reasoned that if she, such a good woman, had cause to doubt whether she was saved, what about himself. It made him go apart and pray for himself for the first time. He vowed to lead a better life and considered his lying, swearing and thieving from other children, which until then, he had never taken seriously. He says that from that time he went on with many 'natural convictions' until he reached the age of fifteen or sixteen, by which time he must have been apprenticed in his trade for some years. Now he confesses to joining up with 'many loose companions' and says he was 'given up to all manner of

---

[2] John Warburton op. cit. pp. 1, 2.

wickedness until my arrival at that time and place which God had purposed, – not to offer but to call by grace.'

He says, 'I was at that time married.' The Parish records show that John Warburton married Lydia Sandiford at Prestwich on 28th December 1795. Lydia was the daughter of James and Alice Sandiford and had been christened at Radcliffe on 4th May 1777. So at the time of his marriage Warburton was nineteen and his wife eighteen. He was living in the first home of his marriage in a cottage near The Dove House in Park Lane, which is between Stand and Whitefield, and now runs beside the playing fields of the present Philip's High School. [Off Park Lane there is a cul-de-sac called Dove House Close.] Here their first child, William was born in 1796, and their second child Sarah in 1797, christened, Sally at Pilkington on 16th April. Another child was born in 1798 who died in March 1800. It was here in the first or second year of their married life that the Lord began His work in the heart of John Warburton. Various references in *The Mercies* show that he had been brought up to attend a place of worship. On one occasion at least he had heard a sermon in his own Parish Church and remembered the effect it had on him.[3] On another occasion he refers to one or two occasions when his mother had taken him to hear Mr Roby preach at his Church in Cannon Street, Manchester.[4] Now the Lord was preparing to work in his heart, and that in a most sudden and unexpected way.

---

[3] John Warburton, op. cit. p. 2.

[4] John Warburton, op. cit. p. 14.

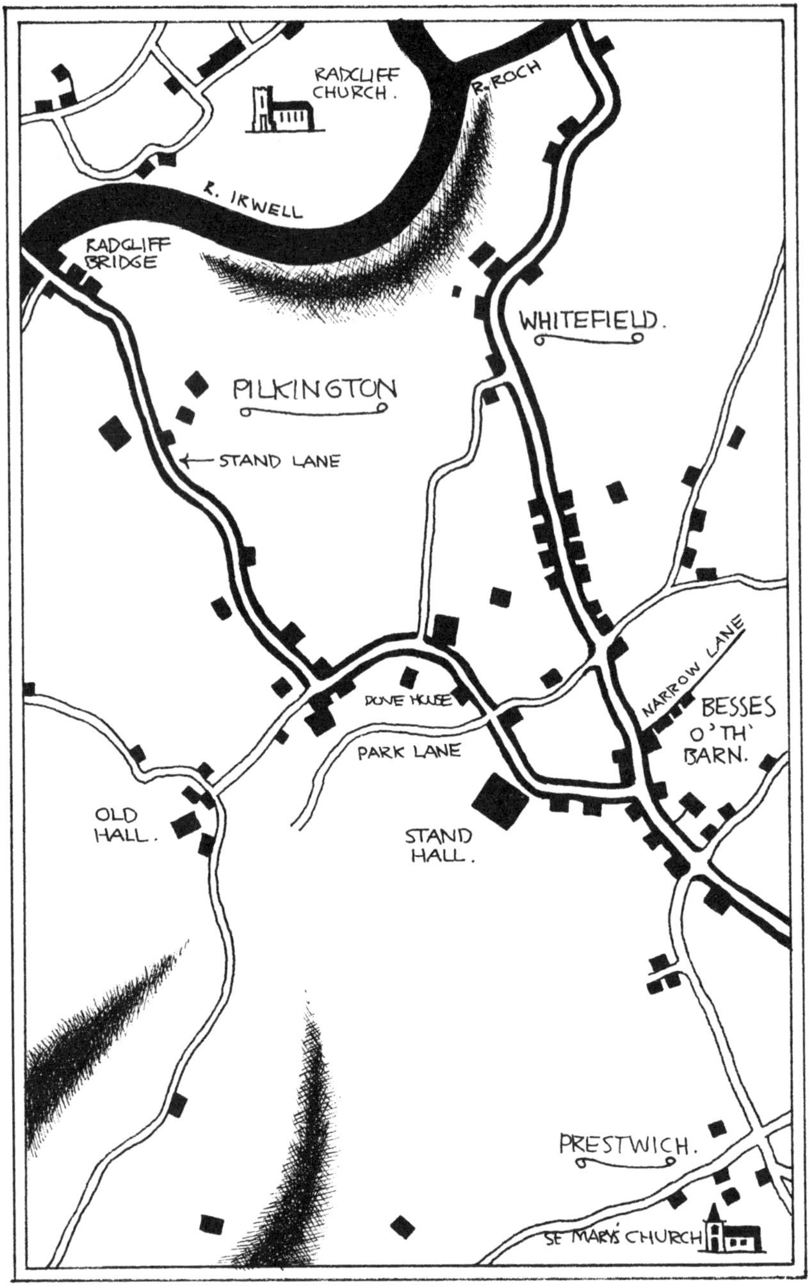

Stand & Besses o' th' Barn

Chapter 3

Saved from his lost estate

I was at that time married, and hearing that a new church, containing a fine organ, was to be opened at Bolton, [distant about six miles,] I made up my mind to go and to enjoy myself by spending a few shillings that I had at the various public-houses on my way home. These houses had been my delight for years; but blessed be the dear Lord, He had designed other things.[1]

Bolton, its population having increased by two-thirds in the last quarter of the 18th century, due to the Industrial Revolution, was in need of a new church. The attraction for John Warburton, was both the architecture and the organ. He says, 'When the day came I went, and was greatly pleased with the appearance of the church.' Knowing that his mother had taken him to Anglican and Independent churches in his youth, it would appear that while poor, she had a degree of culture about her, especially some feeling for music, which she had imparted to him. The Evangelical Awakening had witnessed the composition of many hymns in the 18th century, commencing with Isaac Watts, and going on through great names such as Charles Wesley, Augustus Montague Toplady, John Newton, William Cowper, John Berridge, Anne Steele and William Williams. Nonconformist churches were often led in their singing by a precentor, while the Anglican churches had many beautiful organs. It is of interest that this nineteen year old weaver, recently married, walked six miles for this free

[1] John Warburton, op. cit. p. 2.

entertainment, and though poor was ready to spend a few shillings on ale on the way back. Life being bleak and monotonous, with its constant routine of weaving to eke out a living, John Warburton found a break in the company in the ale-house and in the music in the church.

But the effect of his visit to Bolton was far from what he had anticipated. When the minister entered the reading-desk in the church, Warburton recognised him as a man who had preached in his own parish church 'many years before.' As he was now nineteen or twenty this would suggest possible about 1790 when he was fourteen or fifteen. That sermon he had never forgotten. It had alarmed him to such a degree that he 'had made many vows to live a new life.' But the effect had worn off, the vows had been broken and he had become worse that ever in 'open wickedness.'

Now in this service in the new church at Bolton 'the Lord laid hold of him.' The prayers were read in a striking manner and when the minister entered the pulpit and read his text 'it came from his mouth into Warburton's heart like a two-edged sword.' The text was, 'Be not deceived; God is not mocked; for whatsoever a man soweth, that shall he also reap.' He says, 'All my sins and iniquities from a child stared me in the face and I trembled like a leaf.' The minister described his ungodly life and outlined the mockery of vow making and vow breaking. Warburton says, 'I now saw and felt [what I had never seen or felt before] that I had been mocking God, and deceiving my soul all my life long.' When the minister finally repeated, "God is not mocked, he says, 'As soon as he had concluded, I crept out of the church, as if I had stolen something.'

On his way back to his home at Stand, he went into a field alone, got down on his knees, and prayed with all his heart, 'God be merciful to me a sinner.' As he passed the public houses he says, 'All the dreadful things I had been guilty of in these wretched houses arose before my poor soul,' and he adds, 'I dared not look at them, much less enter them to enjoy the pleasures I had anticipated upon leaving home.' His wife was surprised to see him come home so early and wondered why he was so quiet. He tried to conceal his grief from her. She soon realised however, that something had happened to him and charged him with 'having turned Methodist.' Could she have talked to many people, living up on the moors at Haworth, she would have discovered that his experience was not unique. It was the experience of thousands in the 18th Century Awakening in England and America; it had been clearly portrayed in Bunyan's *Pilgrim's Progress* and by William Huntington in his books *The Bank of Faith* [1784] and *The Kingdom of Heaven taken by Prayer* [1784]. It was also the experience of the Apostle Paul on the road to Damascus. Warburton's wife, Lydia, was not to enter into this experience until 1820, just after the death of their youngest child, Rhoda. John Warburton prayed for her soul's salvation for over twenty years, until the Lord used the death of their three year old daughter to awaken her out of nature's darkness.

The following Sunday, Warburton set out again for Bolton to hear the same minister, whom he now knew to be Mr Jones. He felt 'lost'. and wanted to know the way of salvation, for he knew of no other way but 'by mending his life, doing his duty and trying to please God.' The minister gave him no encouragement, but showed him that all those who were working for 'life' were under the law of God and therefore under its curse. He came back to Stand feeling desolate and his wife told him not to go any more to hear Mr Jones, as he would drive him mad.

The following Saturday evening his partner at cards called for him. Warburton realised if he refused to go he would be mocked all round the parish as a Methodist. He thought he would go just once, and then tell his friends that he would go no more. As he went he felt utterly miserable but dreaded more the stigma of being called *religious* or *Methodist.* At the card table his mind was so taken up with his soul trouble that he was unable to concentrate, was laughed at and eventually professed feeling ill and left early. On his way home he went into the fields to pray alone and says in *The Mercies,*

> And now all my sins, from a child, came before me like an army, with such weight that they actually pressed both body and soul to the earth, and there I lay for a time... But, O, the amazing goodness of an abused God. He gave me a little drop of encouragement: 'Seek, and ye shall find; knock, and it shall be opened unto you.' [Matt. 7.7].... I arose

and looked around to see if anybody was near, who might have spoken these words; but I could neither hear nor see anybody; yet the words were again repeated in my soul with more power..... This so encouraged my poor soul, that I cried again to God to have mercy on me, and told him that if he would but forgive my sins, I would tell all the world what he had done for me. I then went home, resolved that I would seek day and night for mercy and forgiveness of my sins, until I found it.[2]

This 'little drop of encouragement', as he calls it, was in fact his first promise from his God, and all unwittingly he had declared his readiness to go and *preach the Gospel.*

He went to bed early that Saturday night, and getting up the following Sunday morning he set out on his six mile walk alone, leaving wife and family to go and hear Mr Jones again at Bolton, hoping that he might hear something to the comfort of his soul. But 'Mr Jones preached to none but the elect and such as had been born again.' This brought him to cry out, 'O that I were one of those who have been born again.' He now saw that God's holy law required holy thoughts as well as holy actions, and the Scripture came to his mind, 'Thou shalt love the Lord thy God with all thy soul and with all thy heart and thy neighbour as thyself.' Then followed the words, 'Cursed is every one that continueth not in all things which are written in the book of the law to do them.' He says, 'I now saw as clearly as the noon-day, God's holiness and justice in my damnation,' and adds, 'In this miserable state I continued for some months.'

Resolved to take his mind off his sorrows, he went haymaking. The men, he worked with, knew him well and some called out, 'Warburton is turned Methodist,' and laughed at him. He tried to laugh off their mockery and when in that afternoon there was a Wake about four miles away, he went with six of his companions to it. He was resolved to get drunk and drown his sorrows. But when he entered the public-house sounding in his ears came the two texts, 'Because He hath appointed a day, in which He will judge the world in righteousness by that man, Jesus Christ, whom He hath

[2] John Warburton, op. cit. p. 8.

ordained,' and 'It is appointed unto men once to die but after this the judgment.' He says he rose and left the place, his heart filled with horror, crying, 'God be merciful to me a sinner.'

Now, such was his darkness of mind, he began to think about suicide and eventually determined to do it. Several times he went to his bedroom with his razor fully set on cutting his throat. He says,

> I think I shall never forget the night before God delivered my poor soul. Fully resolved to destroy myself, I went on Saturday about midnight to a pool of water, making as I proceeded thither, a solemn vow that nothing should prevent my fulfilling my purpose. When I got to the pool, O the dreadful view I had of the majesty, justice and holiness of God in a righteous law...... After having been for a short time exercised with these thoughts, I rose up to take a leap into the pool, when these words sounded in my ears, as loud, to my thinking, as if a man called them out to me, 'Who can tell?' I made a dead stand, and said, 'What can that be?' 'Who can tell?' The words sounded again and again in my very soul, and something seemed to spring up in my heart, and thus interpret them: 'Who can tell but God may yet have mercy upon my poor soul? Manassah, the thief upon the cross, Saul of Tarsus and Mary Magdalene and many others have experienced his pardoning mercy; and who can tell but that poor wretch, John Warburton, may find mercy yet?' This put a stop to drowning myself. I felt my heart a little softer, and if ever my soul went out in prayer, I believe it was then. I began to feel a little hope shine into me. Who can tell, I thought, but that God will at length hear my cry? I made up my mind that, as the next day was Sunday, I would go in the morning to Manchester and try once more to obtain a little consolation.[3]

Warburton says, 'I had been many times to Manchester and other places far and near, in search of a little comfort for my soul, but all of no use.' It is impossible to tell what journeys he had made previously and to what churches he had been. Manchester from Stand was about five miles, Rochdale about six, Bury four and Bolton six. In terms of return journeys he was walking on a Sunday, on average, eight to ten miles as well as working at his weaving-loom all week. But he was young

---

[3] John Warburton, op. cit. pp. 12, 13.

and strong, a big man from all accounts of him and possessed of a strong character, with considerable will-power, a man of strong passions and feelings. At this time in his life, 1796-7, he was aged twenty to twenty-one. He was working all week at home, so he had no compunction about leaving Lydia and his young family on Sundays.

Now this next Sunday morning he set out on the road to Manchester, which he knew well. But this time his soul was troubled with a sense of hopelessness and many times he considered turning back, but his 'Who can tell,' was the means of keeping him going forward. One text was very sweet to him this Sunday morning, it was, 'This is a faithful saying and worthy of all acceptation, that Christ Jesus came into the world to save sinners, of whom I am chief.' [1 Tim. 1.15.] The constant blessing of Scripture to him in his needs, reveals a young man, who had a very extensive knowledge of his Bible, an uneducated man, who confesses to having had very little education, who could hardly read or write; and yet at the age of twenty-one had an excellent knowledge of the Bible. Following this text in Paul's letter to Timothy came another, as he says, 'with exceeding sweetness and preciousness to his mind,' 'For the vision is *yet* for an appointed time; but at the end it shall speak, and not lie; though it tarry wait for it; because it will surely come, it will not tarry.' [Hab. 2.3.] He says these texts strengthened and encouraged him in a hope that the Lord would meet him in mercy.

In the morning he went to Mosley Street Chapel. He saw a solemn old man enter the pulpit and read Galatians chapter 3. When he came to verse 10, he read, 'Cursed is every one that continueth not in all things which are written in the book of the law to do them.' Warburton says he felt so followed by condemnation everywhere he went, that he paid no attention to the sermon. After the service he wandered in the streets of Manchester until he came to St George's Church and sat down on the steps and wept until he had no more power to weep. Then he got up and thought of going home and putting an end to his life. On his way home he passed through Cannon Street, and noticed a Church into which people were crowding, and remembered it was the chapel of Mr Roby, a place to which he had been previously with his mother. He stopped to consider whether he would go in but felt it was hopeless. He passed by the Church when, 'Who can tell?' echoed in his heart and he turned to enter.

He says, 'If ever I entered a place of worship with the feeling cry that God would, if it were possible, show mercy to one in so desperate a case, I believe I did then.' After the first hymn, Mr Roby uttered a brief prayer in which he asked the Lord that if there was anyone present who had come to make a last trial of His mercy, He would show Himself to such an one as *his* God. Warburton felt like calling out. After the second hymn he watched the minister take the Bible from the cushion to find his text and dreaded what it would be. Would it be, 'Cursed is everyone that continueth not in all things written in the book of the law to do them.' At last after some delay the minister replaced the Bible on the cushion and Warburton could see that it was not opened in the New Testament at Galatians, but was opened in the centre. He pleaded with the Lord to pardon his sins and when Mr Roby read his text he says, 'O the wonder and the glory that shone into my soul.' The text, taken from Psalm 68.18, was, 'Thou hast ascended on high, thou hast led captivity captive; thou hast received gifts for men; yea, for the rebellious also, that the Lord God might dwell among them.'

He says, 'O the love, peace and joy that broke into my heart as the words came out of his mouth.' He wondered with astonishment and said inwardly, 'What can this mean? Where are my sins... Where is my burden and the wrath and terror that I have had so many months ?' Then the text flowed into his soul, 'Thou hast led captivity captive; thou hast received gifts for men; yea for the *rebellious* also, that the Lord God might dwell among them.' He says, 'I looked for my sins.... and could find neither guilt nor sins.... Such a sight of Christ's sufferings and death flowed into my soul as broke my heart to pieces... O the love I felt to my dear Saviour for His unmerited kindness.'

When the service was over he made his way home along the Old Bury Road out of Manchester and got into the fields and shouted and leaped and danced for joy praising God for His mercy. He says he fell on the ground and had such a sight that

God's holy law which had been his terror for months was completely honoured and righteously fulfilled for him by Christ. The words, 'For Christ is the end of the law for righteousness to everyone that believeth,'[Romans 10.4], were very precious to him, as also were the words of Paul, 'Christ hath redeemed us from the curse of the law, being made a curse for us; for it is written, Cursed is everyone that hangeth upon a tree.' [Galatians 3.13.] He says that he saw that Christ had atoned for all his sins and magnified the law and made it honourable. When he got home at a very late hour, his wife was very worried. He told her of the comfort he had received, how the Lord had pardoned all his sins, that he felt sure of going to heaven, because Christ had suffered and died for him upon the cross. To her it was all a great mystery and she thought he was unbalanced. It took another twenty years before the Lord brought her to the same experience as her husband.

Chapter 4

Fed by ravens

It seems that after his spiritual deliverance, John Warburton did not go back to Mr Roby's church in Cannon Street Manchester, but instead went to the Independent Church in Mosley Street.[1] He says in a reference in *The Mercies* dated to about 1801 that he was *a member* there, but his book makes no mention as to when or how he became a member. This would seem to suggest that, while he had Anglican connections before his call by grace, the influence of his godly mother had been the means of leading him in these years, from 1797 onwards, towards the Independents. In 1803 he went for the first time to the Particular Baptist church in Baptist Street [now Dyche Street], which was called Back Lane Chapel, and joined there in 1804, severing his connections with the Independents.

In tracing these years from 1797 to 1803, it is clear that the hardships, penury, sorrows and conflicts that he endured were all part of the Lord's purposes in shaping him for the work of the ministry which he was to enter about the year 1806. This decade of his life, from the age of twenty to thirty, was for him what the backside of the desert was for the Lord's servant Moses, a learning ground for patience, submission and obedience. It was also the trial of his faith in a very practical way and entry into the path of prayer, again in a very practical way.

He says after his deliverance that 'in this happy state of

[1] John Warburton, op. cit. pp. 28, 37.

liberty, peace and praise I lived for months'.[2] He says in another place, 'For nearly twelve months it was little else with my soul but joy and peace.'[3] This was in the year 1796/97. Speaking of it in *The Mercies* he says,[4]

> Three times in particular during the twelve months, the love of God was so powerfully shed abroad in my heart, that for a time I really did not know whether I was in the body or out of the body. One of these times, I well recollect, I was returning from Manchester, on a Lord's day, after service. I felt very happy and comfortable in soul, but languid and faint in body, and exceedingly hungry. And powerfully it came into my mind, 'Yes, and you know you have nothing to eat when you get home, and not a farthing will you have to buy with until tomorrow when you take home your work.' This brought me for a moment to a standstill. What shall I do, thought I; but in came the Lord with some precious portions of his dear word, and dropped them into my soul like honey-comb, and more beautiful, a thousand times, than apples of gold in pictures of silver! 'Man shall not live by bread alone, but by every word that proceedeth out of the mouth of God.' [Matt. 4. 4.] 'Bread shall be given him; his waters shall be sure.' [Isa. 33. 16.] 'The cattle upon a thousand hills are mine, and all the gold and silver.' [Ps. 50. 10.]

He says he had such a sight of God's everlasting love to his soul that he had to lie down on the ground and felt a longing to be taken to Heaven. When he got home his wife had borrowed a few necessities so that they had a cup of tea and enough for breakfast on Monday, which enabled him to rise early, get his piece of weaving finished, all of which he had to do before they could have any dinner.

Soon after this the Lord began to withdraw His comforts, and he began to feel that, 'he had not such meltings

---

2 John Warburton op. cit. p. 18.

3 John Warburton, op. cit. p. 24.

4 John Warburton op. cit. pp. 24, 25.

of heart, nor such free access to Him as formerly.' He found terrible thoughts arising in his heart, which made him tremble and he says, 'My greatest grief was the loss of God's smiles.' He began to fear he had been deceived until the Lord spoke again to him with great sweetness, 'Yea, I have loved thee with an everlasting love, therefore with lovingkindness have I drawn thee.' [Jer. 31. 3.] Then he saw that whatever change he might experience, God's love and faithfulness were the same.

'At this time', he says, 'I had two small children and my wife was near her confinement with the third. Trade was very bad and provisions dear, flour being five pence or sixpence a pound, and other things in proportion. It was what we called *barley times*, for there was scarcely anything for the poor except barley, so that our table was very scarcely provided.' He says there was no money in the house and very little food. He went to get the doctor for his wife and then felt led to go into Manchester about five miles away to see if could borrow half a guinea from his master for whom he worked, knowing that he did not usually lend money to his workforce. To his amazement his master lent him the money, and on his way home from his master's warehouse, he met one of the members of the congregation from Mosley Street chapel, where he then attended, who gave him another half guinea. When he arrived home his wife was safely delivered of the child and he had great cause to rejoice at the Lord's provision for him. The circumstances show that the year was 1798. John Warburton was no historian and so dates rarely figured in his mind, but what did figure always was the number of children he had at any given time, and these facts fixed for him the time in his life of certain events. So at this time he had 'two small children and his wife was near her third confinement.'[5] His first child, William had been born in 1796, his second child Sarah on 16th April 1797 and third child sometime in the early part of 1798.

The next event in his life, that he mentions, was when his landlord insisted that he give up the house he was renting in Park Lane and move with his three children into the cellar The cellar had been the place where previously he had had his loom.

---

[5] John Warburton op. cit. p. 27.

The owner wanted the house for himself and as Warburton owed some rent, he felt bound to comply with the request. He says that, 'My wife having been so lately confined, was so much affected by the dampness of the place, and indeed it was a sad place to sleep in, that for a time she nearly lost the use of her hands, for she was taken with cramp in her hands and fingers, so that she could but seldom either dress or undress herself or the child.'[6] It does not seem at all surprising that this poor baby, raised in such pitiful surroundings, did not live longer that March 1800.

In these early years of his spiritual experience, Warburton was very much misunderstood by many at the Independent church in Mosley Street Manchester. When he related his experience to them at the first Prayer Meeting he attended,[7] some laughed at him and considered his remarkable deliverance to be 'wild fire.' He wondered whether he had been deceived in losing his great burden and feeling the pardon of all his sins. But on his way home to Stand he fell on his knees under a hedge and asked the Lord to show him if he was deceived, and he felt so blessed with a succession of promises that he felt completely delivered. He says, 'Upon rising from the ground, it struck me that it was the very place in which the devil had frequently tempted me to put an end to my life.' At the next Prayer Meeting he related his experience on his previous journey home to Stand, but this the members found quite unacceptable.

They told him that he was turning *Antinomian*, denying the moral law to be the believers rule of life. When Warburton asked whether they meant that law which Paul spoke of when he said, 'Cursed is everyone that continueth not in all things that are written in the book of the law to do them,' they said that was the law to which they referred. Then said Warburton, 'I am one of those Antinomians. Blessed be God He has delivered me from that law. Christ has obeyed it for me and has been made a

---

[6] John Warburton, op. cit. p. 29.

[7] John Warburton op. cit. p. 18

curse for me and has gone to the end of the law for my soul.' He then asked whether they knew what it was to be delivered from the law, but they had never had such an experience and insisted that believers were required to be obedient to the law as well as to believe in Christ. John Warburton insisted that his obedience to the law was in Christ who had kept the law for him. His meat and drink was to do the will of Christ. He concludes that he could not meet with any who knew much of the spiritual pathway in which he had been led. He says that the people were angry with him and warned others to keep clear of him.

Eventually they asked him to leave and told him he was deceived. One of their ministers who lived at Bury, and was in the habit of coming to preach in a house at Radcliffe Bridge near Stand, tried to convince John Warburton of his error. Warburton told him of his deliverance under Mr Roby, and asked Mr Ely how he felt when he was under the law, and what he knew about deliverance from the condemnation of the law. This angered Mr Ely who accused Warburton of trying to be his teacher. But Warburton felt able to stand his ground, and apparently stayed at the Independent church in Mosley Street until he left to join the Particular Baptists in 1803.

The next period in his life which he mentions must be about August or September 1800. He says he had three children and had lost one about six months before.[8] He also says that his wife had an infant at the breast. The three children would have been, William, Sarah and, James born on 10th August 1800. The youngest had died in March 1800, aged about two. It had spent all its little life in the damp cellar in Park Lane. When he lost his last child Rhoda, in 1820, he refers to the death of this little child in 1800. He says, 'The first child the Lord took I was as happy as my soul could hold, and could see and feel He was too wise to err, and too good to be unkind; so that I thought it was but a light thing to lose a child.'[9] One gathers that he felt resigned to the Lord's will in the loss of this, his third child. He

---

8 John Warburton, op. cit. p. 29.

9 John Warburton, op. cit. p. 142.

felt very differently as we shall see, about the loss of Rhoda at the age of three. One wonders what his poor wife felt in her sufferings and sorrows in the Park Lane basement. Probably very differently to her husband.

He records, while living in the cellar that one week the food supply ran out. Realising what was happening he worked at his loom very long hours to try to finish his piece of cloth by Saturday, so that he could get his money. But living mainly on barley and working very hard, he became so exhausted that he had to leave off work on Friday, at the very time when there was no food in the house. That Friday night he prayed the Lord would help the children to sleep though hungry, and they slept. But his poor wife was trying to feed baby James, and Warburton rose very early Saturday morning to attempt to finish his piece of cloth. He worked at his loom until he was so weak that he could hardly walk or stand. His wife, weak and sickly burst into tears fearing they would die of hunger and want.

The finishing stroke for Warburton came, when William, who was about five, looked up at his father with tears running down his little cheeks and cried, 'Father give me some bread; O my father do give me some bread.' Warburton says, 'I thought my soul would have burst with grief.' He then describes how he ran into a little place under the cellar stairs, fell on his knees and asked God to take away his life, rather than witness the death of his wife and children. He says, 'Whilst I was upon my knees, entreating God to take away my life, these words came with great force and power into my mind, "And they did all eat and were filled; and they took up of the fragments that remained twelve baskets full."' [Matt. 14. 20.] He says the words were repeated and he was led to consider how the Lord had fed the five thousand with five loaves and two fishes. But he could not see how the words had anything to do with his present predicament. But the Lord showed him that He would provide for him and he felt the sweetness of the words, 'Jesus Christ the same yesterday, today and for ever.' [Heb.13.8.] Warburton was so strengthened in his faith that he says, 'I rose from my knees as strong as a giant in mind and body,' and told his wife that the Lord would shortly supply their needs.

Warburton says, 'Just upon the back of this, a man knocked at the door.' He was the servant of a factory master who had been sent out with herrings for the work people, and while he had no orders to give any to Warburton's family, he had felt led to offer him a dozen. Warburton was so overcome he could hardly speak. A few minutes later a neighbour came round with two loaves of bread. Warburton says, 'I withdrew into the little place under the cellar steps, the very place where a few hours before I had asked the Lord to take away my life. What a heavenly palace it was. After returning my God thanks, some of the fish was soon ready, and we sat down to the table all crying together. 'Come my dears,' I said, 'we are now dining on the same food as Jesus and the five thousand dined on in the wilderness.' He adds, 'I do believe in my very soul that Jesus sat with us at the table. O the sweetness of that fish and bread.'[10] At this time he and his wife were about twenty-four, William was five, Sarah three to four and James a few weeks old.

The next morning, which was Sunday, Warburton took a walk, very early, in the fields and had a sweet view of his Covenant God, and felt able to call him *Father* and to call Him *Brother* also. Later various friends came to his home and brought provisions, so that they were provided for that Sunday. At the services in Mosley Street, Warburton never ceased to wonder at the ministry which made no mention of the deliverances which he had experienced both in his soul and in his family. He walked with his God and had blessed answers to his prayers. He longed to hear about this in the ministry, but came to the conclusion, that the ministers he heard were strangers to his God and His power. Their ministry consisted about what christians ought to do, and placed much emphasis on duties. Warburton says his heart rose up against this teaching and longed for the power of the Spirit in the ministry.

Now came a major crisis in his life. He dates the event by his remark, 'My wife, who was a fruitful creature, [much too fruitful, many thought for the times and our situation], was again

---

10 John Warburton, op. cit. p. 31.

in the family way.'[11] His next child, Elizabeth, was born on 20th November 1801, so this fixes the period as the early Spring of 1801. Warburton's landlord wanted him out of the cellar so that he could use it for his own loom. He also was afraid that he would not get his rent as Warburton was so poor. As Warburton owed him four pounds in rent, he put the bailiffs in to take an inventory of his few goods, and Warburton saw his bed, loom, even dishes and spoons marked up for sale. Failing to find any help, and feeling the Lord's face hidden from him, in his sorrow and distress he went to see the overseer of the parish of Prestwich. The overseer told him that he did not belong to that parish for assistance, but to the next one. This was three miles away and would appear to be the parish of Bury to the north of Prestwich. Warburton's 'settlement' for parish relief almost certainly rested on his original family home in Stand.

This situation had a profound effect on Warburton. At the end of his life, when living at Dorset House in The Halve Trowbridge, in November 1856, he referred to this time in speaking to his friend John Gadsby. He said, 'O to think of that Park Lane near the Dove House. I remember going with the two children and finding all my things marked to be sold for rent. And now look at me! Here I am surrounded with feather pillows.'[12] The two children will have been William five and Sarah four. James was hardly walking. Eventually with his wife expecting, and carrying James he set out with his family the next day to go to the overseer at Bury. The overseer was out and his wife very rude, but Warburton says he felt so broken that she might as well have wiped her shoes on him. The overseer came home in the evening and listened to Warburton's story. He told him to go home and if his goods were sold to return on the next day and he would take him and his family to the workhouse. So that night the little family trudged back the three miles to Park Lane, the overseer having given him a half-crown.

---

11 John Warburton op. cit. p. 35.

12 John Warburton op. cit. p. 226.

It would appear that his goods were not instantly sold, and Warburton was allowed to finish the piece of cloth on his loom and take it to his master in Manchester a day or so later. There he went to see a deacon of the Mosley Street church, a tailor called Mr Ramsay, who lived in Shudehill. The old gentleman asked him how his family were and he told him amidst his tears that they were all about to go into the workhouse. The old man's response was, 'Never fear, John, your goods will not be sold.' Warburton told him that the following Monday was the day fixed for the sale. Mr Ramsay told Warburton to go to his fellow deacon, Mr Clegg, who had money ready for him and had been expecting that he would come to him for help. Mr Clegg had heard of Warburton's difficulties and had begun collecting for him among the church members. After leaving Mr Clegg's home with the money, he says, 'The first secret place I could find after I got into the street, I crept into; and O what praise, thanksgiving and adoration flowed out of my heart and from my lips unto God.'[13] Now he was able to pay his rent and had a pound left over for food. His landlord made him go and pay the bailiff. He says that his wife and he wept like children. He told her, 'This God is my God, and I believe I shall see the day when He is your God too.'

The situation was now very tense with his landlord and Warburton made strenuous efforts to find somewhere else to live. Finally he got the promise of a house in Narrow Lane, Besses-o'-th'-Barn. He says, 'I packed up my traps on the very same day that I took the house for fear the man should run from his word.' He had two days work on his loom, but he did not stay to finish it. With the help of his brother William, and the use of a horse and cart, he moved about a mile away, just across the Old Bury Road. Almost at once he had to take credit from the publican and the shopkeeper. He says, 'I now had everything that my heart desired; plenty of provisions, a comfortable house, compared with the cellar, and the love and

[13] John Warburton op. cit. p. 38.

smiles and mercy of God enjoyed within.'[14] Warburton had been in the cellar for at least three years. He was to stay in Narrow Lane for ten years, until he left it for Hope Chapel House in Rochdale at the beginning of 1811. His old address had been Park Lane, Pilkington, in the parish of Prestwich. His new address was Narrow Lane, Besses-o'-th'-Barn, Whitefield, in the parish of Prestwich.

Soon after his arrival he records in his *Mercies* a remarkable dream which had a powerful effect on him. He dreamt that he was going to visit his mother and had to pass a farmhouse and turning a corner was confronted with a large black bull. He describes in his dream how the bull rushed him and he thought his end had come, but that he prayed and was able to overcome the bull and woke up with the words in his heart, 'Rejoice not against me, O my enemy; when I fall I shall arise; when I sit in darkness, the Lord shall be a light unto me.' [Micah 7.8.] He then had a strong persuasion that a great trial lay ahead of him and so it proved, for some when after the birth of Elizabeth in November 1801, his wife Lydia was taken severely ill with a fever. This lasted for several weeks and was probably cholera. Nobody was allowed to enter the house and Warburton had to carry on his weaving, look after his wife alone, and feed the children. He dates the illness as 'we then had four children,' William, Sarah, James and Elizabeth a baby in arms. Added to all his troubles he was again desperately short of money. He says that he cried to God to undertake for him and the Lord spoke in his heart with power, 'The ravens brought him bread and flesh in the morning.' [1 Kings 17.6.] He says that he firmly believed that the Lord would appear for him. He says there was a knock at the door next morning. A man came to say that he had had no rest all night thinking of Warburton's family and though he did not like Warburton's religion, he had brought him half a guinea. He says when the man had gone he had such a sweet sight of his Covenant keeping God and said in his heart, 'Who is a God like unto my God, that has sent a raven to feed me.'

---

[14] John Warburton, op. cit. p. 41.

While his wife was still ill and he had the doctor's fees to pay, one of his creditors threatened him with the bailiffs again. Hearing from a neighbour that his friend Mr Clegg had been enquiring about him, he went to Manchester to see him and was given seven pounds to help him with his debts. His text came back to him, 'Rejoice not against me, O my enemy.' Warburton records that this creditor's wife later died of the fever, and he himself went bankrupt, and in less than twelve months was in the workhouse with his children.

After Lydia recovered, Warburton was taken ill himself with what he describes as dropsy. This seems a strange illness for a young man of twenty-five, but possibly it was brought about by all the deprivations he had suffered and the constant work at his loom, using his legs. It lasted for fourteen weeks and at one time he could only just manage to walk with the help of a stick. He describes in his *Mercies* how low and dark he was in his mind. In reading Bunyan's *Pilgrim's Progress* and Christian's description of his passing through the Valley of the Shadow of Death, his soul was softened to think that Bunyan had gone the way before him. He says that on his knees in his affliction the Lord spoke the words in his heart, 'Shall not God avenge His own elect, which cry day and night to Him, though He bear long with them? I tell you that He will avenge them speedily.' [Luke 18. 7,8.] How he managed financially in this illness is not clear, but no doubt his friends at Mosley Street were always in the background watching him. Also his brother and mother were not far away and could help him.

Chapter 5

A sent-servant of Jesus Christ

The next thing I shall notice is my call to the ministry, which was a wonder to many in my own country, but most of all to myself. I believe that the first moving of God in my soul for the work of the ministry was when I was baptized by that dear man of God, William Gadsby of Manchester. I had for several years been convinced of baptism, but had tried all in my power to satisfy my mind without attending to it; for I felt such a reluctance to leave the Independent church, the members of which had proved themselves such kind friends to me. I thought it would seem like base ingratitude to leave them after all their kindness; and as I did not, at that time, know any Baptist church with which to unite myself, I thought it my duty to abide where I was. Sometime after this, Mr Gadsby came to Manchester to supply the Baptist church of which he is now pastor, and I went to hear him.[1]

This is John Warburton's own record in his *Mercies* of the beginning of the work of God in his soul, which *sent* him to preach the gospel as a sent-servant of Jesus Christ. The Scripture was quite clear for him, 'How shall they preach, except they be sent?' [Romans 10.15.] He does not say how or when he became convinced that baptism by immersion of adults was a Scriptural practice. The Independents would have practised infant baptism in common with the Anglican church. It is probable that Warburton was shown the practice of believer's baptism solely by reading his Bible, in such places as

---

[1] John Warburton op. cit. p. 51.

Christ's baptism in the Jordan, and the eunuch's baptism by Philip at an oasis, in the desert. [Acts 8.38.] Carrying in his heart an exercise to be baptised by immersion, he was hindered in going forward simply out of loyalty to the members of the Independent church in Mosley Street who had shown him such kindness when he was in trouble.

In 1803, William Gadsby came to Manchester for the first time to preach at the Back Lane Chapel in Baptist Street and John Warburton went to hear him. He describes in his *Mercies* the prejudice that filled his heart as he took his seat in the old Baptist chapel. The building appeared poor and miserable, he felt enmity towards the congregation, and when Gadsby went into the pulpit his impression was that, 'he looked like an ignorant fool that had not common sense.' When Gadsby prayed [a very short prayer] he felt hatred towards him and came to the conclusion that he would never be able to preach.

But, just as in his visit to Bolton many years before to hear the new organ played, things did not turn out quite as he anticipated. The Lord was watching over him in his poor fallen human nature, and intended to make this man, whom he so despised out of blind prejudice,[and who was a complete stranger to him], to be his best friend for many years to come. William Gadsby gave out his text, Matthew chapter 12, verse 35, and then proceeded to read it very slowly; 'A good man out of the good treasure of the heart bringeth forth good things: and an evil man out of the evil treasure bringeth forth evil things.' The speed at which he read it annoyed Warburton and he says he put his head down and prepared to go to sleep. But then there was a long pause before Gadsby spoke, which caused Warburton to look up. William Gadsby was looking all round the chapel and when finally he began his discourse, the words were such that Warburton could still remember them in 1838 when he came to write the first part of his *Mercies*.

'Perhaps you will be ready to say, that, according to our sentiments, we cannot find a good man upon earth. But by the help of God we will, or we will ransack the Bible from Genesis to Revelation.' This was the first sentence of Gadsby's sermon, and as these preachers knew, the first sentence was all-important to rivet the attention of their hearers at once. Warburton says, 'O how my prejudice was knocked down at a blow. My soul melted like wax before the sun, and I exclaimed, "God bless thee ! The Lord help thee to find the good man!' Gadsby first showed that by nature no man was good and went on to show man's lost and ruined condition. Then he began to describe the good man as he stood in Christ, and the good things which were then brought forth out of his heart. For the first time Warburton heard a clear exposition of the way his God had led him spiritually and says, 'Had he been in my very soul, he could not have opened it up more plainly. I had never heard my ins and outs, my ups and downs, my days and nights, my sorrows and joys, so opened up before.' His heart responded in the words of Ruth to Naomi, 'Whither thou goest, I will go; and where thou lodgest, I will lodge; thy people shall be my people, and thy God my God; where thou diest, I will die.' [Ruth 1.16.] He says, 'My soul was knit to him as closely as Jonathan's to David' and from that day he attended the Baptist Chapel, though William Gadsby was not yet their settled pastor.

In 1804, when William Gadsby came again to preach at Back Lane Chapel, he baptized John Warburton. This marked a major turning point in his life as he left the Independent churches and moved among the Particular Baptist churches which traced their roots back though the line of men like Samuel Medley, Dr Gill, John Brine, the men of the 1689 Baptist Confession, and earlier still, John Bunyan, Hansard Knollys, Francis Spilsbury and William Kiffin. He says he was the only person baptised at that time and goes on to describe his experience in the *Mercies.*[2]

> O the sight I had of the Lord Jesus Christ, when I went down into the water! By precious faith I saw Him sunk in deep waters where there was no standing, and all the waves and billows of divine wrath overwhelming him for my poor soul. I can never describe the solemnity, humility, holy wonder, adoration, self-abasement and godly contrition that I felt whilst I stood in the water. Dear Mr Gadsby, whilst standing in the water, before he baptized me, offered up a short petition to God; and before he concluded, placing his hand upon my shoulder, he begged the

[2] John Warburton, op. cit. p. 53.

Lord to bless me, defend me, stand by me, uphold me and protect me; and what was amazingly astonishing to me, he finished by begging God to raise me up as an instrument in His hands for His own glory and the cause of truth. I believed and felt in my very soul, whilst in the water, that God heard and answered every word that flowed out of his mouth...... After this I was not like the same man. I had no rest nor peace but in reading, searching and praying over the word of God at every opportunity.... Sometimes such light and life would shine and flow into my heart from a text of Scripture that it set my very soul all in a flame of love to God and His people; and I have cried out, 'O Lord, here I am; send me with a message of grace and peace to thy dear children, who are kept in bondage under legal preachers.

When he looked at himself, he felt completely unfit to preach. He had a large family. [William was nine, Sarah eight, James four, Elizabeth three and Leah had been born on 16th April 1804.] He was very poor, heavily in debt, often had not 'half a bellyful of victuals.' He was without human learning except just enough to read the Bible, and hardly able to write his own name properly. He says he felt, 'Surely I must be mad to think of preaching.' One day while weighing up all the things which he felt to be against him going into the ministry and telling the Lord that he could not speak properly, the Lord spoke with power into his heart, 'Who hath made man's mouth? or who maketh the dumb, or deaf, or the seeing, or the blind? Have not I, the Lord? Now therefore, go and I will be with thy mouth and teach thee what thou shalt say.' [Exod. 4. 11,12.] He says his soul was melted and crumbled down at his feet. While praying to the Lord the words in Isaiah chapter 41 verse 10 came with power into his heart, 'Fear thou not, for I am with thee; be not dismayed, for I am thy God; yea, I will strengthen thee; yea I will uphold thee with the right hand of my righteousness.' He says he was now able to commit the ministry into God's blessed hands, for Him to work in His own way, and if it were His good will and pleasure, for Him to open the way in His own time. He says, 'I felt so much the greatness and importance of the work, and the awfulness of running before I was *sent*, that it was my earnest cry, night and day, that I might not be deceived, or attempt it without His blessed approbation and smiles.'

His great concern was now that the Lord would make the matter plain in his heart and give him clear evidences in his soul that the matter was of Him. Going to a Prayer Meeting one night he asked the Lord to confirm the exercise by giving him peculiar liberty in prayer at the meeting. To his amazement the Lord answered his prayer and he went home full of comfort and joy. He then prayed that the Lord would send someone to ask him whether he was exercised about preaching to confirm his exercise. Just as these things were in his mind a deacon called Francis, from Back Lane Baptist chapel, called to see him at Narrow Lane, and asked him to come out for a walk with him in Besses-o'-th'-Barn. During their walk he asked Warburton, 'Have you not John, had some exercises of mind about preaching?' He then told Warburton that ever since he had given in his experience at the Church Meeting at Back Lane Chapel, the members of the Church had felt that the Lord had designed him for the work of the ministry. Warburton then told the deacon all his exercises since his baptism.

Mr Francis then told him that a few friends had agreed to have a meeting at his house once a week, and that each in turn would speak from a verse of Scripture as the Lord enabled them, and he asked John Warburton to join them. To this Warburton agreed and it was fixed that he should speak in a fortnight's time. That next fortnight was a time of many fears for Warburton, but when the evening came, after he had read his text, all fear was taken away and he spoke for the first time with great freedom. The people felt blessed under the Word and it was arranged that he should preach again in two weeks time. Now Warburton felt such blessing in his soul that he longed for the time to arrive. The room was full of people and again he felt great liberty in speaking and the people felt blessed.

But now his poor heart began to fill with pride. He began to have visions of being a great preacher and becoming popular. The Lord intended to give him what he later described as 'a really useful lesson.' In his pride and conceit he went before the next occasion on which he was due to speak to Manchester to the home of the acting deacon Mr Mouncey. When he got to his Warehouse he found a second deacon with him, a Mr Holt. Warburton's object was to draw out from Mr Mouncey whether he thought he was going to become a great preacher. To achieve his object, he told Mr Mouncey and Mr Holt that his ministry was so poor that he felt he could not speak any more. He achieved his object, for their response was to press him to continue and assure him that the Lord had a great work for him to do just as He had for the Apostle Paul. This was just what Warburton wanted to hear and he went back to Narrow Lane, dwelling in his mind on the word *great,* which filled his heart with pride.

Now came the lesson. The next time he went to preach he sought out what he thought was a deep text, Acts 14,22, 'We must through much tribulation enter into the kingdom of God.' He gave out his hymn, spoke in prayer and prepared to preach. But great darkness descended on his mind and after stumbling on for about ten minutes, he was forced to sit down and confess that the Lord had shut his mouth. The room was full, and the people were amazed. Warburton had a solemn and most miserable journey home. Such was his darkness that he felt tempted to give up all, leave family and home, and go to Liverpool and join the Navy. He actually turned along the Liverpool Road, when the Lord spoke in his heart William Cowper's hymn,

> 'Blind unbelief is sure to err,
> And scan His work in vain;
> God is His own interpreter,
> And He will make it plain.'

This stopped him and he turned for home faced with all his hypocrisy and pride. He was met by a very angry wife, for it was midnight before he arrived. For four weeks he was in deep darkness over this sad experience, until the Lord spoke in his heart the words, 'Casting all your care upon Him, for He careth for you,' which brought him into great peace of soul and set him going forward in the work of the ministry again. But this time he had learnt a blessed lesson regarding his dependence upon the Lord in the work. He says, 'O the blessing that trial has proved to me hundreds of times since. It has been a really useful lesson, which has never been forgotten.'

Now he was led to pray that if the work was of the Lord, He would open another door for him to preach. This prayer was answered very quickly when a few friends at Bury opened a room for prayer and invited him to join them and on the second Sunday asked him to speak, which he did with great fear and trembling to a group of six or seven. They asked him again the following Sunday. At 3 a.m. on the Sunday morning he was awake and had no text for the day. When he left Narrow Lane to go to Bury he still had no text. As he walked the four miles to Bury the Bible felt a sealed book to him and he was in darkness. Eventually he stopped and turned back for home, resolved to give preaching up, when the Lord spoke powerfully in his heart, 'No man having put his hand to the plough and looking back, is fit for the kingdom of God.' Now he was resigned to the Lord's will and went on again to Bury. When he got there he still had no text, but while they were singing before the sermon the words came with power and sweetness into his soul, "When the poor and needy seek water and there is none and their tongue faileth for thirst, I the Lord will hear them, I the God of Israel will not forsake them.' [Isa. 41,17.] Then Warburton was enabled to speak with great liberty from this text and afterwards one old man who had known the truth for about forty years, old John Crompton, took Warburton by the hand and said, 'May the Lord God of Abraham, Isaac, and Jacob bless thee! God has thrust thee out into His vineyard, and has sent thee to preach His everlasting gospel. Be strong in the Lord and in the power of His might. Thou art young, and hast many fiery trials to pass through; but God has not sent thee a warfare at thine own charges. Fear not, for He will be with thee, and I am confident He will bring thee through them all.' He says he went home that night much refreshed.

During this time, between 1805-06, he sought further evidences from the Lord of his call to the ministry. On one occasion he wrestled for two days for a token and getting down by his bed asked the Lord for a word. Opening his Bible he came to the words, 'If ye then, being evil, know how to give good gifts unto your children: how much more shall your Heavenly Father give the Holy Spirit to them that ask Him?' [Luke 11, 13.] He says what a remarkable power and sweetness attended the reading of these words, such that he felt a blaze of glory shine into his soul, and now he felt all was right respecting his call to the ministry.

But shortly afterwards he became tempted that fixing his eyes on the first text that he saw when he opened the Bible was a matter of chance, and he might as well have alighted on any other passage and so he could not rest on this passage in Luke. This led him in prayer to ask the Lord for another token. This time he asked the Lord to apply a word with power to his soul that *he never knew was in the Bible.* One night when his family were all in bed he wrestled with the Lord for this special text, and the Lord allowed him to wrestle and heard him with the words, 'Arise and thresh, O daughter of Zion; for I will make thine horn iron, and thy hoofs brass; and thou shalt beat in pieces many people: and I will consecrate their gain unto the Lord, and their substance unto the Lord of the whole earth.' [Micah 4, 13.] He says that he only had a small concordance and could not find the words in the Bible. But searching for several days he eventually came to Micah chapter 4, and found them in them last verse. He says, 'What I felt under this blessing, I can never describe.'

The enemy now tempted him that no one had ever been brought into gospel liberty through his ministry. With this in his heart, he kept praying and watching for the Lord to grant him such a token. Eventually he was invited to preach at a small chapel in Matthew Street, Liverpool. His text was Romans 8, 38-39, 'For I am persuaded that neither death nor life etc.' Warburton describes how he preached in great darkness and bondage, and when he came out of the pulpit left the chapel and went straight to his lodgings determined to take the first coach back to Manchester in the morning. But a lady followed him through the streets and eventually stopped him. He felt cross, but she told him what a blessing the sermon had been made to her soul that morning. She had been for some months under conviction and in deep despair and had resolved to drown herself. Going past the chapel that Sunday she had heard singing and felt an urge to go in and then go and drown herself when it was dark. His sermon that day had been the means in the Lord's hands of bringing her into gospel liberty. She told him that all what he had preached had come into her heart, and God had told her that He had loved her with an everlasting love and that her sins were forgiven. Warburton says, 'My heart was too full to talk much with the poor woman, for I felt my very soul so melted down at the dear feet of a precious Jesus for giving testimony to the word of His grace through such a worthless pipe, that I was not for going home now.' 'How sweetly the old text came, "Arise and thresh, O daughter of Zion.' So he had the token for which he had asked and as the years went by the Lord used this *worthless pipe*, as he called himself, on many more occasions in a similar way to the salvation of many precious souls.

Chapter 6

Preach the Word

Two years had now passed since Warburton had been baptised among the Particular Baptists. In this period William Gadsby had come to Manchester and taken up the Pastorate of the Back Lane Church in October 1805, where Warburton was a member. Warburton dates the period in his usual way, 'We had at that time six children under the age of twelve.' These were William born 1795, Sarah 1797. James 1800, Elizabeth 1801, Leah 1804 and Rachel who had been born on 16th June 1806. This child, Rachel, was to be made a great blessing to him. She never married and stayed in the home looking after him and his wife down to their end, dying herself in 1870 at the comparatively early age of sixty-four. She lies buried with him and his wife in the family grave in the cemetery at Trowbridge.

Warburton was now in his thirtieth year and another decade of his life lay before him in the North before he came south to take up his pastorate in Trowbridge for the last forty years of his life. The Lord was preparing his servant in the 'backside of the desert' as He had prepared Moses many centuries before. Forty years in the court of Pharoah and forty years in the backside of the desert prepared Moses to lead ancient Israel for forty years, out of Egypt to the Promised Land. So John Warburton was being prepared to be greatly used by His Master in His vineyard. The preparation was in the pathway of sorrow, poverty, suffering, temptation, meditation, and prayer, a pathway which the great Reformer, Martin Luther, had outlined many years before as the Lord's way of preparing His servants for the ministry.

Warburton tells us in the *Mercies* that Bury was the first place were he began to preach in a regular way. Gradually as his ministry was blessed numbers increased to about thirty and the small congregation had to rent a larger room in King Street. Warburton continued his work as a weaver, but this little congregation of Baptists agreed to pay him four shillings a week for twelve months for preaching for them twice on Sundays. This must have been a help to him in keeping his large family, though he still records times of extreme need. Often he had to get up very early to finish his piece of cloth on his loom, in order to get money to pay for food that day. On one occasion when it did not appear that he could finish his piece before dinner time, and his wife had a child at the breast and was faint with hunger, he sent Sarah to get some more yarn from his master and she returned not only with the yarn, but also with a bag of food which she had found in the road, containing bread, meat, cheese and a pudding. As Sarah could not find the owner she brought it home. Warburton says how sweet were the words to his soul, 'The cattle upon a thousand hills are mine; the earth is mine; and all the gold and silver are mine,' and also the words, 'Thy bread shall be given thee; thy water shall be sure.' [Isa. 33, 16.].

The poverty of these times and the constant threat of the Poor House, were real for Warburton and his family. Readers of his *Mercies* have sometimes expressed the view that he was not good at managing his financial affairs. Also the view has been aired that possibly his wife Lydia was not a good manager. Even when he was receiving £3 a week as pastor at Zion chapel Trowbridge, [which salary he received unaltered for forty-two years], it is said, he was constantly having to borrow money to pay his debts. On occasions he was merely exchanging one debt for another. But it is well to remember the adverse factors in his life. He came from a 'poor' family; he appears to have been without a father from early in his life; he inherited nothing; he lived in rented accommodation all his life; he had a large family of twelve children, of whom at least eight or nine survived him; he worked hard as a weaver for comparatively low wages, until he went to Rochdale in 1810, and the price of food was undoubtedly high for most of the period that his family was dependent on him, that is from 1795 until 1830. The high price of food was caused by the effects of the Napoleonic Wars, and the Corn Laws, passed in 1815 and not repealed until 1846. The times were far from ideal for rearing large families, and those who criticised had probably never known the harsh reality of Warburton's hunger and that of his wife and children. Equally there was no state social security system to help the unemployed, who were dependent on charity, or in the final resort the Parish poor relief. Warburton never makes any mention in his *Mercies* of having ever received any regular outdoor relief from the parish. But he was often helped by members of the churches where he was a member or where he preached.

He records that sometime in the year 1806-7 he received an invitation to preach one Sunday at a little place in Cheshire about 12-13 miles from his home at Whitefield. He left home on the Saturday to walk the journey, hungry and disconsolate, there being hardly any food at home for his family or himself. His wife's parting remark was that he would preach until they all starved. Such was his hunger that he felt he probably would not be able to walk the long journey. But as he walked the Lord broke into his soul with the words, 'Fear not, for I am with thee; be not dismayed, for I am thy God.' He says that this was enough. In the blessedness of faith he could leave his family in the Lord's hands. He reached his lodgings had a good night's sleep and met on the Sunday morning in a house with a few poor people. His preaching was made a blessing to them that day and when he came to leave them, they in love gave him some of their hard earned money. He says that from one and another on that Sunday, he was given £1.14s and a bundle of cakes to take home for his children. He speaks of the thanksgiving he felt to 'the God of all my supplies.'

On another occasion he received a note from a man one Saturday evening, to whom he owed £2 10s, threatening him with legal proceedings. On the following Sunday he was due to preach at Manchester at Back Lane chapel for William Gadsby. Early on the Sunday morning the words were blessed to him, 'Call upon me in the day of trouble; I will deliver thee, and thou shalt glorify me.' [Ps 50.15.] He records how he walked the five miles that Sunday to Manchester with a heavy heart, full of worry, and yet not without a hope that the Lord would appear. While he was preaching the worry left him. As soon as he left the pulpit it returned. As he left the chapel that morning an old lady put half a guinea in his hand which was a great encouragement to him. In the afternoon service again all his worry was taken away, and when he left the pulpit and returned to the vestry all his worry returned. But he found the old lady back in the vestry to tell him that when she got home after the morning service her heart smote her, because she had not given him enough, and she then gave him another two pounds.

Now he could see how the Lord had provided for his debt and sixpence over, and it caused him to burst into a flood of tears. How great was the burden of poverty and how great the relief when the Lord alleviated it. When he told the old lady what lay behind his tears, she broke down as well and at once emptied her purse on the vestry table, containing ten to twelve pounds, and told him to take it all. But he refused saying that the two pounds and half a guinea were sufficient, and as he left the vestry the words came into his heart, 'The Lord hath done great things for us whereof we are glad.' To the unbelieving world such answers to prayer were not known nor understood, but John Warburton could say with the sweet Psalmist of Israel, 'The Lord *liveth* ; and blessed be my rock; and let the God of my salvation be exalted.' [Ps. 18.46.] Here in these sorrows and blessings lay the authority and substance of his ministry. This was the school of Christ for him. 'Call upon me in the day of trouble; I will deliver thee, and thou shalt glorify me.' [Ps 50, 15.] He says, 'I hated myself for my wretched distrust of God.' With the pound he received for preaching that day, he went home with enough to pay his debt and supply his family needs.

But his needs were constantly recurring and hunger was never far away. He relates in his *Mercies* a time when he had been away preaching about seven miles from Whitefield and was returning home late one night very hungry, fully aware that there would be no food at home when he arrived. But just as he entered the house the Lord spoke into his heart, 'The foxes have holes, and the birds of the air have nests, but the Son of Man hath not where to lay His head,' [Matt. 8, 20.] and with it he had a sweet sight of the sufferings of Christ from the manger to the Cross. Then followed the words, 'And did my Lord suffer, And shall I repine.' [John Newton, *Olney Hymns*, "Begone unbelief, My Saviour is nigh."] He says he felt ashamed of his rebellion occasioned by his hunger, and felt a mourning over his sins and after Christ. The words came to him with great sweetness, 'Though He was rich, yet for your sakes He became poor, that ye through His poverty might be rich.' [2 Cor. 8,9.] He says, 'My little empty house [in Narrow lane] was a palace now in my eyes, full of all sorts of riches.' He then took a candle and searched for an old crust of bread to satisfy his hunger. He found one, hard and not fit to eat. But with a cup of cold water and his crust he sought the Lord's blessing on it, and says, 'O how precious were the words to my soul, 'Man shall not live by bread alone, but by every word that proceedeth out of the mouth of God.' [Matt. 4,4.] He adds, 'I took the dry crust, but it was so softened and enriched with the love and mercy of God that the manna never tasted more sweet to the Israelites than the old crust did to my taste.' His cup of water tasted to him like the richest wine and he never felt his body more refreshed or his appetite more satisfied.

Soon the room at Bury in King Street became too small for Warburton's congregation and they rented a larger room in Butcher Lane where they continued to increase for a time. But trouble appeared as Warburton was criticised for leaving them so much on Sundays, and one of the deacons told him he had always been a burden to them, and he wondered that he had a good conscience in taking 4s a week from such a poor people. Warburton says, 'We had several meetings, but we could not be reconciled, so I gave it up and the place was run for some time by a different preacher each Sunday, but was soon given up.' This was a sad end for the church over which Warburton had had his first pastorate.

He was now forced to travel further afield to preach on Sundays, and one of the places to which he went was Pool Moor in Yorkshire, which entailed a journey of twenty-two miles to reach it, and the same distance home. It is not clear how he travelled, whether he walked, or whether there was a coach route which he could use. It seems more than likely that he walked the whole forty-four miles. His friend William Gadsby walked immense distances, over the Yorkshire Moors in all weathers, to preach the gospel. Equally a friend in later life, Thomas Godwin, used to walk the Wiltshire Downs, journeys of over twenty miles each weekend. John Cennick, the eighteenth century preacher, records walking from London to Bristol and stopping for a night's rest at Sandy Lane, between Chippenham and Devizes, which was at that time a stopping place on the coach route from London to Bath.

Pool Moor Chapel was set in the midst of a large common, and Warburton fell in love with the place and the people. What a difference from the industrialisation of Bolton, Bury and Manchester! No wonder he wanted to go to Pool Moor. Feeling a desire to live there and finding that the Lord blessed his ministry among them, he started to pray earnestly for the church, that he might become their pastor. He went several times and many of his long Saturday journeys were taken up with prayer that a way would be opened for him to go there. Then he found out that there was a minister called Webster from Liverpool preaching there also, and that the church intended to call him to the pastorate. Arriving one Saturday evening to preach the next day, he found that Mr Webster had indeed been called as pastor. Warburton says he went out from Pool Moor that Saturday night and walked in the hills 'like a raging bear bereaved of her whelps.'

His anger continued all night until early Sunday morning he felt the words come into his heart, 'What I do thou knowest not now, but thou shalt know hereafter.' [John 13,7.] He says, 'O the softness these words produced in my heart in a moment!' He felt inwardly, 'It is the voice of my Beloved,' and then there followed the words, 'Ye ask and receive not, because ye ask amiss, that ye may consume it upon your lusts.' [James 4,3.] Now he could see how he had been planning his own way to gratify himself and had not been seeking the Lord's way. That Sunday he went to preach his last sermons at Pool Moor able to pray freely that the Lord would bless them and their new pastor. He describes this lesson as 'the greatest blessing I ever had in all my life. O the use I have found it to me hundreds of times since.' Here was a lesson in the Lord's teaching, 'What is that to thee; follow thou Me.' [John 21,22.] A few of the Pool Moor people later separated and formed a small church of their own and Warburton went occasionally for a number of years to preach for them.

But the Lord had others purposes for him. Soon after this lesson he was invited to go to preach to a few people at Rochdale, who had separated from Mr Littlewood's Church. The reason for this separation had been that William Gadsby's ministry had drawn some of Mr Littlewood's congregation to go and hear him at Back Lane, Manchester. This had annoyed Mr Littlewood, and he had first banned them from going, and when they had defied him, he had suspended them from membership of his Church. They had first met in a farmhouse at Casson Gate and then rented a Schoolroom in Drake Street, Rochdale, and had invited William Gadsby to come to Rochdale to preach for them once a month on a Monday evening, which he did first in May 1807. Warburton first went to Rochdale for a few occasions, and then was engaged, for six shillings a Sunday, to preach regularly for them. The journey was nine miles across hilly countryside from Whitefield to Rochdale. Warburton walked the eighteen miles each weekend. In November 1809 they gave him a call to the pastorate, which he accepted and commenced in 1810, but he was not able to move to live there until January 1811. He says in his *Mercies*,

> O the miserable journeys I had sometimes for about two years [1809-10] from the place where I then lived [Narrow Lane, Whitefield] to Rochdale. I have many times left home with neither money nor provisions in the house, over head and ears in debt, full of carnal reason and unbelief, and not able to see however I could escape bringing reproach upon the cause of God and truth. O how my poor soul has roared like a bear, and mourned like a dove, when I have been passing through the lonely fields on my way on a Saturday night or sometimes on a Lord's day morning, many times without a text, all my debts staring me in the face, no appearance of getting through a single week, and all our clothes nearly worn out..... How many times did I tell the people that I must give it all up..... But they only laughed at me, and told me that if I knew nothing of these trials I should not do for them, and they were at a point that I was in the best school God could put me in for the pulpit.... I was confident that,

if it was the best school, it was a very hard one to flesh and blood. Nevertheless, I always found in the end that they told the truth; and I am as confident of it as I am of my own existence, that there has been a 'needs be' for every trial which my dear God and Saviour has sent me, and that there has not been one too many. They have been all in their place in the hands of God, to empty me and strip me of all my human props, and bring me to God as my 'all in all.'[1]

The first Church book of this congregation of Rochdale Particular Baptists has survived. The date of their formation is given as 16th April 1809. Signed by James Brearley, William Wilson, Benjamin Tweedale, Samuel Lord, Peggy Hardman, Samuel Ormerod, James Brearley [Junior], James Stott, and Mary Brearley, the first entry reads, 'This book is intended for the use of the members of Christ, as a Church Book, that were expelled from the Church at Town Meadows on Friday the 2nd day of December 1808, at a Church Meeting by the unscriptural authority and command of Mr Littlewood their minister, as no one ought to be Lord over God's heritage, for one is their Lord and master even Christ, who is their Lawgiver, and they are all brethren. But it may be asked why they were cut off from the Church; was it not for some bad conduct, or else some gross sentiments in religion. No, it was only because they would not desist from going to hear Mr Gadsby who came from Manchester to preach about once a month, though they acknowledged and believed that he preached the gospel and differed very little in sentiment from them.' Then follows the list of those who had been suspended.

Thereafter the little book records that they elected James Brearley [Senior] and Samuel Lord as their deacons and agreed to meet regularly in the room rented for their meetings at Mr Greenwood's School in the New Road leading to the Canal. Then on that 16th day in April 1809 they added in their Church book, 'And now may the great Head of the Church keep us, and watch over us, and protect us from heresies both in principle and practice, and may we be enabled to vindicate and to contend for that faith which was once delivered to the saints,

---

[1] John Warburton, op. cit. pp. 93, 94.

even for that doctrine which lays sinful man in the dust and exalts Christ as being the Author and Finisher of our faith, and for every doctrine consistent with God's sovereign, eternal, unchangeable, electing love, and for the precepts of the gospel, believers baptism and other ordinances of the gospel, too numerous here to mention.' It was from this group of believers that John Warburton received his invitation to preach at the beginning of 1809 and the Church Book duly records, 'John Warburton, Minister, accepted the Office of Pastor over this Church in the Lord, 1810.'

But all was not easy for Warburton. He says in his *Mercies,* of Rochdale, 'Here I met with many comforts and many sorrows, with some downright real friends as well as some downright real enemies, the latter of whom appeared when I first went among them.' Some of the 'comforts' are recorded in the Church Book. On May 24th 1809 six people were baptised by William Gadsby and added to the Rochdale Church the same day. They were John Stott, Joseph Gee, John Kershaw, James Mayden, John Howarth and Abram Fletcher. [John Kershaw was later to be their Pastor, from 1817 to 1870.] He records in his *Autobiography* the events of that day, it being the Wednesday of Whit-week. He says,

> As we had neither chapel nor baptistry, the question arose as to where the ordinance [of baptism] was to be administered. One of the friends, a farmer, said, he had a small stream of water running through one of his fields, which could be made use of for that purpose. This was agreed to. When the day came, nearly 2,000 people were assembled. Professor and profane were gathered together to witness the ordinance of baptism by immersion. Mr Gadsby stood on the bank of a reservoir, which served as a kind of gallery where many sat, the great body of the people being before him in the field. He preached from John 5, 39, 'Search the Scriptures etc.' At this time he was about thirty-six years of age, and such was the power of his voice that the sound of it was heard nearly a mile off, but not to distinguish the words. After the sermon he baptised six persons. In an hour after, we met together in the farmhouse, were formed into a church and partook of the Lord's supper. This was similar to the apostolic custom, when the churches met in private houses for breaking of bread and prayer.

I have a sweet and solemn remembrance of that day when fifteen souls were thus united together. [1]

John Kershaw, born at Lower Fold, Healey in the parish of Rochdale on 25th August 1792, was a weaver like Warburton. He was a lad of seventeen at the time of his baptism. Warburton soon had further encouragements as the Church Book records he baptised Mary Butterworth on 13th November 1809, just at the time he had accepted the call to the pastorate. But he was still not free from his poverty. He records in his *Mercies* that on one occasion in these years 1809-10, that he went backwards and forwards from Whitefield to Rochdale, that he was short of one guinea in the payment of his rent. His hope was that on the next Lord's day, he would be able to borrow it from one of his friends at Rochdale. But these people were for the most part very poor. John Kershaw records in his *Autobiography,* pp.69, 'John Warburton being our principal minister, we had to enter into a weekly subscription to support his coming among us.' He reveals that he subscribed three pence a week, and to do this went without his dinner on Sunday. So it was not easy for them to find a guinea among themselves.

That Sunday no one was able to help Warburton and the rent at Narrow Lane was due the next Monday morning. He returned that Sunday evening on his long walk back to Whitefield very disconsolate. When he came to Heywood village, through which he had to pass, he remembered he had to call on an old lady to deliver a message from Willam Gadsby about a visit he proposed to make to her. The old lady insisted that he should come in and have something to drink. They entered into spiritual conversation which was greatly blessed to a young girl who was listening. Then the old lady asked him to read and pray before he left. He felt the Lord's presence and says, 'When I arose from my knees and was taking leave of them, the old lady left me a guinea in my hand, at which I burst into a flood of tears in the room, and could not help it.' Then he explained his circumstances with regard to his rent the next

---

[1] John Kershaw, *Autobiography of an Eminent Lancashire Preacher,* Gospel Tidings Publications, 1968, p. 68.

morning. He left the house for his long and lonely journey in the dark, rejoicing in his heart. He says that that night as he walked he sang Cowper's hymn, 'God moves in a mysterious way,' especially the verse beginning, 'Ye fearful saints, fresh courage take,' and the lines, 'God is His own interpreter, And He *has* made it plain.' In his *Mercies* he quotes the whole of the Twenty-Third Psalm as his sweet experience that night. So these years saw a 'balancing of the clouds' in his life, with mercies mingles with his sorrows – 'a time to weep, and a time to laugh; a time to mourn and a time to dance.' [Eccl. 3, 4.]

Chapter 7

Begun in hope

Some little time after this, [1810] we began to build a new chapel at Rochdale, where I then laboured, and had done so for some time; and the Lord having blessed my labours, we were crowded in the room in which we then met, and therefore began a new chapel. It was truly wonderful and amazing to see how the Lord opened a way for us, for we were a very poor people. But O how many times did we prove that portion of God's word, 'The cattle upon a thousand hills are mine, and all the gold and silver is mine.' For He opened the hearts of people far and near to communicate towards the raising of Hope Chapel, which we called it, for we say, it was begun in hope, carried on in hope, and a hope too which will never make ashamed. So we called it Hope Chapel. Through many toils and difficulties, at length we got the Chapel up, but with a considerable debt upon it, which was very heavy on our shoulders.'[1]

Within a few months of commencing his pastorate at Rochdale the congregation decided to venture and build themselves a chapel and a house for their pastor. The Lord blessed Warburton's ministry among them and in his first year as pastor he baptised Daniel Eastwood and Samuel Stott on 6th May, Martha Taylor on 9th May, Betty Ashworth on 4th August, and on 7th October John Howarth and Jacob Wolfenden joined them, and on 2nd December John Cockcroft joined. Subscriptions were commenced for the new building which cost well over £1,000. A site was bought in 1810 and the foundations laid. It was opened in the following year in Whit-week by William Gadsby when he preached from the words, 'I will glorify the house of My glory.' [Isa 60,7.] In 1811 Warburton had five baptisings. On 6th June he baptised James

[1] John Warburton, op. cit. p. 97

Wild, on 6th October David Moffitt and Mary Holmes, and on 3rd November Sarah Chadwick and Hannah Lord. The Church book shows that he baptised his old friend the Scotsman Thomas Niven on 31st May 1812 and the last person he baptised before he left Rochdale for Trowbridge in April 1815 was Jenny Berry. When he left them in 1815 they were still in debt to the sum of about £600. While he was there the Church paid him twenty-five shillings a week.

A few months after the opening of the chapel Warburton was able to leave Whitefield and move to live in the new chapel house attached to the Chapel. For some months after the opening he was 'so stuck fast [at Whitefield] with many little debts' that it appeared impossible for him to move. He says that for years the devil had tempted him that if ever he left Narrow Lane it would be to go to the Poor House. But now friends moved to pay all his debts and he says, 'When my traps were put in the cart, not a dog was able to move its tongue,' 'So off we went with six children, we having seven in all, but the eldest [William] did not then live at home.' Presumably William had left home to take up an apprenticeship, or possibly to live at Whitefield with his Uncle William. In 1811 when this move took place he was about fifteen. Of the others, Sarah was thirteen, James ten, Elizabeth nine, Leah six, Rachel four, and Gideon two. Mrs Warburton was expecting again and within a week or two of their arrival, on 23rd January 1811, another boy arrived in the family.

Almost immediately they arrived in Rochdale Warburton was forced to go on credit at the local shop for the things that they needed. Again he found himself having to borrow from one to pay another. Extra expenses came as the time of the delivery of the new baby drew near. It would seem that he was still working at his loom, because at the moment Lydia went into labour he was forced to make a journey to Manchester, which was about ten miles each way. It would seem that he was taking a piece of cloth back to his master there at the warehouse, which would give them a little more money. He had a long and anxious journey thinking of the situation back at Hope Chapel House. But in Manchester he met a friend [presumably from Back Lane Chapel], who helped him financially, and as he left Manchester to return to Rochdale the words came into his heart with sweetness and power, 'The angel of the Lord did wondrously and Manoah and his wife looked on.' He says,

> It was a looking on indeed. I verily believed it was well with my wife, and that the child was a boy, so I cried out in the way as I went, 'His name is Manoah.' What a different journey I had home. All the way to Manchester the devil roared, but all the way back the Lord smiled. When I arrived at home, all was well; my dear wife was safely put to bed, and the child was a boy. How sweetly did I take the dear child up in my arms and bless it in the name of the Lord and said, 'His name is Manoah and may the angel of the Lord do wondrously for him, and his poor soul look on,' which God grant may be the case in his own time.[2]

Nothing more is known about Manoah. He came to Trowbridge with his parents in 1815, and presumably worked there, when he was old enough. He died on 4th November 1839 at the age of twenty-eight and lies buried in the family grave at Zion Chapel which is described in the burial record as 'In front of the chapel under the footpath nearest the door.' His little sister Rhoda had been buried in the same grave in October 1820 when she had died at the age of three years three months. Warburton had published the second part of his *Mercies* in 1839, dealing with the years of his life from 1815 to 1839, but it came out too early for any reference to be made to Manoah's death. All that survives, regarding Manoah, is this blessing that his father had at his birth. From the absence of any further mention of him in the *Mercies* Warburton leaves the reader to assume that the boy led a quiet life and did not cause his parents any great sorrow.

One blessing which Warburton experienced in his new home at Hope Chapel House Rochdale, with the Chapel next door, was to have his family with him on Sundays. He says, 'Ever since the Lord had opened my poor mouth in His dear name, there was one request I had made, that He would open a place for me where I might have my family with me on the Lord's day..... but little did I think that the Lord would favour

---

[2] John Warburton, op. cit. p.100.

me with a habitation adjoining the chapel. But so it was! And I verily believe on the Lord's day when my wife and children entered the Chapel, I should have fainted away in the pulpit had not the Lord supported me. O with what power did I feel the words of David, 'Thou hast caused men to ride over our heads; we went through fire and through water, but thou broughtest us out into a wealthy place.'

But Warburton's peace of mind did not last long and he soon found himself in some more trouble. As he put it, 'We got behind at the shop.' They were in debt for provisions upward of seven pounds and only had two pounds to meet it. The real trouble came when one of his two deacons, either James Brearley [Senior] or Samuel Lord, went to the shopkeeper and out of *kindness* let him know that if he did not get his money back from his pastor soon, he would never get it at all. Warburton says of this deacon that he professed such love to him when he first went to Rochdale, but after a little while he began 'to manifest his hatred and enmity against me, by trying to harass, perplex and distress me.' The result of the deacon's efforts was that the shopkeeper put pressure on Warburton to clear his debt at once.

This pressure was put on him on a Saturday and he hardly knew how to go and preach the following day at Hope because of the worry. He says, 'But through the tender mercy of a covenant God, I had a good day in the courts of our Lord.' That night his wife asked him how he thought they would get through the week with only two shillings, and the two pound they had set aside for their debt at the shop. He suggested she leave tomorrow till it came. In the morning the postman called and there was 1s -11d to pay on the letter. His wife brought it up to him in bed and threw the letter and the last penny of her last two shillings on the bed and said, 'Now you have such a stock of faith you have a whole penny to go to market with,' and went downstairs in a rage. Warburton opened the letter and there was a two pound note and a one pound note. When he went downstairs to show her she was amazed and when his old Scots friend from Hope Chapel, Thomas Niven called in shortly after to see him, and heard the story, he went home and brought back the two pounds needed to make the seven. So that day

Warburton says, 'My old dame dressed herself up in her best gown and off she goes with the seven pounds and discharges the debt with honour.' He himself went alone into Hope Chapel to thank the Lord, only to have the thought enter his mind, 'Why did not the letter contain five pounds instead of three!' This ingratitude grieved him. He says, 'I learned that thankfulness was a gift that cometh down from above.' But a few days later walking in the street, the Lord gave him a sweet sense of gratitude for this remarkable deliverance.

Not only did Warburton have debts in his family, he also had a heavy debt outstanding on the chapel. John Kershaw says in his *Autobiography* that the estimated cost of chapel and chapel house had been £1,000 or £1,100 and that in fact it cost several more hundreds than that when finished. He says that when Warburton came there to live he brought a large family, that trade was bad, food prices rose, and he needed more support than the church could afford to give him; this at a time when the church also had a heavy chapel debt and ground rent to pay. Often at church meetings poor members, who could hardly make ends meet at home, were asked to give money to the church they could not afford. Kershaw adds that, 'While I thus speak, I feel very much for a man of God in the ministry who has a large family, a poor people, and a heavy church debt.'

There seems little doubt that some of the friction between Warburton and the deacons centred on the anxiety generated in their minds, by the overwhelming debt which hung over them all. The Lord provided Thomas Niven, a Scotsman and prosperous business man and a man of property, to help in this hour of need. He had joined the church in May 1812 and been baptised by Warburton. Now in this time of crisis he stood by the young church. Kershaw says that Thomas Niven 'took the temporal affairs of the place into his own hands for a time....he received from the deacons what the pew rents and other collections made, making up the deficiency from his own pocket. He took Warburton his salary every Friday, paying interest, ground-rent and other matters that came against us.'

Warburton also took his part in the responsibility for the church debts. In 1812 he says, 'The Church wished me to go out begging, as two hundred pounds was wanted, and we were threatened with the law if we did not get it. So off I set round the different counties, till I got to London.' It would be of interest to know exactly were he went, and how long he was away. In the light of future events in his life, it seems possible that he might have got as far as Maidstone in Kent, for he was later given a call to a pastorate there, and there is no information as to how they knew him, or where any of them had heard him. But the record of what was certainly a preaching tour round various chapels, to ask for money to help pay for Hope Chapel Rochdale has not survived. All that has survived is the details of his visit to London during that tour and his meeting with William Huntington.

Huntington was within a year of his death, he died at Tunbridge Wells on 1st July 1813 at the age of sixty-nine. At the time Warburton was thirty-five. He had come into contact with the writings of William Huntington early on in his life. He says in his *Mercies,*[3]

> Many years before I began to preach, being one night at a prayer meeting, [probably at Mosley Street Independent Chapel in Manchester about 1797-8] which I was in the habit of attending, a person who was there offered to lend me a book, the title of which, he said, was *'The Kingdom of Heaven Taken by Prayer,'* written by Huntington a coalheaver... He said it was exactly my experience and he was sure I should like it. So I took it, and O what a night I had in reading that blessed book! Never can I relate a thousandth part of my feelings. Sometimes I was crying, sometimes laughing, sometimes blessing and praising God, till my very soul was so overpowered that I hardly knew whether I was in the body, or out of it. I read it till nearly daylight in the morning, and O what a union of soul did I feel to that dear man of God! I made a solemn vow to God that if ever He brought me in His providence any where near to him, I would go and tell him the blessing which I had received from reading his book.

As he arrived in London that day in 1812, so the words echoed in his heart, 'Pay thy vows unto the Lord,' and he knew that he must find Huntington out at his home at Hermes Hill, at Pentonville and visit him, and tell him what a blessing his book

---

[3] John Warburton, op. cit. pp. 130 – 134.

had been made to him ten or fifteen years before. Accordingly he went to his house and requested an interview, which was granted. At first Huntington was cool, but when Warburton began to tell him how he had been brought into condemnation in his soul, and then how he had come into gracious liberty under the ministry of old Mr Roby, and what he had felt of joy and peace in his soul, he says, 'Huntington looked up with tears running down his cheeks and blessed God for what He had taught me.' After what Warburton describes as a long and savoury conversation, he told Huntington why he was in London, and how he was pastor at Hope Baptist Chapel, Rochdale. Huntington told him he could not beg at his chapel as they had had a big expense with their chapel, but he took out all the silver he had in his desk and gave it to him especially for his family. Then as they shook hands in parting the old patriarch blessed him with the words, "May the Lord God of Abraham, of Isaac and of Jacob, bless thee and go with thee.' 'And,' says Warburton, 'the Lord did go with me in a most wonderful manner, for I got the £200 in my journey, and went home to Rochdale with joy and peace.' This must have brought down the debt considerably, though John Kershaw reveals that when he became pastor, in March 1817, the debt was still £600, the membership twenty, the congregation small, and his salary £20 a year. He had himself to carry on his weaving in order to keep his family.

Sometime between 1810 and 1813 at a Church meeting when John Kershaw had been absent, the church had come to the unanimous view that the Lord intended him for the ministry, and had sent one of the deacons to speak to him about it. This had led to him revealing his exercises in the matter, but asking his pastor not to act immediately. In the intervening time Kershaw passed through a period of much poverty in his circumstances. Eventually one Sunday evening at the end of 1813 a group of two or three friends were in the parlour of the Chapel House with Warburton, and John Kershaw came in to join them. Kershaw records in his *Autobiography,* 'In the course of conversation, in which he appeared to be in a very humble frame of mind, Warburton said, "Friends, if the Lord spares us until next Wednesday week, we shall have a preaching instead of a prayer-meeting. One of the friends inquired who was to be the preacher. Warburton replied, "The lot will fall upon Jonah; and looking earnestly at me, he said, "John you do not need to open your mouth any more by way of excuse; it must not be put off any longer. I already have a guilty conscience, when upon my knees before the Lord, for allowing it so long...... I am determined that, God helping, you shall speak amongst us at the named time.'

Accordingly on Wednesday evening, 9th January 1814 John Kershaw preached his sermon from Psalm 110. 3, 'Thy people shall be willing in the day of Thy power.' He preached a second sermon from Roman 8.14, 'For as many as are led by the Spirit of God, they are the sons of God,' on Wednesday evening 23rd January 1814. He tells us that, 'On the very day I preached my second sermon, our minister set off to supply the people at Trowbridge for six Sabbaths.' Hope Chapel, Rochdale was to have a supply minister from Manchester on the next Lord's day 27th January, but a very heavy fall of snow prevented one from coming and eventually it fell to John Kershaw at the age of twenty-one, to take his pastor's place, and preach for the first time in Hope Chapel pulpit. When Warburton returned, a Church Meeting was called and Kershaw was unanimously sanctioned to preach. After Warburton had left for Trowbridge in April 1815, John Kershaw was called to the pastoral office, which he commenced in March 1817, at the age of twenty-four, and continued in it for nearly fifty-three years until his death on 11th January 1870.

Events were now moving for Warburton to leave Hope Chapel Rochdale. He says in his *Mercies*, [4]

> Soon after this I had trouble upon trouble at Rochdale, and began to see that I could never stay there long; and I was firmly persuaded that God never intended it, for every way kept closing up, till at last, my old friend the Scotsman said he could not promise to communicate so much to the cause, and, indeed, I wondered he did what he had done for years. Then the deacons, [James Brearley and Samuel Lord] told me that it was plain the Lord meant me for some other place, and, if Providence opened a

---

[4] John Warburton, op. cit. p.104.

way, they considered I should be right in embracing it. O how my soul did sink down within me. I had eight children; [another child Ruth, had been born at Hope Chapel House on 27th October 1813] I was over head and ears in debt and nothing but clouds and darkness within and without.

Now within two days, Warburton received two letters. The first was an invitation to go to Maidstone in Kent on a month's probation for the pastorate there, and the second was from Trowbridge in Wiltshire to do the same there. After only four years in his new home at Hope Chapel House, Rochdale, and in his new Church, again the cloudy pillar was going before him, and this time it was to lead him away from his beloved Lancashire. But his union with William Gadsby and John Kershaw was to remain as strong as ever, in fact it was to increase. For these three ministers, together with men like William Huntington, had been led deeply into experimental truth and were men of the calibre of Martin Luther and John Knox when it came to standing against the errors of Andrew Fuller, which had spread among the Particular Baptists at that time, and were becoming a cause of division among them in the Manchester area and elsewhere in the country. 'William Gadsby always considered, and often stated publically, that Andrew Fuller was the greatest enemy the church of God ever had, as his views were so much cloaked with sheep's clothing.'[5]

[5] *Memoir of William Gadsby* 1847, p. 27.

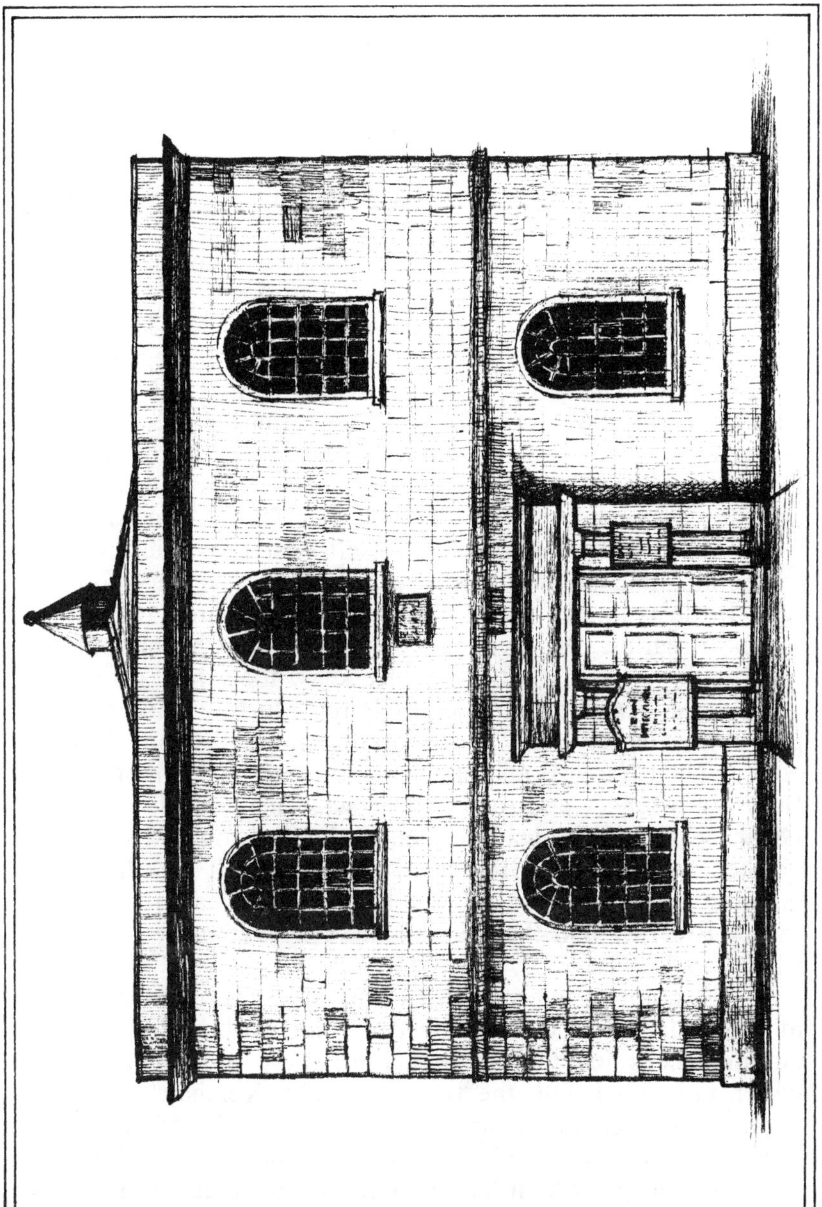

Zion Chapel

Chapter 8

Much people in this city

Looking back on his brief pastorate at Hope Chapel, it is not easy to see what went wrong. Warburton was a strong, forceful, and at times, emotional man. In later life J.C.Philpot his close friend, [formerly Fellow of Worcester College Oxford, Co-Editor of *The Gospel Standard Magazine* 1840-1849 and Editor 1849-1869] refers to 'his fine portly person, commanding look and loud voice, that struck terror into the timid and silenced the talkative.' He also refers to his temper and obstinacy. Equally he refers to his tender-hearted spirit, which frequently manifested itself in his life. So his temperament contained some strong traits in a very forceful mix. Little is known about the characters of Samuel Lord and James Brearley, the two deacons at Hope Chapel, but the records do show that after John Kershaw took the pastorate in 1817 there was often trouble at Church Meetings, and that the peace was largely kept by the godly old Scotsman, Thomas Niven. The Church Book makes mention of the death of Abram Brearley in 1842, and says that he was 'the son of old James Brearley [one of the leading men in the division of 1826], and brother to Thomas Brearley [who also left in the 1826 division.]' This reveals that John Kershaw also had trouble with James Brearley and that he and his son eventually left Hope Chapel in 1826.

A point of interest which now arises is how the people of Trowbridge first came to hear of John Warburton, and what circumstances led to him preaching there in January 1814, which coincided with the time that John Kershaw started to preach. The separation at Mr Littlewood's Church at Town Meadows had occurred over the distinctive preaching of William Gadsby, which had commenced in Rochdale in 1807.

Mr Littlewood, whom Kershaw considered a godly man, regarded William Gadsby, who had come to Manchester in 1805, as an Antinomian. An Antinomian, in a strictly technical sense, was a person, who professing to be a Christian, at the same time lived a licentious and immoral life. Mr Littlewood knew this was not true of Gadsby, so it is necessary to look further to understand why he referred to Gadsby as an 'Antinomian', and refused to allow him to preach in his pulpit, eventually excommunicating those members of the Town Meadows church, who regularly went to hear him; which in turn led to the formation of the congregation at Hope Chapel, Rochdale.

Many of the distinctive features of Gadsby's preaching were not confined to himself. They had characterised the ministry of some Particular Baptists in the eighteenth century and were apparent in the ministry of William Huntington, a very powerful preacher in London between 1783 and 1813. Mr Littlewood called Gadsby an 'Antinomian,' because he did not believe that the Moral Law was the believer's rule of life, rather he [and others] saw the Gospel as the rule of life of a Christian; 'the Gospel containing the sum and substance and glory of all the laws which God had ever promulgated from His Throne.' The pattern set by Christ in the Gospel precepts was a perfect law of liberty to be kept by all Christians in love to Christ and in no way did it ever lead to licentiousness, witness the exemplary life of Gadsby, [until his death in 1844] and those who believed like him. The charge of Antinomianism was malicious and without foundation.

But there were other points in which Gadsby stood out. In 1781 the Baptist, Andrew Fuller, had published a work entitled *'The Gospel Worthy of all Acceptation,'* in which he had attempted to prove that all unconverted men and women were able to accept the Gospel in their unconverted state, because their inability to do so rested solely on the fact that they did not want to accept it. To establish his point he quoted from Psalm 2, verse 12, 'Kiss the Son,' which he said was a command to all mankind. Assuming that he was right, he then was able to show that the manner of preaching the Gospel should be firmly to offer the Gospel to all mankind, on the warrant that it is clear in Scripture that it is the duty of all mankind to, 'Kiss the Son.' From this it was then shown that faith and repentance were the duty of all, and that men and women would be condemned for refusing the offer of the Gospel.

William Gadsby had responded in his day with a number of books, stating the Scriptural viewpoint, and was not alone, as William Huntington had also entered the lists against Andrew Fuller before him. In the period just after December 1804, William Gadsby published an article entitled, *The Gospel, The Believer's Rule of Conduct,* and at other times published works such as, *The Present State of Religion- What are the people miscalled Antinomian* [1809]; *The Perfect Law of Liberty [1811]; Hints to Messrs Bogue and Bennet [1823]; Controversial Works on the Law.* In these he made it clear that the believer's rule of life must be the Gospel, that the Gospel according to the Scriptures was to be *preached* and not *offered*, and that faith and repentance, far from being legal duties were in fact graces of the Spirit. The Scriptures never once made any mention of the *offer of the Gospel*, but rather referred with great distinctiveness to '*preach the Word*,' as the commandment given to God's servants, and referred to the work of the Spirit in the New Birth in terms of 'a call' rather than an *offer*.

John Warburton had himself been branded as an Antinomian in his early days at Mosley Street, Independent Chapel, when he attempted to tell his friends how the Lord had delivered him from the curse of the law under the preaching of Mr Roby. When, sometime, about 1804, William Gadsby went to Liverpool to preach, he fell foul of Richard Davis, the pastor of Byrom Street Baptist chapel, which had been the scene of the pastorate of the minister and hymn writer, Samuel Medley. Davis had been ordained there as pastor in 1800, and Mr Littlewood of Rochdale had preached the ordination sermon Richard Davis had for three years preached at a church at Thorn in Bedfordshire, and had been closely connected with the Baptist Mission and John Ryland, John Sutcliff and Andrew Fuller. When he went to Liverpool, he was fully convinced that the position of Andrew Fuller was the Scriptural one. When William Gadsby began to preach in Liverpool quite a number of

Richard Davis's congregation, including two of his deacons, used to go to hear him, and this caused Richard Davis considerable annoyance. Eventually such was the division in his church that he felt he had to leave Liverpool, and he accepted an invitation in 1810 to the pastorate at the Baptist Chapel, in Back Street, Trowbridge, known as the Little Meeting.

Sometime in 1811 or 1812, William Gadsby was invited to preach at Bath. At this time there was already trouble in the Baptist Chapel in Back Street, Trowbridge because Richard Davis had begun propagating the ideas of Andrew Fuller regarding *the offer of the Gospel.* By 1812 a group of nearly fifty members were preparing to leave Back Street Chapel and meet together, as they objected to the new teaching of Richard Davis. The Church had had as their former pastor, Nathaniel Rawlings, who had come to them in 1763 and eventually became their pastor in 1769. Due to some trouble he had left and gone as pastor to Broughton in Hampshire where he remained from 1771 to 1778, when he returned to Back Street, and stayed as pastor till his death in 1809, at the age of seventy-five. His ministry had united the church and he had baptised 175 people in his pastorate. It is clear that he never preached in the same way as Richard Davis either at Broughton or Back Street. It was the change of pastor that caused the trouble and the members, who left, resented the teachings of Andrew Fuller and Richard Davis, and preferred the ministry of Nathaniel Rawlings.

William Gadsby records in his writings that while he was at Bath, two men approached him and invited him to go to a place seven miles away. He promised to go if they would arrange transport. They were two members of this group which were in process of separating from Back Street, Baptist Chapel. They were wondering whether Richard Davis would let William Gadsby preach in his pulpit in Back Street. Gadsby assured them, once he heard his name mentioned, that Richard Davis would refuse. So after every other chapel had been refused him, William Gadsby came to Trowbridge for the first time and preached in the Unitarian Church on the Conigre. His text that night was 'Lord teach us to pray, as John also taught his disciples.' [Luke 11.1.] Gadsby says in his writings, 'I went and it proved to be Trowbridge. I preached; and that night was the beginning of the interest there, over which John Warburton is now placed.'

The two men who had approached Gadsby at Bath were almost certainly two of the leaders of the breakaway group, William Eacott and Samuel Hurd, who later became John Warburton's deacons. In *A Brief Memoir of William Eacott,* by Joseph Rudman, it states that it was Mrs Eacott who first heard William Gadsby at Bath and was the means of recommending that he be asked to preach in Trowbridge. It also says, that the time was, 'Before the warehouse was taken and the large upper room furnished..... After the opening of the room by William Eacott, no further difficulty was experienced as to where men of truth should preach.' It appears from this last remark that Richard Davis was not regarded as a 'man of truth,' but William Gadsby was.

The Zion Baptist Chapel, Trowbridge, first Church Book goes on to relate events:

> We whose names are herein subscribed were members in full community of the Particular Baptist Church meeting for divine worship in Back Street, Trowbridge, under the pastoral charge of the late Mr Nathaniel Rawlings, whose ministry we believe was according to the divine word and made a blessing to our souls.
>
> On his removal by death, it was our earnest prayer to God that He would graciously provide and send to us a minister of the Spirit by whom our souls might be edified as by our late minister. It gave us much sorrow of heart that it was not so and after near three years [1809-1812] attending the ministry now introduced [Richard Davis, Pastor 1810] and finding no comfort or satisfaction, lamenting our painful situation, we frequently consulted what steps it would be most proper to take, and after spreading our cause [secretly and socially] before God by prayer, we concluded that it would be most conducive to peace and our spiritual profit to withdraw from the Church of which we stood members, and form ourselves into a distinct Society, and seek such a ministry as we thought was most spiritual. Providence presenting an opening, we engaged with Thomas Timbrell Esq., to rent some premises of his situate near the Bridge, Trowbridge, and having fitted up the same for a place of Divine Worship on the third day of January 1813, [being the first Lord's day of that year] we began public worship, believing the steps we have taken are of God and that Christian Society is of

divine appointment we mutually and heartily agree to join together and to be a distinct Church of Christ of the Particular Baptist Persuasion.

There then follows a group of twelve articles of faith the fifth one of which quite explicitly states,

> We believe in the Fall of Man and that by it the whole of the Human Race became Original and [as they were born into the world] Actual Transgressors against God, and that by the Fall they were rendered both unable and unwilling to deliver themselves.

Here they stated the difference between themselves and Fuller and Davis in that they maintained that man was *unable* to come to Christ on account of the totality of the Fall in Adam. Andrew Fuller in Volume II of his works, page 83 says, in his concluding reflections at the end of his book, *The Gospel Worthy of all Acceptation,*

> If the inability of sinners to perform things spiritually good were natural, or such as existed independently of their present choice, it would be absurd and cruel to address them in such language. [that is an offer]. No one in his senses would think of calling the blind to look, the deaf to hear, or the dead to rise up and walk; and of threatening them with punishment in case of their refusal. But, if the blindness arise from the love of darkness rather than light; if the deafness resemble that of the adder, which stoppeth her ear, and will not hear the voice of the charmer, charm he never so wisely; and if the death consist in alienation of heart from God, and the absence of all desire after Him, there is no absurdity or cruelty in such addresses.

The view of the new Baptist Church at Trowbridge was that the fall of Man had rendered the sinner utterly unable to return to God. He was born, 'dead in trespasses and sin.' Andrew Fuller was in error in his theology and had a totally different view of the effects of original sin. Christ's teaching had been, 'Except a man be born again he cannot *see* the kingdom of God.' They believed that until a man was born again of the Spirit of God no amounts of offers or tenders could reach their heart. It was only the 'new creature in Christ Jesus' that could respond and that under the Scripture, 'No man can come unto Me except the Father which hath sent Me *draw him.'* And so they believed like Warburton, Gadsby and Huntington that the Gospel invitations were only made spirit and life to 'sensible sinners,' i.e. those, who born again of the Spirit of God, had been brought under the condemnation of God's Holy Law.

It was from this group of fifty members and their congregation that John Warburton received his first invitation to come and preach in January 1814, and it was to them he came as he left Rochdale to travel the long journey by stage coach, via Manchester, Birmingham, Bristol and Bath. He left home on Wednesday 23rd January, when there was heavy snow about in the North and preached at Trowbridge in the warehouse by the Bridge,[still there today, though much restored - formerly known as the Bonded Warehouse, now an Estate Agents Offices]. It seated about four hundred people. William Eacott had provided £100 toward the cost of fitting it out for worship. The Church book records that William Marvin [one of the five deacons elected on 13 April 1813] was paid £2 to look after John Warburton while he was in Trowbridge.

Trowbridge, a West Country Woollen Cloth Mill town, was in the throes of becoming industrialised, a situation which would eventually lead to it becoming known as the 'Manchester of the West.' At this time the Kennet and Avon Canal was complete, linking the town by 1805 with the coalfields at Radstock, via the Somersetshire Coal Canal. This had led in 1805 to the installation of the first steam engine for the Cloth Industry in the town. By the time Warburton arrived to preach in the Bonded Warehouse in January 1814, there existed just between the warehouse and the Town bridge, Trowbridge, Bridge Cloth Mill, the first purpose-built cloth mill, run by a twenty horse power steam engine, installed in 1808. Warburton was later to baptize twenty-four people on 1st August 1824 at Bird's Coal Wharf on the Kennet and Avon Canal at Hilperton Marsh, at the place where the coal was unloaded to fire these steam engines in Trowbridge. Courts Mill in Polebarn Road also boasted a twenty horse power engine installed in 1812. The town was beginning to follow the pattern set earlier by the cloth industry in Yorkshire.

Warburton the weaver, was coming among a people, mostly cloth workers, which was for him a familiar environment, and one can imagine that in his six week stay, he probably visited Bridge Mill, which was under an hundred yards from the Bonded Warehouse, where his congregation met and where he was preaching, to see the powerful new engine. He preached on Sunday 27th January 1814, then each Sunday in February, and finally on Sunday March 3rd, before he left to return to his congregation at Hope Chapel, Rochdale. He had plenty of time to get the feel of Trowbridge, see how poor many of the people were and experience the winter weather, the grime from the factories and the odours from the streets, though he was already used to this in Rochdale. It is clear from what he says in his *Mercies* that Trowbridge was too similar to Rochdale and Manchester for him to want to live there.

When at the end of 1814 he received his letters to go on trial for the pastorates from Maidstone and Trowbridge, he decided to go to Maidstone first and preach there for a month, and then go on to Trowbridge to preach for William Eacott and his friends. As regards the final decision as to which pastorate he would accept, in his own mind, it was clearly to be at Maidstone. It seems that at Maidstone there was a church building, whereas at Trowbridge a new church would have to be built, and Warburton had fresh memories of all the problems associated with the building of Hope Chapel, Rochdale, such that he had no desire to experience the same problems a second time. Also the Maidstone people generally were much more prosperous. He describes the Trowbridge people as 'a poor people.' He himself had a large family, and by the time he had to decide which church to accept, his wife was already expecting another baby. He could see he would be needing much financial support, nor could he see how it would be forthcoming in Trowbridge.

Early in 1815 he left Rochdale for Maidstone and stayed four weeks. The people gave him a call to be pastor and everything he says,was 'as pleasant to flesh and blood as he could desire.' He determined to go to Maidstone, but he had first to go to Trowbridge to fulfil his month there. He says at Trowbridge, 'The room was crowded [on Wicker Hill in the

Bonded Warehouse], and God blessed the word abundantly.' But he was set on going to Maidstone. The Trowbridge people gave him a call to be their pastor and he adds, 'My time being out, it was necessary to give them an answer.' Then he sought the Lord to give him a command to go to Maidstone, 'For to pray to stay at Trowbridge,' he says, 'I could not; for I could see nothing but difficulties, trials and miseries; for I saw plainly the toils of a new chapel, and these I dreaded as knowing what sorrows and miseries Hope Chapel had caused me.'

The night before he had to make the final decision was the evening and night of 4th – 5th March 1815. He accepted the call to Trowbridge according to the Church Book on 5th March 1815. He spent most of that evening and night in prayer alone, his wife and family far away in Rochdale and himself alone with strangers. What a momentous time it was for him! In his *Mercies* he reveals the conflict of that night showing how he wrestled with his God, like Jacob did at Brook Jabbok. [Genesis 32. 22-32.] In it is revealed the sacred reality of spiritual experience and the divine leadings which time showed were so right. He says,

> O what a night I had the night before I was to settle the business whether I was to go to Maidstone or stop at Trowbridge. I *wrestled* and prayed, and cried to God until about three o'clock in the morning, to let me go to Maidstone; and O how I sunk down when He spoke these words into my heart: 'Abide in this city, for I have much people here.' [Acts 18.10.] 'O', cried I, 'Do Lord, let me go to Maidstone; do Lord: do not be offended with my poor petition; do let me go to Maidstone.' But the text sounded again and again, 'Abide in this city, for I have much people here;' but still I wanted Him to let me go to Maidstone. At last the dear Lord settled the matter at once by speaking these words to my soul: 'If His children forsake My law, and walk not in My judgements; if they break My statutes and keep not My commandments; then will I visit their transgressions with the rod, and their iniquity with stripes;' [Ps. 89. 30-32.] and I could see it as speaking all this to my soul. You may go to Maidstone; but here is the rod, and you shall have nothing else, if you go.
>
> I fell down and cried out, 'Not my will, but Thine be done.' But cried I, 'How can I get on here? How can I live here, when I come with ten in family, and my wife in the family way? How can I possibly live here and *the people, a poor people*?' O how God condescended to settle the

matter in my soul. 'The cattle upon a thousand hills are mine.' 'The earth is mine and all the gold and silver is mine.' 'Thy bread shall be given thee and thy waters shall be sure.' 'Fear thou not; for I am with thee: be not dismayed, for I am thy God; I will strengthen thee; yea I will help thee; yea I will uphold thee with the right hand of my righteousness.' [Isa. 41.10.] I cried out, 'It's enough, it's enough: Amen to it.'

Maidstone from that moment, was as completely taken away from my mind, and the feeling of any desire to go there to settle, as if I had never heard of such a placc. And here I am at Trowbridge; a poor worm, and have proved the word of the Lord to be truth nearly twenty-two years.[1]

He now returned home to Rochdale and prepared to relinquish his pastorate, leave his recently built home, beside Hope Chapel, and all his friends. He says that it was cutting work when he came to say goodbye to his old friends, especially such friends as Thomas Niven, the Scotsman; Jacob Wolfenden [deacon 33 years and member 35 years]; Hannah Lord [member 30 years] a great friend of Thomas Niven and John Kershaw's wife Margaret; the young minister John Kershaw, and Jenny Berry who was the last one he baptised in the early months of 1815 just before he left, and who was a member 38 years until her death in 1853. He says in his *Mercies* that he had hoped to live and die at Rochdale and never expected to have to leave them. He says it was a weeping time as he committed the little flock into the hands of the Great Shepherd.

He goes on, as he wrote in 1837, to say, how he has lived to see that those prayers, for Hope Chapel, Rochdale and the people there, have been fully answered, as the Lord placed his own son in the faith, John Kershaw in the office of pastor within two years of his departure. His text for his farewell sermon, preached on Sunday 26th March, was from Acts 20.32, 'And now, brethren, I commend you to God, and to the word of His grace, which is able to build you up, and to give you an inheritance among all them which are sanctified.'

On the following Monday, he and his family left Rochdale for Manchester, where they arrived in the evening

---

[1] John Warburton op. cit. pp. 105,106.

and stayed for two nights. On Tuesday evening 28th March Warburton went to hear William Gadsby preach at Back Lane Chapel. The text was Proverbs 5. 15-17: 'Drink waters out of thine own cistern, and running waters out of thine own well. Let thy fountains be dispersed abroad, and rivers of waters in the streets. Let them be only thine own, and not strangers with thee.' He felt the whole sermon that night was for him, given as a solemn charge for him to take to Trowbridge, 'Which,' he says, 'I found some hundred times after, to be for my soul's encouragement in very deep waters of despair, respecting my ministry.' Many times when feeling he could never preach again, the words of that text would return as an encouragement to go on, 'Drink water out of thine own cistern, etc.' He says, 'I have indeed reason to believe that God designed that sermon for me; and I must confess I never heard a sermon in all the days of my life that was for such a length of time made so great a blessing, for it never failed me, when I was brought to despair that I should ever be able to preach again.'

On Wednesday morning 29th March 1815 Warburton left Manchester with his wife [who was expecting a child in August], and their eight children on the stage coach for Birmingham. It was a seventy mile journey and would take about ten hours. At the time Sarah was eighteen, James fourteen, Elizabeth thirteen, Leah ten, Rachel eight, Gideon six, Manoah four, and Ruth one and a half. William the oldest boy was being left behind. He never came to Trowbridge. He had been away from home for some time, almost certainly on an apprenticeship. He had John Warburton's brother, William, at Whitefield, who could keep an eye on him. John Warburton Junior, who was born at Trowbridge in August 1815, visited him many years later at Whitefield when he grew up. The family almost certainly split up as they travelled, Sarah and her mother, the girls and little ones travelling inside the coach, while John Warburton, James and possibly little Gideon travelled on the roof. No doubt there was much excitement as they made their three day journey at an average speed of seven miles an hour! which was 170 miles, taking 25 hours travelling time.

They stayed at an inn in Birmingham on Wednesday night and set out again on Thursday morning for Bristol, which was a journey of 80 miles taking eleven hours. No doubt they were all very tired when they arrived at Bristol on Thursday evening, where they stayed the night. On Friday morning 31st March they set out by coach for Trowbridge, on the last twenty miles of their journey, catching sight of the beauties of Bath as they passed through, and reaching Trowbridge via Bradford-on Avon in the evening. Warburton says,

> My poor soul was indeed melted with gratitude to the God of all mercies, for His kind protecting care over such a poor worm and his little tribe, in bringing us safe nearly two hundred miles. But when I arrived at Trowbridge, I was quite overcome to see how the hearts of the people had been opened, and their kindness manifested in fitting me up a house, with everything needful, from beds to dishes and spoons. Surely, thought I, the Lord is here; for the people in general were a very poor people; but what cannot be done when God undertakes? There are no impossibilities with Him.[2]

No doubt, the coach arrived at the George Inn that Friday evening, in the Market Place in Fore Street, Trowbridge, all new to his family, but not to John Warburton himself. William Eacott, Samuel Hurd and their fellow deacons and members would have been there to welcome their new pastor and his family, and would have provided some form of transport to take them and their luggage to the house in The Halve, which was to be their home for the next two or three years. Setting his home in order on Saturday 1st April, Warburton preached his first sermons on Sunday 2nd April in the Bonded Warehouse on Wicker Hill.

Writing to a friend, George Greenough [a deacon at William Gadsby's Church at Manchester,] on 14th May 1815, [3] Warburton says, 'The place is well attended,' and adds, 'We all got safe to our habitation, which God, for a time, has fixed. How long, it is to be, is unknown to me; but for anything that I can see, it appears that the Lord has designed it for good, and I

---

[2] John Warburton op. cit. p.108.

[3] *Gospel Standard* 1878. pp. 207, 208.

pray that it may be to His glory. Mr Gadsby preached for us the week but one after I got here [week beginning Monday 10th April], upon the subject of people and ministers uniting together, from two texts. One was: 'Preach the word;' and the other: 'See that ye refuse not Him that speaketh;' and a very solemn time it was indeed. He had precious liberty.' This shows that William Gadsby followed Warburton to Trowbridge in April 1815, and within a fortnight of his arrival, preached in the Bonded Warehouse on Wicker Hill, what was undoubtedly Warburton's recognition services as pastor.

Another letter, dated 27th July 1815,[4] was written by John Warburton to his young friend John Kershaw in reply to a letter he had written to his former pastor. In it Warburton refers to having received Kershaw's kind letter and speaks of Kershaw as, 'my dearly beloved son in the faith.' Then Warburton speaks of his admiration for the Lord's 'wonderful goodness though all my travels, for He has brought me by the *right* way.' He tells Kershaw that, 'Three have joined us from the other Church [Back Street], and three more have applied for their dismission; that makes six, and fourteen are to be baptised in a fortnight. As for the congregation, we are so crowded on a Lord's day that it is quite uncomfortable. The Fullerites are all in a rage, and say I am a downright Antinomian, a robber of Churches, a fool, and a firebrand; and think the people are all beside themselves, or else they would never come to hear me.' He goes on to say that he has sent a letter to the Church at Rochdale but does not expect a reply, and adds, 'The less I am loved of them, the more I love them.' Finally he sends his 'particular love' to Samuel Lord, and his love from himself and his wife to Hannah Lord, and says, 'Very often we talk about her, and should like to see her come into the house to have a chat with us.' He sends his love to James Brearly and says he has not yet received his letter. In conclusion he asks John Kershaw to write again soon. This letter makes clear that it was the error of Andrew Fuller, which divided the Particular Baptist Churches at the end of the eighteenth century and the beginning of the nineteenth, and led to the eventual formation of the

[4] *Gospel Standard* 1878, pp. 33,34.

Gospel Standard Churches, through the leadership of William Gadsby, John Warburton and later John Kershaw.

The birth register of Zion Chapel records the first major event in their lives in the new home in The Halve. A son was born there on the 4th August 1815. He was named after his father, and called John. He was to cause his father many sorrows by his waywardness, but was to balance it later, as he was called to be a minister like his father, and be made a blessing to him. Without any doubt, his entrance into the world was heralded by the screeching of the swifts, as they chased each other round the clothiers houses [built in 1793] in The Halve, with their beautiful eighteenth century facade, just as they had returned every year for centuries from Africa, and winged their way around Trowbridge Parish Church with its old spire, and in former centuries around Trowbridge castle; and still come back today. It is highly likely that this house which John Warburton was to rent in The Halve was owned by William Hayward, a local clothier, who was to be a great supporter of the new congregation and loan money towards the building of the new Zion Chapel in 1816. His family owned property in The Halve and elsewhere in the town.

The year 1815 was to be a momentous one. John Warburton Junior, in his *Memorials*[5] describes it as, 'a year in the annals of history of remarkable occurrence, peace being restored after a long, cruel, destructive and murderous war.' On the 18th June, the Duke of Wellington and Marshal Blucher had led their armies to defeat the Emperor Napoleon at the Battle of Waterloo, and after twenty-two years of war, Europe was to be at peace. But sadly this did not spell instant prosperity, as the result of the peace initially meant some reduction in demand in the cloth trade, and the Corn Laws were passed in 1815 to protect farmers who had overproduced in the war and now faced a cut back in the demand for corn. The Government moved to protect them and in so doing forced up the price of bread to artificially high prices, which hit the poor most.

[5] *Memorials of John Warburton of Southill*, 1892. p. 2.

John Warburton says that soon after arriving in The Halve that last day of March 1815, the words echoed in his mind with power, 'Abide in this city, for I have much people here,' and also, 'The cattle upon a thousand hills are mine, and the gold and silver at my disposal.' It had been a great mountain to come to Trowbridge. Now he saw a house furnished and, amazingly, stored with food and provisions. Love had provided all. The congregation were meeting in the Bonded Warehouse on Wicker Hill just near the Bridge Cloth Mill. Warburton was thirty-eight at the time and in the full vigour of life. He was a big man and a strong one in body and in his personality.

Regarding the acceptance of the pastorate by him on 5th March 1815, the Church Book says, "Mr John Warburton accepted the call of this church to be their pastor, as long as the majority of the Church and him should agree.' The Church was composed of the original forty-one members who had left Back Street Chapel. On 28th August 1814, before John Warburton's arrival, but after his first visit, John Dymott, the pastor since 1810 of the Hilperton Baptist Chapel, had baptised six new members for the Wicker Hill Church; probably in the Canal at Hilperton Marsh, where he usually baptised his own members. Then on 18th June 1815, three more members were received by transfer from another Church. On 13th August 1815 Warburton baptised twelve new members, a few days after the birth of his son John. One of these was William Hayward who was father of John Hayward, who later married Warburton's daughter Elizabeth.

Warburton records that the room on Wicker Hill held three to four hundred people and was full. He says,

> 'I believe God met with us in that room in a most wonderful manner, and bore testimony to the word of His grace, for it was evident by signs following. The congregation increased to that degree in a few weeks, that it was with difficulty that the people could get in; and it went on increasing so much that we found we must begin a chapel, for the souls of the people were truly alive and the word of God ran and was glorified...... We soon had a goodly number that came to tell what God had done for

their souls and cast in their lot amongst us, who were not ashamed to take up the cross and follow their dear Lord through good report and evil report.[6]

There was no lack of evil report as Warburton was accused of being 'a bigot,' 'an enemy to all holiness,' 'an Antinomian,' 'presumptuous, and destitute of charity.' He refused to unite with Arians and Socinians said the reports, and this seemed to suggest that he stood separate from the Unitarian Church on the Conigre, which in its early days, 1700-1725, had been the first Particular Baptist Church in Trowbridge. It had thereafter denied the doctrine of the Trinity, which caused those believing in the Trinity to secede in 1736, and eventually build themselves 'the Little Meeting' House in Back Street in 1754,[7] over which Nathaniel Rawlings had been Pastor from 1778-1809. Richard Davis had finally left Back Street Baptist Church in 1816, and had gone to Devonport, but it seemed there was considerable opposition from this quarter also to the members who had seceded from their midst in 1813. It also appeared that some were still leaving Back Street and joining the Wicker Hill congregation. Some of the members who Warburton received by *transfer*, [already baptised] probably were Back Street members.

So the Church of Warburton's grew and very soon commenced to build a Chapel in the Lower Courts. This was at the bottom end of the town at river level. A lawyer passing the builders one day inquired what the building was and why it was being built in a back part of the town. When told, he offered the Church the first refusal on a plot of land in Union Street, not far from the Parish Church and in a much higher position. This land was purchased for £124 6s, a large area at the back being reserved for a burial ground. The building of the chapel, called 'Zion,' cost £1,231 12s, a large sum for such poor people. It was capable of seating up to 700 people. The deacons at the

---

[6] John Warburton op. cit. p. 116.

[7] *Twenty Golden Candlesticks*, W. Doel, 1890, pp. 111-113.

time were Samuel Hurd, William Chapman, William Eacott and William Marvin. On 28th September 1816, William Hayward, whom Warburton had recently baptised, loaned the Church £500 at 5% interest. The following March,1817 Samuel Hurd, William Eacott and James Hayward all loaned the Church £100 each at 5% interest. This money [£800] represented the outstanding debt after the building was completed in 1816, and all bills paid, which suggests that the congregation had raised by then something over £500 towards the cost from their own resources. These debts were not finally paid back until 1841, when the last settlements were made. When William Hayward died in 1835, £440 of his loan had been repaid and the rest was transferred to his son John Hayward. Warburton started his pastorate with this heavy debt, and spent much time travelling, collecting money from other churches, trying to clear it.

As the plans for the building progressed so the Church increased. On 10th September 1815 two joined by transfer, and on 5th November Warburton baptised four and received three more by transfer. On 3rd December five more joined by transfer, which meant that in the first nine months of his pastorate twenty-nine new members had joined the Church. While he had such blessings attending his ministry, Warburton was not without his misgivings as he watched the Chapel going up. He says in his *Mercies*,

> Being quite crowded out of the room in which we met, we began to build a chapel which would seat between seven and eight hundred people. O the sinkings down I had at times for fear we should never be able to finish it! One day in particular, as I was looking at the building when it was up to the first window, I sank within, and feared it would all come to nothing, and that our enemies would have to say, "Ah, so would we have it, for many declared it would be impossible for us to finish it, and others were pleased to think it would make a good factory. I got home into my room [in The Halve] as full of unbelief as ever I could hold...... O the groans and sighs I had for some hours that the Lord would appear and give me a testimony that His hand was in it, and that He would prosper us, and be with us; and how sweetly did He apply the precious words of Psalm 2. 1-6, 'Why do the heathen rage and the people imagine a vain thing.... He that sitteth in the heavens shall laugh at them...' O what humility, joy, peace and confidence dropped into my heart from those words...How

sweetly did the words which nailed me at Trowbridge sound in my soul, 'Abide in this city, for I have much people here.'[8]

In 1816, when the Chapel was finished, opening services were conducted by John Dymott pastor of Hilperton Baptist chapel since 1810, and John Warburton. Four new members were received into the Church that year, and in the following year, 1817, John Warburton baptised eight in April and received three more members by transfer. So the Lord continued to bless his preaching and establish His promise that He had 'much people in this city.'

[8] John Warburton, op. cit. pp. 116, 117.

Chapter 9

Deep Waters

In his *Mercies* Warburton records what he describes as 'a most lamentable and trying circumstance which happened in my family, which I feared would prove my death,' and goes on to explain why he was putting it in print in 1838. He says, 'I feel that I cannot help writing it down purely from this motive, that if ever it should come into print, it may perhaps fall into the hands of some poor child of God that may have been, or is now, in the same trying affliction.' 'The circumstance' appears to have taken place just before the completion of the building of Zion Chapel, which places it toward the middle of 1816. It concerned his daughter Sarah who had had her nineteenth birthday on 14th April that year. She was the oldest child in the family to have come from Rochdale. Whether she had any work there is not clear. The Trowbridge marriage register shows by 'her mark' at her wedding on 22nd March 1819 that she was unable to write. Without doubt her father's move south had had a great effect on her life, causing her to leave all her friends behind at Rochdale, where she had lived since she was thirteen, when she moved from Besses-o'-th'-Barn. Her father's moves in the course of her life had affected her considerably, more so probably than the other younger members of the family.

Now this Lancashire lass arrived in Trowbridge and was forced once again to make new friends. She no doubt was 'disturbed' by the change. As with all their family, her broad Lancashire accent would have stood out among the Wiltshire dialect of Trowbridge. [It would be of interest to know how well John Warburton was understood among his congregation on account of his accent]. Sarah found a friend in a young lad, who was almost certainly the same one, as she married in

March 1819. His name was John Earle. John Warburton records in his *Mercies* that one week he had been out preaching in several places in the country [presumably this means locally in the villages] and had had great liberty in preaching. Coming home on the Friday, when about a mile from Trowbridge, the words dropped into his mind, ‘In the day of prosperity be joyful, *but* in the day of adversity consider. God also hath set the one over against the other, that man should find nothing after him.’ [Eccl. 7.14.] He felt persuaded that there was some bad news waiting for him when he reached home. His wife Lydia was in tears when she met him, only to tell him ‘that the young man that kept company with his eldest daughter had left her in a disgraceful state.’

For seven days Warburton was in dreadful anguish of mind and felt his preaching was at an end. His congregation were deeply shocked. His real friends were clad in mourning. Some thought it was a judgement on him for preaching ‘particular election, imputed righteousness and atoning blood for none but the sheep.’ Some agreed privately with these doctrines, but thought they should not be preached, as they might frighten poor sinners from coming to Christ and closing in with the Saviour. Others said he was an Antinomian, who did not believe that the Law was the believer’s rule of life, and therefore had not brought up his children properly. Many thought he could never preach again. But with the Lord’s strength he managed to preach the next Sunday. But he felt great anger against Sarah.

One day in the following week going up stairs to his bedroom, he was halted on the stairs with the words, ‘Who maketh thee to differ from another, and what hast thou that thou didst not receive?’ [1 Cor. 4.7.] In a moment he saw that he had not a stone to throw at his child. He saw that if God had left him to his ungodly nature, it would have been him instead of her that had fallen. This broke his heart at the thought of the mercy of God that had kept him, and led him into a deep sense of love for his child and earnest prayer for her. He felt led to plead that God would save her soul and manifest her as a vessel of mercy. He felt the force of the words, ‘Be still and know that I am God.’ He says, ‘O what a calm there was, How still was everything in a moment.' Now he felt able to go and preach again with liberty and freedom of spirit.

What happened to Sarah is not entirely clear, but certain facts are traceable. She married John Earle. [The child was *probably* born in 1817 and she *possibly* lived at home with it for two years before her marriage.] Her father's prayer was answered. She came forward in 1823 and was baptised by her father, with her sister Elizabeth, in the Mill pool at Ladydown Mill on 13th July, with eighteen others. It must have been a day of rejoicing for her father. Her husband, John Earle, had been baptised the previous year on 21st July 1822, together with twenty-four others, one of which was John Warburton's own wife, Lydia. These occasions were almost certainly marked by congregations of several thousand standing watching on the rising hillsides around the Mill pool and listening to the open air preaching, which John Warburton had been so used to in the North.

The Zion Baptist Birth Register contains the record of the birth of a girl Mary Anne Earle on 11th October 1835. Her parents were John and Ann Earle, who were living in Union Street, Trowbridge. This John has all the *appearance* of being the child born out of wedlock to Sarah in the Summer of 1817, now married and having his first child. What is certain is that the 1841 National Census returns show John Earle and Sarah living in Prospect Place and having a son Manoah, who was over fifteen years old and was an apprentice blacksmith. Also the same Census shows a Martha Earle aged fifteen plus, staying at Waterloo Terrace at John Warburton's home with Warburton's two daughters, Rachel and Ruth. It also shows a James Earle and his wife Elizabeth, both aged twenty, living in Prospect Place, *probably* another son of Sarah.

The Zion Burial register records that John Earle died on 17th March 1853, and was buried at Zion Chapel, having been excluded from Church membership at Zion Church in 1835. Sarah had resigned as a member of the Church at the same time in September 1835. There seems to be some *possibility* that there is a connection between the writing and publication of the *Mercies* at this time, and the departure of John and Sarah Earle from Church membership. After all, at the time of the publication of the *Mercies* in 1838 and 1839, Sarah certainly had a boy and a girl in their teens, and it is possible that the boy born out of wedlock had just married. If this were the case, what a bitter trial it must have been for the family to have their mother and father's sin of their youth, brought out into the open again. It would *seem* that when Sarah resigned her membership at Zion in 1835, she may have been aware that her father was proposing to publish an account of her fall in her youth. Whatever justification Warburton may have felt for publishing the account from his own side of the sorrow, it seems that he had not fully considered what Sarah, her husband and their family might feel. Sarah lived on until the age of eighty, dying on 13th November 1877, after a widowhood of twenty-four years. She was buried in an unmarked grave in the same row as her father, seventeen graves away, by Edwin Porter, the Pastor of Allington Baptist Chapel, near Devizes, which suggests that she continued to attend Zion Chapel until her death. Warburton's *Mercies* became widely known and passed through many editions, but for Sarah it contained a bitter sorrow, one might almost say a stigma, which followed her all her days, though no doubt when she joined the Church in 1823, one for which she had felt the Lord's forgiveness.

In July 1817 Warburton's wife gave birth to their last child, which as Warburton put it 'made up the dozen.' One had died in March 1800, William had been left in the North and so there were now ten at home. The new arrival was a girl and was called Rhoda. The year and place of birth are recorded in Zion Chapel Register of births. Just prior to her birth the Warburton family had moved house. It was not many yards away, in an area of three rows of houses, with passages in between, called Brick Plat, at the north end of The Halve. The 1821 National Census return shows them still living in Brick Plat. It seems probable that the move had been made in order to have a larger house for his large family. But it was not long before Warburton was in financial difficulties, as he had been in Rochdale He owed about ten pounds and was paid by Zion Chapel £3 a week. Weighed down with worry, he went up Back Lane [now St Thomas's Road] into the fields one day, just beside Brick Plat, where he happened to meet a friend from Zion chapel who gave him a ten pound note. He says when the friend had gone he went aside into the fields and had such a sight of the mercy and faithfulness of his God and again felt the force of the words, 'Abide in this city, for I have much people here,' and, 'Thy bread shall be given thee, and thy water shall be sure.' Very quickly he was able to pay his debts.

But he soon found it necessary to tell the deacons at the Church that the financial pressures were very great, and ask them to pay his rent for his house in Brick Plat, in addition to his salary. This they agreed to do and the Church records show that they paid £11.10s on 25th March and on 29th September 1818, and also the same again on 25th March 1819. But the Church at Zion were themselves in a difficult situation. The financial balance for the Church at the end of 1818 was 2s and at the end of 1819, 6s.

So in 1818 the deacons, Samuel Hurd, William Chapman and William Eacott came to Brick Plat one day to tell Warburton that to pay his rent, was more than the Church could afford. Their plan was that he should pay his own rent and the Church would give him two months in each year to go away and preach in other churches, one month in the Spring and one month in the Autumn. They would pay the ministers that took his place while he was away. This he agreed to do, though he began to be tempted that a similar situation was arising as at Rochdale, where their affection would cool and he would soon be unwanted. But it must be remembered that the Trowbridge people were for the most part poor, and the Church debt was very heavy.

About five weeks after this meeting with the deacons, Warburton received a letter,[1] dated 28th May 1818, from London, inviting him to supply for a few Lord's days for his old friend and brother, Mr Edmund Robins [former Pastor of York Street Chapel, Bath, 1811-1815], who preached at Conway Street Chapel to a number of William Huntington's former hearers, who had separated from New Providence Church after Huntington's death on 1st July 1813. Warburton was rather

---

[1] *Gospel Standard* 1873, pp. 410 – 412.

1. Hope Chapel, Rochdale

2. Site of first Meeting Room on Wicker Hill, Trowbridge.

3. Warburton's home, Park Lane, Stand

The first home in Trowbridge, in the Halve.

4. Brick Plat, Trowbridge.

Yerbury Street, Trowbridge.

5. The Cottage at Trowle Common, Trowbridge.

6. Ladydown Mill & Bird's Coal Wharf, The Canal

7. The Coach Road, Marlborough to Devizes & Milestones.

Roundstone Street, Trowbridge

Devizes - Beckhampton

8. Downgate

Waterloo Terrace [No.31, 2nd from right]

anxious about going to London to preach to such a congregation. He had preached to them once before, and had not felt very much at ease. However, remembering his interview with William Huntington in 1812, he felt he would accept. Their pastor was seriously ill, and William Gadsby was preaching five Sundays for them from 17th May until Sunday 21st June. Their request was that Warburton would come for Sunday 28th June and pay them 'another visit.'

He says that as he set off by coach, he was anxious. 'All the journey from home to London was with tears, cries and prayers that God would be with me; all the way from London home again was nothing but praises and thanksgiving at His goodness and mercy in giving me a door of utterance and opening the hearts of his people to communicate to my necessities.' *Piggots Directory* [1822-3] shows that the London coach left the George Inn, Trowbridge, in the Market Place at 4pm every Sunday, Tuesday and Thursday and went via Devizes, Marlborough and Reading to London, taking about 13 hours. The milestone, in Roundstone Street, Trowbridge, told the traveller that it was 99 miles to London. The road was clearly marked with milestones many of which still survive on the road from Devizes to the A4 on its west side, and are also to be seen along the A4 [The Great Bath Road] to Marlborough on its north side.

Another letter [2] dated July 1818 written by the Conway Street Church deacon, J. Gautrey, to William Gadsby explains that John Warburton had come to London and had preached for two Sundays. 'He has been well received in His Master's Name here, and the word has been blessed to many. Although the weather has been and is so very hot, the place is full as it well can hold. There has been a collection for the Church at Trowbridge.' In fact that collection had amounted to £52; added to which Warburton had been given ten pounds by a friend for himself. The Zion Church records show that Mr Handsforth, the pastor of the Old Baptist Chapel Devizes, and Mr Knights had each supplied one Sunday at Zion, and were paid £1 each. The

---

[2] *Gospel Standard* 1874. pp. 104-106.

Church accounts at Zion show that William Hayward was paid back on 28th August 1818 £100 of his £500 loan. Part of this obviously came from the Conway Street Chapel collection.

No doubt John Warburton travelled on top of the coach as he come home, on that hot July day in 1818, from London, down the Great Bath Road, and was aware of the possibility of highway robbery as he carried the £62 home for his chapel and family debts. Highwaymen executed at Devizes after the Assizes were hung in the gibbet at Cherhill between Calne and Beckhampton on the Great Bath Road. The letter to William Gadsby also reveals that Warburton had been into Kent to preach for two Sundays while in London. Mr Gautrey told Gadsby, 'Warburton is heartily sick of his Kentish journey.' It is possible he had been to Maidstone. Warburton says in his *Mercies*, 'O the pleasure and joy that I felt when I got home, that I could go and discharge most of the debts that had bound me up so fast, and which, about a month or six weeks before, I believed, would be my ruin.'

The Conway Street Church eventually built themselves a new Chapel in Gower Street, London, which was opened on 9th July 1820. Henry Fowler became their pastor on 1st January 1821 and stayed until his death on 16th December 1838. The Chapel cost £4,000, of which £1,400 was borrowed on mortgage. From 1820 onward John Warburton and William Gadsby regularly preached for them for a month each year, when two special collections were taken, realising about £120-£130 annually to defray the interest on the mortgage and the cost of the ground rent. Here was the commencement of a wider ministry for Warburton, which helped him towards overcoming the financial difficulties at home in his Church and the family; and at the same time allowed many more people to hear his ministry in London and other parts of the country.

These were difficult years in the country, both locally and nationally. The aftermath of the Napoleonic wars which ended in 1815, brought large numbers of servicemen home from the Army and Navy, with little prospect of finding work. The progress of the Industrial Revolution with its very gradual transposition of work from the home to the factory, especially as it concerned the North and the West, had resulted in unrest among the working people. A combination of bad harvests and the effects of the Corn Laws passed in 1815 to protect the farmers, resulted in erratic movements in the price of wheat and therefore of bread. Wheat priced at 52s 6d a quarter [4.5 cwt] in January 1816, giving a price for a 4lb loaf of 7.5d, then due to a severe winter followed by a bad harvest in 1816, rose to 111s 6d a quarter in June 1817, resulting in the price of a 4lb loaf rising to 15.5d. Here was one of the reasons for Warburton's debts as he attempted to feed a family of twelve. As he used to express it, 'The cost of provisions was high.'

Hunger, debt, and the prospect of unemployment had already had its effects in Trowbridge. Every time Warburton walked through the Parish Churchyard on his way from Brick Plat to the Market Place, he passed the grave of Thomas Hilliker, a lad of nineteen, who had been hung at Salisbury for supposedly taking part in the burning of Littleton Mill on Whaddon Brook, just to the east of Trowbridge on the Devizes Road. Shearing frames had been installed there in 1802 to be run by water power. The Trowbridge shearmen, fearing unemployment, because of mechanisation, had gone out on the night of 21st July 1802 and attacked the Mill and burnt it to the ground. Hilliker fitted the description of one seen at the riot, and though many thought he was innocent, he was hung after his trial in 1803. His fellow shearmen went to Salisbury, brought his body back to Trowbridge and buried him in the Parish Churchyard, erecting a costly gravestone to his memory, which is still beautifully maintained to day.

A similar destruction of machinery, seen in the Trowbridge area in 1802, had been already witnessed by Warburton in 1811, when he was pastor at Rochdale, in the Luddite riots in Lancashire, Yorkshire, Derbyshire, Nottinghamshire and Leicestershire. On 2nd December 1816, a riot started in London known as the Spa Field Riot, in which an attempt was made to seize the Tower, but it failed. On 28th January 1817, the Prince Regent's coach was attacked and the windows smashed as he was returning from the State Opening of Parliament. The King, George III, was insane, so his son had been appointed Regent in his place. The Regent himself was a dissolute man living apart from his spouse, Queen Caroline.

The Government reacted through the Home Secretary, Lord Sidmouth, [A street was named after him in Devizes, near Trowbridge, by the law-abiding corn merchants, who feared unrest, and supported the Government] by suspending Habeas Corpus throughout 1817, so they could arrest and detain suspects for long periods without trial.

In March 1817 a large body of Lancashire workers set out to walk to London to protest to the Prince Regent at the suspension of Habeas Corpus, each carrying a blanket. It was known as the March of the Blanketeers. It was stopped at Stockport and many were arrested. But then came a mass meeting in St Peter's Fields, Manchester [right beside Mosley Street, which Warburton knew so well], in August 1819. 50,000 to 100,000 people gathered to hear Orator Hunt, a Wiltshire farmer, speak on the question of political reform, and the great injustice suffered by the poor. The meeting was declared illegal. The magistrates tried to send the yeomanry to arrest the speaker, and when this failed, panicked and sent the 15th Hussars, who charged the crowd on horseback with drawn sabres. The result was eleven dead and 400 injured, with seventy taken to hospital, the injured lying in 'several mounds.'

The country was enraged at what became known as 'The Peterloo Massacre.' Warburton, Gadsby and Kershaw in their respective homes at Trowbridge, Manchester and Rochdale must have been deeply angered by the whole event, in an area which they all knew. William Gadsby must have had eye-witness accounts of the massacre from members of his congregation. [In that same year, Gadsby had already helped the poor hand loom weavers of Manchester in petitioning Parliament for a repeal of the Corn Laws.] The reaction of the Prime Minister, Lord Liverpool and his Home Secretary, Viscount Sidmouth, together with the approval of the Prince Regent, was to pass The Six Acts restricting public meetings, allowing magistrates to search for arms, and putting a duty on pamphlets similar to the duty on newspapers. These measures were not exceptionally severe, but they demonstrated that the Government feared some sort of revolution. In February 1820,The Cato Street Conspiracy was exposed by an informer, which was a plot to assassinate Cabinet ministers at a dinner in

London, and seize the Bank of England. Five conspirators were hung and five transported.

The country was in turmoil, politically, socially and economically. All moderate people wanted Parliamentary reform, to increase the number with a right to vote and bring in reforms through Parliament. At least eleven of Warburton's congregation at Zion Chapel were on the Electoral Register of 1818 [in the Poll Book], including Samuel Hurd, William Eacott and William Hayward. John Warburton himself appears [in the Poll Book] on the Electoral register of 1819, after he had moved to live in Brick Plat. Wiltshire had two MPs before 1832, which were elected on a very limited franchise. It is surprising therefore to find the Lancashire weaver's name in the Poll Book, though it must be remembered that his salary of £3 a week, paid by Zion Church, was quite substantial compared with local manual workers in 1819, and his rent for the house in Brick Plat, which was being paid by the Church in 1818 and the first half of 1819, amounted to £23 a year.

The year 1819 was marked in the Warburton family in Brick Plat by two weddings, within a week of each other. The first to marry was Sarah. She married John Earle on 22nd March at the Parish Church of St James, Trowbridge, with its beautiful spire, the second highest in the country to Salisbury Cathedral. She lived to see it come down and be rebuilt in 1846, as it came down again in the hurricane, in recent years. She was twenty-one and was married for nearly thirty-four years, her husband dying five days before the thirty-fourth anniversary of their marriage, on 17th March 1853. Her brother James married Martha Edwards on 28th March 1819 at the Parish Church in the presence of her father's deacon William Eacott and William Nightingale, the parish clerk. At neither wedding was John Warburton himself a witness, though this is probably explained by the fact that at that time weddings were very low key affairs. What is clear is that both Warburton's daughter, Sarah, and James's wife Martha were unable to write, and so put their 'mark'[x] on the register.

James Warburton was a weaver like his father and the family lived for many years after their marriage in Shail's Lane, Trowbridge. He had two sons, John, named after his grandfather, born 19th November 1819, and James born 1st January 1825. John became a weaver and James was a dyer. Their mother, Martha died in 1868 and their father in 1874. The family are all buried in Trowbridge cemetery just a few yards away from John Warburton senior's grave, and not far from Sarah Earle.

1820 was a year that John Warburton never forgot. In it he suffered one of the greatest, if not *the* greatest sorrow of his life. He says that his little girl, Rhoda, had just turned three years old at the time, so this dates the month as August or September of that year. He was about to leave Trowbridge and go on one of his monthly preaching tours to Wallingford, [between Reading and Oxford] London and Brighton. He had allowed his little girl Rhoda to become the great idol of his life. Being the youngest, and having had sorrow with his eldest girl, she had become his favourite. Like Jacob and his favourite Joseph, the Lord was about to move in his life. In his *Mercies* he describes the circumstances as he left Brick Plat to go to the George Inn in the Market Place to board the stage coach,

> O how my very soul was knit to that child! Everything it either said or did was beautiful in my eyes and pleasant to my feelings. My dear wife often told me that she was sure I should be stripped of that child, and quite wondered I made such work about it. When I left home, the dear little girl kissed me, and bade me goodbye, and a second time followed me into the passage [Brick Plat], calling, 'Father do give me another kiss;' and after I got to the door, she came again with tears in her beautiful eyes, 'Father do give me one more kiss,' and looking with such an anxious look as pierced my very heart, she said, 'Father shall I ever see you again?' O how this cut my very soul, and into my feelings like a dagger. I was obliged however to leave the child and family, and all the way down the street [Union Street] I could not help weeping, fearing I should never see the child again in this world; and, true enough, it was the case, for I never saw her more.[3]

[3] John Warburton, op. cit., p. 139.

He travelled to Wallingford, to preach and stay with his friend, Thomas Clowes, and then to London, where he received letters from home to say Rhoda was not well. His prayer was constantly that the Lord would spare the child. He went down on the stage coach from London to Brighton and the morning after he arrived in Brighton a letter came for him, sealed with black. When he opened it, it was to say that Rhoda had died, and that night he was due to preach in Brighton. In the midst of all his sorrows he was given his text, 'Heaviness in the heart of man maketh it stoop, but a good word maketh it glad.' [Proverbs 12.25.] He was helped to preach in the face of all his grief and then took coach the next day for Trowbridge. When he arrived home [Oct. 1820] the funeral was over and Rhoda had been buried in the minister's grave 'in the front of the chapel under the footpath nearest the door.' She was three years and three months old, and his home was desolate. But in his sorrow he felt the Lord speak in his soul, 'Be still and know that I am God.' [Ps. 46.10] Now a calm descended on his soul and he adds, 'Not a rebellious thought moved its tongue.' Then he could say with Job, 'The Lord gave, and the Lord hath taken away; blessed be the name of the Lord.' [Job 1.21.] The first child he had lost, in 1798, had not caused him such a degree of sorrow and he had thought it was a comparatively light matter and he says, 'I have given many a poor child of God some hard blows because they fretted against God in taking their children.' Now the Lord had dealt with him in a way which had mellowed him and would make him a more useful minister. Equally, Lydia, his wife had passed through a harrowing experience in losing the child while he was away. No doubt the deacons and members of the Church, such as William Hayward, who lived a few yards away in Union Street, turned to help her arrange the funeral. Also there was, James, her married son aged twenty, John Earle, her son-in-law and his wife Sarah, Elizabeth, her daughter aged eighteen, and the other children, Leah 16, Rachel 14, Gideon 12, Manoah 9, Ruth 7 and John 5.

The sight outside Zion Chapel that day, as they laid little Rhoda to rest in her grave under the main pathway into the chapel, with all Warburton's family gathered around [but her father absent], must have been a fairly common sight at that time. Although there had been a dramatic drop in the infant mortality rate, which between 1700-1750 had stood at 75% of children, dying before the age of six, now between 1800-1820, it still stood at 40%, dying before the age of six. The improvement was largely due to better roads, enabling more meat and milk to reach the towns, less scurvy, and better farming methods. But in Trowbridge sanitary conditions were bad and the water supply was from wells, whose source was often polluted.

Now in that Autumn of 1820 John Warburton had a sight of the significance of the hymn of the poet, William Cowper, of which the first line is, 'God moves in a mysterious way.'

> Ye fearful saints, fresh courage take;
> The clouds ye so much dread
> Are big with mercy, and shall break
> In blessings on your head.

He says in his *Mercies,*

> 'O the blessings that broke through these clouds that I had so much dreaded. I can never tell a thousandth part of them, for there broke forth a blessing that I had prayed for, for nearly twenty years; I mean the salvation of my dear wife. When the dear Lord first set my soul at happy liberty, how her soul was laid upon my mind! O the wrestling that I had with the Lord that He would be pleased to open her eyes.'[4]

He goes on to record that at times in prayer, it was as though he already had the answer and assurance that he was heard, but at other times he felt it would never come to pass. About 1804, when they had five small children and his wife was carrying one at the breast [probably Leah, born 16th April 1804], [also the year in which he was baptised and joined Back Lane Baptist Chapel, Manchester], his wife had a bad fit and in spite of his many prayers for her recovery she continued to have a series of them. It caused him deep anxiety as he feared he

---

[4] John Warburton, op. cit. p.143.

would not be able to cope with his family and have to put them in the workhouse.

He records in his *Mercies* how one night returning from a prayer meeting to their home in Narrow Lane, Besses- o'- th'- Barn, through the fields, he fell down on the ground and wrestled with the Lord.

> I told Him that I must either have my request or die on the spot; when these words came to my mind, 'Let me go for the day breaketh;' [Gen. 32. 26.] but my soul cried out and my mouth too, 'I will not let Thee go, except Thou bless me.' [Gen. 32.26.] ... By and by He came with such glory, 'Be it unto thee even as thou wilt.'[Matt. 15.28.].... My poor soul answered Him with such humility, 'Lord my request is that my dear wife have no more fits.......' He answered me with such a smile, 'It is done as thou hast requested.' O what confidence I felt that God had heard and answered my cries.[5]

He returned home late that night and told his wife that she would never have another fit. Her response was, 'I wish you may tell true.' He adds in his *Mercies,* 'It is now between thirty and forty years ago, and she has never had one fit since.' Following this answer to prayer for her health, Warburton again felt great liberty in prayer that the Lord would open her eyes. She thought that her husband was far too religious. She told him that he went to preaching and prayer meetings enough for twenty people. Her religion was that if people would mind their families, and do their duty, and trust to the mercy of God, it was quite enough. The words of Christ, 'Except a man be born again, he cannot see the kingdom of God,' [John 3.3.] were meaningless to her.

Warburton says that after he returned from Brighton in October 1820, he saw a great difference in his wife, but thought it was the result of their bereavement, until one day she burst into tears before him and said, 'I am lost, I am lost for ever.' He asked her if it was connected with the loss of Rhoda, but she assured him it was not, and added, 'It is my never-dying soul

---

[5] John Warburton, op. cit. pp. 145, 146.

that will be lost for ever.' When he asked how such thoughts had ever come into her heart, she told him that just before he had left home and before Rhoda had become ill, he had preached at Zion concerning the awfulness of the ungodly being cut down in their sins, and the awful eternity that these poor souls would have to suffer... and came out with this word three times, 'O eternity, eternity, eternity!' She told him it had entered her heart like a sword and she saw, and felt that she was one who must endure eternal wrath for ever and ever. Warburton says, 'O the joy that entered my heart when she told me these feelings.' Lydia Warburton walked in great spiritual darkness for some long time, but a day came, when under her husband's ministry, as he was preaching at Zion from Ephesians 3. 18,19, 'May be able to comprehend with all saints what is the breadth, and length, and depth, and height, and to know the love of Christ which passeth knowledge,' the Lord blotted out all her iniquities as a thick cloud and she came out of Zion Chapel that day with her heart full of joy and peace. Warburton says, 'What struck me with wonder above all the rest, was that He should make use of my poor mouth to pluck her out of the devil's kingdom, and likewise to lift her soul from off the dunghill, and set her among the princes of His people.'

Warburton records that when this took place that the family 'lived out of town.' He says in his *Mercies*, 'We then lived out of the town, and generally called at one of our deacon's houses for a short time after the evening service before we went home.' He describes how the deacon's wife asked Mrs Warburton to come to tea with her on the following Tuesday, before the evening service. She replied, 'If the Lord enables me.' Warburton in his blunt way, knowing in what soul darkness she had been, said, 'How can you think of coming on Tuesday evening? What is there for you? You say you are out of the secret.' To his amazement she responded, 'Bless the Lord! I know what it is to feel the love of God, and I am sure that I am one of those that are interested in the love of God, for I feel its preciousness in my heart.' Then Warburton knew that the day had come, for which he had waited twenty years.

This dates her soul deliverance to the period that they were at Trowle Common, which was between May 1821 and

February 1822. The Church Book shows that she was baptised shortly afterwards by her husband, together with her son-in-law John Earle and twenty-two others, at Ladydown Mill on 21st July 1822, and what a day it must have been for Warburton as he took her down into the waters. There were all her children there to watch the sacred scene on that July day with a great congregation to hear Warburton preach, and perhaps it was on this occasion that her two daughters, Sarah and Elizabeth, felt led to follow in their mother's footsteps, which they did at the same place the next year, on 13th July 1823, together with sixteen others. John Warburton junior, the youngest son, in a letter written in April 1891 to a friend in New York U.S.A., says, 'Zion Chapel was built in 1816, and I, myself, have some faint remembrance of my father baptising at Ladydown Mill.'[6] He would have been within ten days of his seventh birthday at the time of his mother's baptising.

Now all was peace and happiness in Warburton's home as he and his wife walked together in a union they had never known before. But within a short while Mrs Warburton was tempted as to the reality of all she had felt in her soul and a great darkness of unbelief settled in her heart. In it she began to criticize Warburton's preaching and took offence at one of his expressions in the pulpit, 'devil-dragged.' She described it as crude, and told him that in all her reading and hearing of other ministers, such as Huntington and Gadsby, she had never heard them use such common expressions.

Then she decided to go one week evening and hear a minister at another church in Trowbridge, probably Mr Macfarlane at Back Street, Baptist chapel. When Warburton asked her how she had got on, she replied, she preferred 'devil-dragging.' Later Warburton preached from, 'For the oppression of the poor, for the sighing of the needy, now will I arise, saith the Lord; I will set him in safety from him that puffeth at him.' [Ps.12.5.] That sermon was made such a blessing to her soul

---

[6] *Memorials of the late John Warburton of Southill*, Publ. F. Kirby, London, 1892. pp. 233.

that she never again was critical of her husband's ministry, but now realised a little in her own heart, that Satan's temptations were a reality in the heart of every child of God, to teach them that without Christ they can do nothing, and with Him they can do everything.

While his wife was suffering temptation so was Warburton himself. When he returned from Brighton in October 1820 his finances in the family were in a crisis situation once more. He lists the causes and names school bills, rent, taxes, clothing and provisions, which were very dear at the time. He also mentions the fact that the children were now 'men and women at the table.' In fact at the turn of the year 1820/1821 Elizabeth was 19, Leah 16, Rachel 14, Gideon 12, Manoah 9, Ruth 7, and John 5.

Although there is no accurate knowledge of the height of Warburton, various references suggest that he was a big man, probably at least six feet tall, and if this is so, it is quite probable that his family were following him in height. It is clear from various pictures, that his son, John, later grew to be tall. J.C. Philpot, who wrote about Warburton senior, and describes his 'weighty foot' and 'fine portly person' and 'commanding look,' was himself well over six feet tall. So Warburton's family, no doubt, had good appetites. They certainly grew to be strong and healthy. Of the twelve, four lived to be over eighty and three over seventy. Only two died in childhood. One granddaughter, the youngest child of John junior, died in February 1961 at the age of 101, making an amazing span of time from the birth of her grandfather in 1776 to her own death in 1961 of 185 years for three generations.

At the end of 1820 Warburton was looking for an easy way out of his financial troubles, when one appeared on the horizon, in the shape of a house to let, out in the countryside to the north of Trowbridge, at a place known as Trowle Common. It was an extensive thatched cottage with a large yard, common land nearby on which to graze one or two cows, and a good sized orchard, as well as garden. For Warburton it seemed an ideal way of reducing his expenses, growing his own potatoes and vegetables, fattening his own meat, keeping cows and pigs, making a little money in selling some things, and giving his family a fit and healthy life away from the cramped quarters in Brick Plat, with its poor sanitation and bad water supply.

He went to survey the place and met Thomas Rumming, Licensed Malster, the owner. [The thatched cottage is now demolished, but the Malt House to the rear is still there and is now a dwelling. The present owner is a direct descendant, and retains the family name, Rumming.] This meeting must have taken place in the late Spring of 1821 for by May, Warburton was ready to leave Brick Plat and go up onto the higher, open ground of Trowle Common, away from the smoke and grim of the Trowbridge factories, with its lovely views extending to the south, ten miles toward Salisbury Plain, and toward the north over Bradford-on-Avon and on to the hills around Bath. Knowing the area well, it is easy to see the attraction for Warburton, who had lived in the countryside at both Stand and Narrow Lane, Besses-o'-th' -Barn.

It is interesting to know that on Trowle Common an hundred years earlier, there had lived a Baptist and his family, Thomas Cator. His daughter Anne, had married William Steele, the Baptist minister of Broughton in Hampshire, and become stepmother to his daughter, the hymn writer, Anne Steele, who was at Trowbridge at school in 1729, at the age of twelve, and no doubt was often on Trowle Common herself at the home of her step- grandparents. Old Thomas Cator died in 1733 at the age of eighty-two. Also Anne Steele's pastor at Broughton in her later life, 1771-1778, was Nathaniel Rawlings, who had been pastor at Back Street Chapel, and whose 41 members now formed the nucleus of Warburton's congregation. So it is quite likely Warburton was aware of Anne Steele's connections with Trowle Common.

All Warburton's closest friends and his wife warned him that he was making a foolish move. His wife told him, 'I am confident whatever you take in hand, except preaching the Gospel, will never prosper, for I believe you must live upon the Gospel.' Here is manifest the new found grace in her heart,that now faithfully warned him, whereas up till 1820, she would have considered that he was over-occupied with religion. Here also is seen the strong vein of stubbornness and obstinacy in his nature. Against all advice, he pressed on and says that it turned out that she was right, but he himself would not admit it until he had proved it. [It is interesting that A.B.Taylor, who succeeded William Gadsby as Pastor at Back Lane Chapel, Manchester in 1848, later took a little farmhouse called Moss Cottage, at Middleton, where he kept a few cows and carried on a small farm.][7] But for Warburton the move proved to be nothing else but wrong, and everything he put his hand to failed utterly. He borrowed £20 and went to market and bought fifteen pigs to put out on the Common. When he had fattened them and tried to sell them the market price was such that all profit had gone. So he kept them and bought barley to fatten them further. When he eventually sold them the price was barely a third of what he had hoped he would get. When after about six months he took stock, he found that he was forty pounds deeper in debt than when he was living in Brick Plat. He says that in the eventual winding of it all up, 'I thought I must have been turned on the Common myself.'

The pigs were a hopeless venture, the potatoes rotted in the ground, the apples in the orchard were a failure. How he got through his preaching for several months he did not know. His heart was full of anger against God and man; everything was wrong in the house, and the pigs often got out of the sty into the garden in front of the cottage and routed out the few potatoes and cabbages left there. One Saturday night they escaped into the garden several times while he was reading his Bible seeking a text for the next day. When news reached him that they were out in the garden again, he says. 'O, thinks I, the very devil must be in the swine; and I believe he was not very far from them when I got near them...... How I got through the preaching the following day I cannot tell.'

In the midst of all his trouble the Lord began to teach him. The words were applied to his heart, 'Do ye not know that they which minister about holy things live of the things of the temple? and that they which wait at the altar are partakers with the altar? Even so hath the Lord ordained that they which

---

[7] *Further History of Gospel Standard Baptists*, Vol. 4, S.F.Paul, 1961, pp. 26, 27.

preach the gospel should live of the gospel.' [1 Cor. 9. 13,14.] Another word used to teach him was, 'No man that warreth entangleth himself with the affairs of this life; that he may please Him that hath chosen him to be a soldier.' [2 Tim. 2.4.] The questions in Scripture came to him, 'Who goeth a warfare anytime at his own charges?' [1Cor. 9.7.] and, 'Doth God take care for oxen?' [1 Cor. 9. 9.] 'When I sent you without purse and scrip and shoes, lacked ye anything? and they said, Nothing.' [Luke 22. 35] Warburton knew, in answer to the last question, he must respond, 'Nothing, Lord.' And so as he sat under the apple tree in his garden a blessed change came over him and in quietness he prayed for the Lord to make a way to leave Trowle Common.

At the end of January 1822, two months to rent day, when he owed £22, after he had been there about ten months, a man came out from Trowbridge to ask if he could take over the property; to which Warburton readily agreed. He wanted to come in soon to get the ground sown in the Spring and wanted Warburton and his family out within two weeks. Warburton went into Trowbridge and found a house standing empty in Yerbury Street,[8] owned by Thomas Jarvis a clothier from Bratton. He says, 'In about a week we moved and took possession of our habitation.' It was relatively new-built, about 1793.

Then came the reckoning up of his debts. It appeared impossible to pay them. But some of the members of the church had a collection for him and collected about £20. Then a letter came one morning, the postage costing 1s-11d, and it was from William Gadsby from Manchester and contained a £10 note. At that moment Warburton had a £10 debt waiting payment at once. He describes how it made him go to his bedroom and get on his knees and thank the Lord. Gadsby had in fact been given £20 for him, but had kept ten pounds to discharge debts still existing in Manchester and Rochdale. He says, 'I was brought to a settled point in one thing at Trowle Common, that God was

---

[8] *Trowbridge Poor Rate Books*, 1822, 1823, 1824.

determined I should live by the gospel. He concludes with the words, 'Necessity is laid in me to vindicate a feeling religion.'

Chapter 10

The wind bloweth

The wind bloweth where it listeth, and thou hearest the sound thereof, but canst not tell whence it cometh, and whither it goeth: so is every one that is born of the Spirit. [John 3. 8.]

Warburton knew these words of Christ well. In his heart, their fulfilment was at the centre of his ministry. Since his arrival in Trowbridge on the first Sunday in April 1815, his ministry had been greatly blessed. The wind of the Spirit had blown where it listed, and he had seen its spiritual fruits. In August and November 1815, he had baptised sixteen, and received thirteen into his Church. In 1816 four more had been received and in 1817 he had baptised eight and received another five. These baptisings of August and November 1815, and of April 1817 had probably taken place in the Canal at Hilperton Marsh, which was used by John Dymott and the members of his Baptist Church in Hilperton. This was at Mr Bird's Coal Wharf, where the coal from Radstock coal mines was off-loaded from the barges for transport by horse and cart to the Cloth Factories in Trowbridge, to fire the steam engines. By 1820 Trowbridge had at least a dozen large steam- driven factories, beside other workshops with smaller steam engines.

When on 2nd October 1818, Warburton wrote to his friends at Conway Street Chapel, London, to thank them for their kindness to him in his visit to them in May and June that year, he was able to tell them, 'The Lord appears to be with us at Trowbridge. We have an addition to our Church, since I came home, of nine persons, and six of them God owned poor me as the unworthy instrument of bringing to happy liberty.'[1] The Zion Church Book records that on 4th October, for the first time in the history of their Church, the baptising of these nine people, by John Warburton, took place at Ladydown Mill.

This was a Fulling Mill for the Cloth Trade on the lowest stretch of the River Biss, before it joined the River Avon. It was not far from Zion Chapel, being approached from Down Gate, along Canal Road, on the northern side of Trowbridge. It was owned by the Elton family of Bristol and let to Edward Franklin. When he died in 1817 it was probably let to William Franklin. In 1828 it changed ownership when it was bought by William Stancomb.[2] The name Franklin appears in the membership of Zion Church and also in the Burial Register of Zion Chapel. It is possible that William Franklin or his relatives attended Zion Chapel. Warburton was allowed to use it once a year from 1818 to 1823 when permission was withdrawn, probably due to the fact that a change in ownership was in sight. It had been put up for sale in 1817 but had not sold.

Here in the mill pond, beside the old Fulling Mill, which dated back to 1726, with the gently rising ground ascending gradually from the meadows, either side of the River Biss, John Warburton came with his church and congregation to lead them publicly in the ordinance of believer's baptism, which Christ had instituted, when He had Himself been baptised by John the Baptist in the River Jordan. What an exact example it was of the teaching of Christ. A visible witness before the whole community in which they lived, that they were now followers of Jesus Christ and were ready to take up their cross and follow Him. A few hundred yards away to the north on its embankment, with its aqueduct over the River Biss, ran the Kennet-Avon Canal, with its constant procession of horse-

[1] *The Gospel Standard* 1874 pp. 232-234.

[2] *Wiltshire & Somerset Woollen Mills,* K.Rogers, 1976, pp. 147, 148.

drawn barges. In a letter dated 5th November 1822 [3], John Warburton says, 'We are going on at Trowbridge very well. I believe the Lord is with us, and is blessing His word abundantly. We are quite crowded with people, there being not much less than a thousand.'

If this was indeed the number of his regular congregation, then at these baptising services, its seems likely that there was at least double that number, as many of the towns people would have come out from Trowbridge to watch the baptising. Zion Church had a choir and precentor, who led the singing in their normal services in Zion, and it would have been customary for them to have a normal service at the waterside, with reading of the Scriptures, a prayer and a sermon of an hour by John Warburton, as well as the singing of several hymns. *The Trowbridge Advertiser* for 10th April 1857 records that at the funeral of John Warburton in Trowbridge cemetery on Good Friday 9th April, an estimated congregation of two thousand, led by Mr William Keats and Zion Chapel Choir, sang the six verses of Hymn 468 of *Gadsby's Selection* [The hymnbook used at Zion Chapel], beginning, 'Death is no more a frightful foe, Since I with Christ shall reign.' If this was the practice then, it is certain that in their baptising services at Ladydown Mill, Zion people would have been used to singing, prayer and preaching in the open air. Such services were common place in the eighteenth century in the days of George Whitefield, who regularly for over thirty years preached in the open air. Warburton had himself seen such congregational worship in the North when William Gadsby often preached in the open.

The Church Book records these annual events over several years. The first such occasion at Ladydown Mill was on 4th October 1818, when nine were baptised. There was no baptising there in 1819, but on 25th June 1820 twenty-three people were baptised by John Warburton, one of whom was Richard Knee, who was elected a deacon in 1825 and died in 1864. On 23rd September 1821 nine people were baptised at Ladydown by John Dymott the pastor of the chapel at

---

[3] *Gospel Standard* 1853, pp. 207-209.

Hilperton. For some reason unknown, John Warburton was unable to conduct the service himself. On 21st July 1822, the following year, John Warburton baptised twenty-four new members of his Church, which included his own wife Lydia and his son-in-law John Earle, husband of Sarah. On 13th July 1823 was the last occasion when Zion Chapel used the Weir pool at Ladydown, and on this occasion John Warburton baptised eighteen, including two of his own daughters, Sarah Earle, and Elizabeth Warburton, who later married John Hayward, who became a director of Salter's Cloth Mill.

No contemporary record of these remarkable gatherings survives, so far as is known. No newspaper seemed to regard them as sufficiently significant to comment. But records tell us something about John Warburton. In the *Historical Account of Zion Chapel* published in 1913 to commemorate the centenary of the Church, its says, [p.20],

> 'There are still those among us who are now Church members, but who in 'Old John's' time were but thoughtless youths, who still remember the good old man, and his solemn, clear and incisive style of preaching, and how at each service the Chapel was so filled with worshippers that every seat, was occupied and at the evening service seats had to be placed in the aisles. Also what a charm there seemed to be in his wonderful voice which was so clear and strong that every syllable could be heard without effort.'

These words tell something of the services in the valley at Ladydown Mill as Warburton's clear, strong voice rang out from the water's edge and carried all round the large crowd, while he preached the Gospel of Christ. Warburton was then aged between forty-two and forty-seven, a strong man, over six feet tall and preaching the Gospel from the fullness of his heart. What an evangelist he was as his ministry reached out to the hearts of his own people and to the hearts of those who never went inside his chapel. How many a heart must have been touched by his homely, warm-hearted preaching of the Gospel, so real to him in the experience of it in his own soul. He spoke as one that had authority like his Lord and Master, Christ. And it was quite easy afterwards to creep into Zion Chapel, lost in the crowd of his hearers, and sit unnoticed, to find out more about the truths he preached. Possibly one or two of the godly noticed a new hearer, for the town was not large and it was a very close community. [In 1811 the population was about 5,800, and in 1821 it had increased to about 9,500.] The decade, from 1815 - 1825, with its open-air preaching was blessed of the Lord in the fulfilment of His promise to Warburton that night in March 1815, as he led him to come to Trowbridge, 'I have much people in this city.' Warburton's congregation included a substantial number of the inhabitants of Trowbridge, and he himself would have been a well-known figure in the town.

The town itself was increasing at the same time as Warburton's congregation was growing. *The Book of Trowbridge* [1984] by K. Rogers, details that expansion, and shows that when the congregation of Warburton made its way to Ladydown Mill in the years from 1818 to 1823 it was passing along newly built streets and by new areas of housing. A wide, hygienic, new street, called Timbrell Street, had been built after 1814 in front of Zion Chapel leading out of the town to the north [replacing Frog Lane], via Islington, Down Gate and Canal Road to Ladydown Mill and Staverton. Off it, to each side was a large area of development including Cross Street, Thomas Street, Charlotte Buildings, Prospect Place and York Buildings, all built just after the Napoleonic wars, in which many of Warburton's congregation and some of his own family were to find homes for themselves. Other streets that were developed included Castle Street, Court Street, Mortimer Street [1821].

The town had seen at the end of the eighteenth century the building of several large houses such as Bellefield House [1794] on the main road out to Devizes, and Rodney House [1789] in Roundstone Street, beautiful stone-built, Georgian houses in the Bath style. Also in 1794 the Cavalry Barracks had been built on the Frome side of the town for the Army. They were later sold at the end of the Napoleonic Wars, but repurchased by the Army at the time of the Chartist risings in 1839. Later in 1819 two large houses were built in Hilperton Road, Sunnyside, and the house, now the Hilbury Court Hotel. Near to Zion Chapel, in Union Street, a lovely terrace of

Georgian Houses was erected about 1815, and called Waterloo Terrace. Warburton was later to live for ten years in one of these houses. So the town continued to develop and by the time of the next National Census in 1831 it had reached nearly 11,000 inhabitants. More Georgian terraces had appeared along Hilperton Road and in Stallard Street opposite Holy Trinity Church, beautifully faced in Bath stone, simple and elegant in style. Between 1817 and 1822 five hundred houses were reported to have been built in Trowbridge and many more were under construction. Equally while there was much real poverty and unemployment among the workpeople, the factories were expanding and working day and night to keep up with demand for cloth.

While Warburton's ministry prospered amidst the industrial activity and expansion of Trowbridge, so he travelled at the same time, to preach the gospel in surrounding towns and villages, and to open churches; sometimes meeting initially in cottages or converted buildings, often at a later date, when they could afford it, building their own chapels. In 1817, within two years of coming to Trowbridge, John Warburton was preaching at Calne on 1st January at the opening of a new Church, calling itself Zion Chapel, which met in a house in Castle Street just in front of the present Zion Chapel. Sixteen members of the Old Baptist Church [the present Castle Street Chapel] had seceded and formed a Church of their own. The reasons for their secession are not altogether clear. One reason was that they could not profit under the ministry of their pastor, Joseph Stennett. The fact that they called upon John Warburton to preach the opening services in the morning and evening [Mr N. Milford in the afternoon], is in itself an indicator of where they stood.

The 'Modern Question', as the teaching of Andrew Fuller was called, was all the talk of the times. Warburton was a noted preacher against it, attacking the Offer of the Gospel, duty faith and duty repentance, and denying that the Law was the Believer's Rule of Life, but rather the Gospel.This was the difference between Somerset Street Chapel in Bath, and York Street. This was the difference between Zion, Trowbridge, and Back Street,Trowbridge. Studley Chapel had been built near

Calne in 1814, by Martha Wiltshire and her friends. Martha Wiltshire stated in her writings, that John Warburton had first preached at Studley in 1813. Both Warburton and Gadsby had preached at Devizes in the period 1814-15. It is clear that Zion Chapel, Calne, was formed for the same doctrinal reasons as Zion, Trowbridge, namely to come away from Fullerite error. Warburton's presence at the opening amply demonstrates this. In 1818, this Church called to the Pastorate, Mr N. Milford, and his ordination services were preached by Mr Handsforth of Devizes. Mr Handsforth was the Pastor of the Old Baptist Church at Devizes from 1813-1819, and Zion Chapel Trowbridge records show that he preached at Trowbridge for Warburton in 1818. So it is quite clear that Devizes Old Baptist; Zion, Calne; and Zion, Trowbridge were united as regards the truth.

Much later in 1837, the Church and congregation at Zion, Calne, built themselves a chapel, the present Zion Chapel, and again they showed where they stood. For the opening services on 17th May, they invited John Warburton and J.C.Philpot; again demonstrating exactly where they stood doctrinally, [though in fact Warburton could not attend and William Cowper of the Dicker, Sussex took his place]. In 1835 the *Gospel Standard* magazine had been started by William Gadsby, and Churches supporting the anti-Fullerite position grouped themselves together and became known as Gospel Standard Baptists. William Gadsby, John Warburton and John Kershaw were the principle architects of this group of Baptist Churches. The situation at Calne is a good example of how this came about. J.C.Philpot, distinguished Editor of the *Gospel Standard*, and John Warburton preached at the Calne Anniversary services in May every year together, until 1856 when through age and ill-health Warburton had to decline.

In 1821 John Warburton found himself in very similar circumstances to Calne, but this time at Melksham. A group of nine people had done, what some had done at Town Meadows in Rochdale in going to hear William Gadsby preach, only this time it was John Warburton. They had according to the Melksham Baptist Church Book, 'absented themselves from their own place and attended an interest commenced by Mr

Warburton of Trowbridge.'[4] The Melksham Church regarded them as supporting 'Antinomians,' and for doing this they were expelled from the Church on 27th May 1821. They approached Mr John Curnick for a place which was formerly a bakehouse, to use the ground floor only, which would seat an hundred. Here they met and invited John Warburton to come over from Trowbridge to preach for them. This he did and soon the place was crowded. Again it is clear, exactly what had happened. The Fullerite error had divided the existing Particular Baptist Church in Melksham under its Pastors Thomas Ward [1797-1818] and John Shoveller [1818-1823]. Thomas Ward had been a student at the Bristol Baptist College under the presidency of John Ryland, and was a friend of Andrew Fuller. The group rejecting Andrew Fuller's error had left to form a new Church. Later in 1835 they built themselves a chapel in Union Street and John Warburton was asked to come over to preach the opening services, which he did. One of the first seceders and founders of the new Church was John Taylor. His grandson, Harry Taylor, joined the Church in 1886 and was chosen deacon in 1894 and held the office until his death in 1944. Here was the foundation of what was later [1835] to be a Gospel Standard Baptist Church.

In 1821 John Warburton was even further afield at Wantage in Berkshire. The Particular Baptist Church there had become divided under their Pastor John West, and a group of people had separated to meet in a house at Grove, just outside Wantage. Among the ministers who they invited to come to them was Edmund Robins of York Street, Bath. Later they built a Chapel at a cost of £250 which was opened in April 1821 by John Warburton and Mr Weldon of Marlborough, a former Sergeant Major in the Army in the Napoleonic Wars. [He preached for Warburton at Zion in 1826.] Again the presence of John Warburton, so disliked and despised by the Fullerite Baptists indicated the position of Grove Chapel at its foundation, as did the presence of Edmund Robins, who was later Pastor at Conway Street Chapel, London. These people

---

[4] *Strict Baptist Chapels of England,* Vol. 5, R.W.Oliver, pp. 50.

were lovers of the works of William Huntington and William Gadsby and welcomed Warburton all the way from Trowbridge to preach for them.

A solid group of churches was building up in the Wiltshire, area, radiating out from York Street, Bath initially, under William Gadsby's influence; taking root under Warburton and John Dymott in the Trowbridge, Hilperton area; spreading out to Devizes under William Gadsby's influence, and moving across to Melksham, Studley, Calne and Grove, near Wantage, through the influence of John Warburton. This was the beginning of the Baptist churches in the West Country, that were later to identify themselves with the Gospel Standard after its inception in 1835. The members of these new churches had seceded from the old Particular Baptist Churches of the eighteenth century in response to the error of Andrew Fuller which had spread widely among them. The Churches they left behind them frequently lost their Calvinism altogether and also their strict communion, and went on in the nineteenth century to cease to believe in Particular Redemption. They eventually formed the General Baptist group of Churches.

One case of such separation in the Trowbridge area is of more than usual interest. This was the case of Hilperton Church. This was formed as a *natural* separation from Back Street Chapel, Trowbridge, by their Pastor Nathaniel Rawlings in 1806. It was the custom of Mr Rawlings to send gifted members of his Church in Back Street, to preach the Gospel in the 'highways and lanes' of Hilperton.[5] The first convert was William Lindsey, who was baptised by Mr Rawlings and joined Back Street in 1797. After nine members had been baptised from Hilperton, in 1806, Mr Rawlings decided to form a Baptist Church and build a chapel there, which was done, the Church being formed on 9th February that year. This Church prospered and on Sunday 2nd August 1807 Mr Dymott baptised seven new members in the Canal [called the New River] at Hilperton Marsh. In 1808 John Dymott received a call to the Pastorate and was ordained Pastor on 7th November 1810. The register of

[5] *Twenty Golden Candlesticks*, W.Doel, 1890, p.142.

baptisms show that eight were baptised in June 1808, five in June 1811, eleven in July 1813, and five in August 1814.

On 20th August 1815, John Warburton baptised fourteen members of the Hilperton Church for John Dymott, almost certainly in the Canal at Hilperton Marsh. Only a week before, on 13th August, he had baptised twelve of his own people. On 13th July 1817 John Dymott baptised five members for his own Church, and on this occasion John Warburton spoke at the water. In September 1818 John Dymott baptised four more members. On 28th July 1822, nine were baptised by John Dymott, and John Warburton preached at the water. This was exactly a week after John Warburton had baptised twenty-four of his own members at Ladydown Mill on 21st July. It would seem possible that Mr Dymott, [who had already baptised for John Warburton in September 1821 at Ladydown Mill,] was baptising his own people there. On 14th September 1823 John Dymott baptised seven more members, when William Eacott, John Warburton's former deacon, who had gone out to preach in 1818, spoke at the water. On the following Monday evening, William Gadsby preached at Hilperton. Zion Church records show that William Gadsby also preached at Zion Chapel, Trowbridge that same September, and that he had previously preached there in September 1821 and on 21st February 1822.

One of the early members of this Hilperton Church was Henry Rawlings, probably some relation of the late Pastor of Back Street. The great interest in this case lies not only in the spiritual prosperity, similar to that at Zion, Trowbridge, but more particularly in the blending between the Zion and Hilperton Churches, considering that Hilperton was a natural offshoot of Back Street under Nathaniel Rawlings. It reveals that these Hilperton people had not imbibed the errors of Andrew Fuller and Richard Davis. It equally reveals that Nathaniel Rawling's ministry had not been infected with the errors of Andrew Fuller and Richard Davis, for an offshoot to come from Back Street during his pastorate, and then at a later date to blend so closely with Warburton's Zion.

Various extant letters of Warburton show, that it was not only at Zion Chapel, Trowbridge that his ministry was being blessed. At Hilperton, he was working closely with John

Dymott and was in close contact with Churches at Melksham, Calne, Studley and Grove. They also reveal his movements on a much wider level. A letter dated 12th May 1819 concludes with the words, 'Next week I leave Trowbridge for Manchester, and, perhaps may be two or three months before I get home again.'[6] A second letter of 1819 dated 20th August [7] is in response to a letter from Conway Street Chapel, London. Warburton explains he could not answer it sooner, as he had been away from home. Then he goes on say, 'When I was at Conway Street,' which suggests that he had been there preaching in 1819, possibly on his journey to and from Manchester, to preach for William Gadsby. Another letter dated 29th April 1820, [8] refers again to leaving London and suggests a possible visit has already taken place in that year to Conway Street. It is probable that William Eacott preached at Zion when Warburton was away in 1819 and 1820.

A letter dated 4th May 1821,[9] says in its second sentence, 'Since I came home from Plymouth Dock, I have been very much engaged in blowing the trumpet in the different villages round the country.... Through mercy my family are well. I have been but poorly, but am now better.' He had been in April, on a long coach journey to Plymouth. David Denham, the minister and hymnwriter, was Pastor at Rehoboth Chapel Plymouth from 1816-1824.[10] He had previously been at York

---

[6] *Gospel Standard* 1881, p. 321.

[7] *Gospel Standard* 1875, p. 120.

[8] *Gospel Standard* 1876, p. 482.

[9] *Gospel Standard* 1851, p. 403.

[10] *Strict Baptist Chapels of England,* Vol. 5, R. Oliver, p. 127.

Street Chapel in Bath in 1815. He was a young man of twenty-four when Warburton first knew him at York Street, Bath. Now six years later he had invited Warburton to preach at Plymouth. Warburton was in the area of Arthur Triggs, who preached for Denham at Rehoboth for the first time in September 1821,[11] and became pastor of Denham's congregation, when it moved to Trinity Chapel in York Street, Plymouth, in 1828. Later Warburton was to come into close contact with Triggs in July and August 1837, when Warburton's youngest son, John, ran away and joined the Army at Exeter [12]

Now, no doubt, in 1821, Warburton took coach to Salisbury, and joined the London- Devonport Mail Coach, 'The Quicksilver,' which, having come from London, via Basingstoke and Stockbridge, proceeded via Blandford Forum, Dorchester, Bridport, Axminster, and Honiton, to Exeter and Plymouth/Devonport. From Salisbury the distance was about 140 miles, and from Trowbridge 170 miles. The average speed was about 10 -12mph and the cost 6d a mile, making the time of the whole journey about seventeen hours, and the cost about £4 5s single, plus tips for the coachman. The 'Quicksilver' would have had an armed guard, with blunderbuss, cutlass and two pistols, to protect the Royal Mail, which the Coach was carrying. Sadly, on 20th October 1816, the guard had failed to stop an escaped lioness from killing all the horses of the 'Quicksilver, just outside Salisbury at Winterslow, on its way to Stockbridge! Highwaymen were also a hazard, as were snow and floods. The guard had his horn to be sounded on approaching towns and villages, and a timepiece in a leather case. It was his duty to keep the Coach on time, and in case of accident, snow or flood, to take one of the horses of the team and ride on with the Mail. Two passengers were allowed on the box with the coachman, and six other passengers on the roof. The coachman always wore an ornate uniform, and the Coaches themselves had a beautiful livery. Remembering Warburton's

---

[11] A Memorial, Arthur Triggs, 1838, p. 111.

[12] *Memorials of John Warburton of Southill*, 1892, p. 24.

journey took place in the Spring of the year, it was probably a very pleasant ride, in very beautiful country with many glimpses of the Channel.

The letter of 4th May 1821 goes on to refer to Warburton preaching the gospel in the villages of Wiltshire, while at the same time it shows that he was undertaking some very long journeys. This was the year, on 23rd September, that John Dymott baptised for him, at Ladydown Mill, so possibly he had exhausted himself with his constant preaching and travelling. Two letters survive for the year 1822. One dated 4th June,[13] in which he says, 'I got home safe and found my family and friends all well,' and a second dated 5th November, [14] in which he explains, 'I had thought to have come to Eastbourne and Brighton, and have sent a letter to Mr Grace to have been there next Lord's Day week; but, since your letter came, I have sent a line to postpone it until after Christmas; and I think it will be better, as Mr Gadsby has been there lately.'

John Grace, who later became a well-known minister in the nineteenth century, was at the time of Warburton's correspondence with him, aged twenty-two. He and his wife, with a group of friends had prior to 1822, set up a chapel in a converted bakehouse in Eastbourne. Between 1822-23, John Grace had at his own cost, and on his own land beyond the bakehouse, built a substantial chapel, capable of holding an hundred people. This was at the extreme north-east end of Seaside Road. This chapel was in constant use from 1823 to May 1857, when Cavendish Place Chapel was opened. William Gadsby, John Warburton, Henry Fowler and John Vinall, minister of Jireh Chapel, Lewes, and Providence Chapel,

---

[13] *Gospel Standard* 1852, p. 216.

[14] *Gospel Standard* 1853, p. 207.

Brighton frequently preached there.[15] If Warburton kept to his suggestion in his letter of 5th November 1822, then it would seem that he preached at Providence Chapel, Brighton and John Grace's new chapel in Eastbourne sometime in the early part of 1823.

A letter dated Trowbridge, 15th June 1825,[16] says, 'Through mercy I got home safe, and found family and friends all well.' It goes on to say, 'Give my love to Mr V.' He then mentions various friends and adds, 'The Lord bless them, for I found the Lord with me among you at B; and I do hope the Lord blessed the word, which is the greatest comfort of my soul in seeing the word of the Lord run and be glorified. I hope, if I should be spared till next Spring, to pay you another visit; that is if the Lord will.' This letter is referring to Mr Vinall of Jireh Chapel, Lewes and Providence Chapel, Brighton. It is clear that in the Spring of 1825 Warburton was again in Brighton and probably Eastbourne with John Grace, and hoped to go again, 'if the Lord will,' in the Spring of 1826.

A long letter survives dated Trowbridge, 7th December 1826. [17] It reads,

> Yours I received, and was truly glad to hear from you. I certainly did think my journey into Norfolk had been of little use; but I am glad to hear the Lord did bless it to some of the poor souls there. My dear friend, I am experimentally taught where to ascribe the glory. I am confident of it, that the treasure is in an earthen vessel, that the excellence of the power may be of God, and not of us. I certainly did feel pleasure in my journey, and found myself much at home among you.

This letter reveals another extensive journey, this time, into Norfolk. It is difficult to be certain exactly where this was,

---

15 *Recollections of John Grace,* 1893, pp. 27, 28.

16 *Gospel Standard* 1848, p. 77.

17 *Gospel Standard* 1871, p. 155.

but having regard to the fact that two of his sermons, reprinted in *The Gospel of a Covenant God* [1976], were preached at Norwich, on 22nd August 1841, it is possible that this was an early visit to Norwich. But the letter is of wider interest as it goes on to say,

> I have been in the furnace pretty keenly since I saw you. We have had a separation in our Church. Those that are gone have taken another place, and are doing all they can to overthrow us.

Then he goes on to open up the feelings of his heart, and says,

> When the Lord draws, I can run; when He holds up, I can stand; when He pours into my heart the grace of supplication, I can pour out prayer unto Him; when He gives faith, I can believe and rest upon Him; when He calls me His child, I can call Him Father; when He softens, I can melt down at His feet; when He strengthens me by His Spirit in the inner man, I can glory in tribulation; and when He drives out the enemy before me, I can shout 'Victory' as well as the boldest; but generally it is when the enemy is running away. O what a blessing it is to have such a Covenant God......... I stand alone. There is not one settled minister in all the county of Wilts, but what looks upon me and considers me a man of mischief, a bad spirit, and dangerous to have anything to do with me; and since we have had the separation the whole town has been in ferment; and some, that have been as dear to me as my own life, have turned against me with all their might. Yes, my friend, and added to this, sometimes I get up on the Lord's day morning and have no text, three times to preach, and as dark as a dungeon.....

This letter reveals a division in the Church at Zion Chapel, Trowbridge, which had finally resulted in a group of members withdrawing and forming a new congregation. When Warburton wrote to his friends in Norfolk, after his visit there in 1826, the Church trouble had resulted in a breach which could not be healed. The Minutes of Zion Church Meetings from September 1825 to May 1826 tell the sequence of events, and some of the causes of the trouble, and give the actual date of the final separation as, 24th May 1826.

In Part II of the *Mercies* first published in 1839, Warburton gives an account of the causes of the separation, as he saw them. He says that from the time of his arrival in Trowbridge in 1815, he always had a dissatisfied minority among his congregation and members of his Church. He says,

> We had a great deal of patching and mending for many years, but it never answered any other end than only to make the rent worse; for I perceived soon after I came to Trowbridge, that there were a few in the Church that were not long together satisfied or quiet about one thing or another, though they professed to receive me as a minister of God, and many of them thanked the Lord in public [18] that ever he sent me to Trowbridge. But I believe in my heart that some of them, if it had been the will of God to have sent me out of Trowbridge, could have thanked Him with more freedom, for the word of God will ever stand true, 'By their fruits shall ye know them.[19]

Some criticized his salary of £156 a year, which he was paid quarterly, except from 1829 – 1841 when he was paid annually. Most thought £3 a week was far too much. This salary remained unaltered from 1815 to 1857. His friend William Gadsby was paid £125 a year when he first went Manchester in October 1805.[20] This was increased to £230 [21] in 1820 and stayed the same until his death in 1844. It must be remembered that Warburton had a far larger family to feed and clothe than Gadsby. When William Gadsby found himself unable, in 1807 to exist on his salary, and asked to be allowed to return to his

---

[18] This reveals that Zion Church had public Prayer Meetings.

[19] John Warburton op. cit. p. 170.

[20] *Memoir of William Gadsby,* 1847, p. 29.

[21] *William Gadsby*, op. cit. p. 99.

hosiery trade, he was asked how much he required. His response was, 'I'll do with as little as any of you, at least, any of you who are in business. I'll not be measured by a journeyman shoemaker or tailor; but whatever you find enough to support yourselves and families, I'll be satisfied with.' He adds, 'I have never had a dispute with them about my salary from that time to this.'[22] It is also worthy of note that in 1818 - 1819 Warburton was paying £23 a year rent for his house in Brick Plat Trowbridge, whereas K. Rogers, in the *Book of Trowbridge* [1984], p.98, quoting from a writer in a Devizes newspaper for 1826 says, that the town of Trowbridge then covered twice as much ground as it had in 1814, and adds, 'At that time [1814] the poor people were crowded into small close tenements, and a whole family occupied a single room, paying for it 3s 6d a week. [£18 2s a year] But now, little snug houses are erected on the outskirts of the town, and a comfortable entire house can be procured for from £6 to £8 per annum.' Trowbridge Poor Rate Books show that John Warburton and his family were living in Yerbury Street renting their house from Thomas Jarvis from 1822 until 1824, but in January 1825 Warburton had moved to one of the 'little snug houses erected on the outskirts of the town' at Down Gate, on the road out to Staverton, quite close to Ladydown Mill, where the family was to stay until 1832.

When all the circumstances are considered, it is very difficult to tell whether Warburton was overpaid or underpaid, or determine whether the criticisms levelled at him were justified. He himself was of the opinion that it was a lever used by some to attack the content of his preaching. Another criticism laid at his door was that his ministry lacked variety. He was said to have a fresh text each Sunday, but preached the substance of the same things over and over again. His response to this criticism was that it was perfectly true. He says in his *Mercies,*

---

[22] *William Gadsby*, op. cit. pp. 29,30.

> It was all perfectly true, for let the text be whatever it might, I was sure to be on the old spot, or not far from it, attempting to show the lost, ruined state, and utter helplessness of man, whether saint or sinner; and exalting free, sovereign, electing discriminating grace in the Holy Trinity, in the salvation of the elect, made manifest in the heart by the teachings of the Holy Ghost; and bearing fruits in a conduct and life that adorned the doctrines of God our Saviour; and giving testimony to all around that the grace of God teacheth the denying of ungodliness and worldly lusts; and to live soberly, righteously and godly in this present world. This has been the substance of my preaching ever since my mouth was opened.[23]

One morning, a member of his Church came to unburden himself to Warburton and tell him, that he and many more were tired of the monotony of his preaching. He offered the suggestion that Warburton might find more variety if he commenced a series of sermons on the Parables. Warburton felt that the man's motives were far from friendly, but felt willing to try out his advice. He tried to study to prepare these sermons, but says the more he studied the darker it all appeared, until the whole Bible seemed like one parable from beginning to end. But late one Saturday night, feeling his days at Trowbridge were coming to an end, the Lord spoke into his soul, 'I will bring the blind by a way that they knew not; I will lead them in paths that they have not known. I will make darkness light before them, and crooked things straight. These things will I do unto them, and not forsake them.' [Isa. 42.16] He says that he went down to Zion Chapel the next Sunday morning, 'hanging upon the Lord like a child,' and preached from, 'Whether we be afflicted, it is for your consolation and salvation, etc.' [2 Cor. 1. 6-7.] He says what liberty and sweetness flowed into his soul, and he prayed for the man who had suggested he get into the parables, for he felt he had learnt the lesson that, 'no one could spiritually understand one text but as the Spirit revealed it.'

He says, 'I have blessed the dear man scores of times since for coming and telling me that I ought to get into the parables; for I have been brought hundreds of times like the

---

[23] John Warburton, op. cit. p 171.

dear disciples, 'Lord, declare unto us this parable.' He says that it taught him that in preaching it was useless to go to Dr Gill, Dr Doddridge, Dr Goodwin, Dr Hawker, Dr Huntington for help, and that he had to go to the never-failing Doctor, Jesus. He says he learnt that he never could nor ever did get anything out of other men's works that was of any use to him in the pulpit, for however he loved their writings, and they had been made good to his soul in private, it was of no use to him for pulpit work.[24] He concludes, 'I cannot carry another man's line of things into the pulpit,' or else he would be forced to confess, 'Alas, Master, it was borrowed.'

Finally the undercurrents of criticism surfaced when in 1825, Zion Chapel was barred from using the Ladydown Mill pool for their baptising services. It was the place were all the other Baptist Churches in Trowbridge were accustomed to baptise. Zion Church was refused permission,because the man who had the right to grant permission, felt that Warburton and his Church showed an exclusiveness, and a narrow minded, separatist spirit, which he resented. One of the Zion deacon's went round the town searching for another place to baptise in the open-air, but failed to find anywhere convenient. So a Church Meeting was called at Zion on 14th September 1825 and by a narrow margin of 84 for and 74 against, it was agreed by a majority of ten to build a baptistry in the chapel, 'being denied baptising in the river.' A baptistry was quickly built and on 9th October 1825, Warburton baptised six new members, the first to be baptised in the chapel.

But the matter did not end here. Warburton was called a 'pope' for acting with such a small majority. He received numerous anonymous letters criticising him for taking away the open witness of the Gospel in the town. Many felt it was an entirely wrong decision to take the baptising services indoors. It is interesting to see that the Church was equally divided on the subject. Warburton says that he was quite agreeable to have the baptistry in the Chapel. This seems surprising, since he had

---

[24] Cf. Dr John Kennedy's comments in *The Days of the Fathers in Ross-shire,* Christian Focus, 1979, p. 35.

seen remarkable open air services in the North, such as the baptising at Rochdale, when William Gadsby baptised John Kershaw, before two thousand people. It seems strange that he did not value these occasions more highly, and continue the Zion baptisings at Mr Bird's Coal Wharf at Hilperton Marsh, where he had held the baptisings for Zion in 1824. It appears that he only looked for another place to baptise, in Trowbridge itself. But he says, 'All (the opposition) had no effect upon me; for I went straight forward according to their own rule, which they had in the Church Book before I settled amongst.' Rule number one read, 'Any debate or difference that may arise in the Church, to be settled by the majority; that is the greatest number shall decide.' This appears somewhat unwise as a rule, in that changes of considerable importance could be decided by a majority of one.

Originally, in 1813 the Church had had only four rules, of which two to four concerned those who were allowed to take communion and attend Church Meetings. On 1st June 1825 a Church Meeting had been held which had endorsed a further four rules. [These Rules are given in full in Appendix F.] The fifth rule agreed in June stated, 'After the ordinance of the Lord's Supper has been administered and the spectators dismissed, [25] the members shall remain in their places to answer to their names which shall be called over by one of the Deacon's to ascertain if any are absent, in order that the cause of such absence may be inquired into.' The group of members who had disagreed over the question of building a baptistry in Zion Chapel, now disagreed with the new rule five. This rule according to Warburton in his *Mercies* [26] had been passed by a unanimous vote. When the leaders of the group who opposed the baptistry agreed to drop that issue, they then refused to answer their names after the Lord's Supper was over.

---

[25] This shows that Warburton allowed unbaptised members of the congregation to watch the Lord's Supper.

[26] John Warburton, op. cit. p. 179.

A Church Meeting was called at Zion for 24th October 1825 at which it was agreed that all the church members should sign the eight rules, and from the list of names in the Church Book, it appears that about 130 signed, leaving just under thirty who refused to sign. The Church Minute for that meeting reads, 'We whose names are undersigned have agreed that no member shall come to any of our Church Meetings or sit down at the Ordinance of the Lord's Supper, until they sign the above rules, as a number of members have objected to sign. We have agreed to give them 6 months to consider it, and if at the expiration of 6 months they have neglected to sign their names, we shall consider them as not being in union with us as a Church, and shall at the expiration of the time take such steps as the majority of the Church shall decide.'

There then followed further trouble, or as Warburton refers to it in his *Mercies* 'Contention upon contention.' Another Church meeting was called for 21st November 1825, at which the Minutes state, 'It was unanimously agreed upon, not one dissenting voice, that Samuel Hurd and William Chapman be dismissed from their office as Deacons. Our reasons are two. First, we believe there is not that union betwixt them and our Pastor which is needful for peace. Second, being out on a Lord's Day preaching, they are very seldom at home to fill up their office. Also agreed unanimously, without one dissenting voice, that if any of our Deacons should ever go out to preach, he shall give up his office as deacon.' This was a sad day because these men had been among the original five deacons appointed on 14th January 1813, after the Church was first formed on 6th January that year. The deacons then appointed were, Benjamin Marshman, [dismissed to Broughton Gifford Church 21st October 1813]; William Marvin, [excluded 15th October 1816 with his wife Hannah, for leaving England in a way not becoming their profession]; William Eacott [dismissed with his wife Pheby in 1825, after he went as Pastor to Chapmanslade, where he was Pastor 1824-1840, and then went to Southwick as Pastor 1840-1850. He had gone out to preach in 1818, his first sermon being preached at Little Zoar Chapel Studley] ; Samuel Hurd and William Chapman.

It is not clear when these last two deacons became ministers. But certainly, three of Warburton's original deacons had gone into the ministry. It is possible that some of these difficulties might have been avoided if the Church at Zion had had the Church offices of Elders and Deacons, then the ministers who were not Pastors could have stayed in the Church as Preaching Elders, a distinction which some Presbyterian Churches have maintained. On 5th December another Church Meeting was held and Thomas Ball, James Porter and Richard Knee were chosen as Deacons in the place of Samuel Hurd and William Chapman.

The following year, on 24th May 1826, when the 6 month time allowed to sign the rules had expired, the dissenting members still being of the same mind, Zion Church unanimously separated from them, as the Church minute says, 'they being a minority and not submitting to the will of the majority.' The Church Book lists twenty -seven members, eight man and nineteen women. The list is headed by William Chapman and Samuel Hurd. For a time the group met in the old Bonded Warehouse on Wicker Hill, but later they built a Chapel in the Lower Courts, which they called Little Bethel. It continued until 1863, when it was sold and was bought by the Church of England and became St Stephen's Church.

This was a rather sad end to the first decade of Warburton's ministry at Zion. It was also a cause for considerable concern as there were now many empty seats in the Chapel. About six months after the group had left, the Deacons called a meeting of the Pastor and a few male members to discuss the finances of the Church, as the Church appeared to be in financial trouble. They had borrowed £800 in 1816 and 1817 and had paid back £200 of the capital by 1818. But up until 1826 they had paid very little of the 5% interest, which had accumulated as extra debt. So in his *Mercies* Warburton gives the outstanding debt at the end of 1826 as £700, which probably includes, rather than excludes, the outstanding interest. At the meeting they each agreed to subscribe 2s a week, and Warburton agreed to subscribe 4s. This was put to the Church and they accepted it. The Church Finance book shows that in 1826 the subscription raised £14 13s 11d, in 1827, £28 12s 8d, and in

1828 £27 18s 3d, making a total in three years of just over £77 towards clearing some of their outstanding debts. There was no subscription in 1829, but in 1830 they agreed to a penny a week subscription, as well as seat rents and seven monthly collections. By these means they raised their income from £175 in 1827, to £274 in 1831, £255 in 1832, £216 in 1833, £241 in 1834, £271 in 1835 and £270 in 1836. In that year the penny a week subscription appears to end. The 1d subscription mostly brought in just over £50 extra a year.

Warburton felt to have 'many sweet testimonies' in his soul in 'the midst of all the fire and water' he and his Church passed through in these years. The Lord spoke many 'precious promises into his soul.' He felt he could see the needs be for it all, and was satisfied that 'it was all working together for good, for the future peace and prosperity of them as a Church.' He says the Lord was with him in public and that what the Lord gave him in secret he was able to proclaim on the house-top. He says, 'We soon had an increase in Church and congregation,' and adds, 'Many of the poor dear sheep that had run away from the fold came creeping back, poor things! half starved to death...' He himself felt much of the Lord's presence in all the turmoil, what he describes as 'much sweet fellowship and communion with my covenant God and Father.' The Church Book shows that eighteen were baptised in the Chapel in 1826, twenty-four in 1827, ten in 1828, thirty in 1829, besides seven received as members from other Churches.

But still there hung over the Church the outstanding capital debt of £600 plus interest and Warburton speaking of the year 1829 says, 'It was absolutely necessary for me to go out begging.' Warburton's figures given in the *Mercies* do not tie up with the Church Accounts of the times. Writing in 1838/9 he does say, 'If I recollect right.' He quotes the outstanding capital debt as £700,[27] but in 1817 and 1818 William Hayward had been repaid £100 each year, and overall only £800 had been borrowed. But, be this as it may, Warburton felt a need to try to reduce it. It is not quite certain when he went to London 'begging.' Zion Church records show that he was away from

[27] John Warburton, op. cit. p. 183.

Trowbridge preaching in April and October 1829 and in May and June 1830. It would seem probable that this visit to London 'begging' was in April 1829.

The Deacons of Gower Street Chapel, where Henry Fowler was Pastor, warned him that he must not beg there as they had a heavy debt on their Chapel which their people were still trying to clear. Henry Fowler was a friend of Warburton and had preached for him at Zion Trowbridge in 1822. But Warburton felt the Lord had set before him 'an open door' in London and so he took his subscription book and went around among his friends asking for their support. He received £35 at the end of the first day and so it went on until after much preaching and 'begging', he came home to Trowbridge with £182 7s 3d. He says, 'I arrived home [to Downgate], very poorly and weak in body, but strong and happy in my soul.' The Lord had preserved him also, with all this money on him from highwaymen. He says, 'After a few months at home, I went down into Sussex to Brighton and Lewes and a few other places with my begging case.' This time he collected £150 14s.

Now the Church began to make interest payments and capital repayment to the four men to whom they owed money. In May 1830, William Hayward was repaid £158 of his £300 outstanding capital and £7 interest, and in December 1830, he received another £41 capital repayment and £5 interest. Samuel Hurd was repaid £43 of his £100 capital loan, and £5 interest, William Eacott received the same as Samuel Hurd, and James Hayward received £15 capital repayment and £5 in interest. Now the overall capital loan stood at £300 half of what it had been, and some of the interest at 5% had been paid. Warburton says, 'When I returned home, and told the brethren of the good hand of our God that had gone before and opened the door, it was truly a time of thanksgiving and joy...... We had a true reviving time indeed, to see how the Lord had gone before us in the way, and brought our debt down to about three hundred pounds.'[28]

None of Warburton's letters survive over the period from 1827 to 1831. The Zion Chapel Account book, however, after the departure of Samuel Hurd in 1826, was taken over by

---

[28] John Warburton, op. cit. p. 192.

one of the new deacons who meticulously recorded the dates that each minister preached, who stood in for John Warburton, when he travelled away to preach. So it emerges that in 1827 Warburton was away from Sunday 8th April to Sunday 29th April, and from Sunday 30th September to Sunday 7th October. In 1828 he was absent from Trowbridge from Sunday 20th April to Sunday 25th May, and from Sunday 19th October to Sunday 9th November. In 1829 he was away every Sunday in April preaching at Gower Street Chapel in London, and other Churches in the vicinity of London, and then went to Brighton and Lewes for three Sundays in October. In 1830 he was away most of May and June, whilst in 1831 he was away in May and October. While it is known that he regularly preached at Gower Street Chapel London, it is not always possible to know where else he was preaching.

In his *Mercies,* he records that at this period 1830/31, he suffered a period of great darkness of mind for about six or seven weeks. He describes it in the words, 'The Lord began to try me sorely in withdrawing the light of his countenance from me.' [29] He had to preach to a large congregation and yet felt the Lord's absence in his own soul. A large congregation was no comfort to him. He felt with Jeremiah, 'Surely against me is he turned.' [Lam.3.3] He says, 'Such seasons as these, though they are cutting to flesh and blood, are valuable lessons, not designed to destroy us, but to purify us, and to strip us from our idols, to bring down the cursed pride of our nature, and let us see that the Lord can do as well without us as with us.' He says his cry continually was, 'Bring my soul out of prison that I may praise Thy Name.' [Ps. 142.7.] The Lord heard his prayer and spoke into his heart the word, 'For the oppression of the poor, for the sighing of the needy, now will I arise, saith the Lord; I will set him in safety from him that puffeth at him.'[Ps. 12.5.] He says, 'O what a lift this was to my heart.'

So he came to the end of the first fifteen years of his Pastorate. The Lord had fulfilled His word, 'I have much people in this city.' He had a regular congregation of a thousand and well over two hundred baptised members in his Church. In

---

[29] John Warburton, op. cit. p. 192.

1830 he baptised ten and received one, and in 1831 he baptised twenty and received four. But the great period of blessing which centred around the baptisings at Ladydown Mill, was beginning to decline, though there remained still much prosperity in his ministry at Zion. These years, in the Lord's hands, had been a building time in his Church. Now while the years ahead were to witness further growth, they were to be years of establishment. Equally there was under his ministry in the area, the development of a group of Churches which had separated from the errors of Andrew Fuller, and were to form at a later date the nucleus of the Gospel Standard denomination in Wiltshire. A little Baptist Chapel had been opened at Allington in 1829 by a local farmer, Joseph Parry and the son of a Naval Officer, Joshua Carby Tuckwell, which was to prove in time of considerable significance.[30] In the country at large, they were times of considerable turmoil, as George IV died, William IV succeeded to the Throne in June 1830, and the campaign for the Reform of Parliament developed, resulting in the West Country, in serious rioting in Bristol on 29th October 1831.

---

30 *Further History of Gospel Standard Baptists,* S.F. Paul, Vol. 6. p.1.

Chapter 11

The balancings of the clouds

John Warburton concludes his *Mercies of a Covenant God* with a long account of the trial he had with his youngest boy, John. It extended from Shrove Tuesday, 6th March 1832, when he first ran away from Down Gate, until Warburton baptised him at Zion Chapel on 29th April 1838. He describes it as, 'One of the keenest trials he ever had in all his life,' though near the end of his life, on his last visit to his son John at Southill, his father told him, 'You have been both the greatest joy and the greatest sorrow of my life.' John had been apprenticed in 1829 at the age of fourteen to a tailor. As was to be expected, there were a good number of tailors. working in this West of England cloth town. John appears to have preferred an outdoor life. He was about sixteen and a half when, on Shrove Tuesday 1832, he went to work as usual in the morning from Down Gate, but did not return home in the evening. It was the usual week-night preaching service at Zion and amidst great anxiety Warburton had to go and preach. Many enquiries were made and the family stayed up until 2 a.m. Wednesday morning and had no sleep all night. But there was no news of John. Not until the following Friday morning at 11a.m. did any news reach Trowbridge, and it was then to report that he had been seen in Salisbury on either Wednesday or Thursday.

This boy was the youngest of ten and again it appears that Warburton had made an idol of him. He says, 'My soul was wrapped up in the lad.' Also, knowing how often Warburton, in the course of his preaching engagements was absent from home, often for a month at a time, it is clear that there had been times, when as the lad grew, he had missed a father's control and discipline. Mrs Warburton, taking her rather unobtrusive roll in the Warburton home, had had to carry much responsibility in the rearing of eleven children both while the family was in the North and now in the West Country. In 1825 for example when John was a lad of ten, when the family went to Down Gate, Ruth was twelve, Manoah fourteen, Gideon seventeen and Rachel nineteen. Mrs Warburton, left alone for weeks at a time, no doubt had her problems with them, especially the three boys.

As soon as Warburton had the news of his son, he went to his son-in-law, [probably John Hayward] hired a horse and gig, borrowed £10, and after dinner on Friday, they set out for Salisbury. On route, via Westbury and Warminster, they met a Trowbridge man, who told them he had seen John on the road to Winchester. They stayed at Salisbury on Friday night and early Saturday morning, 10th March, set out for Winchester, which they reached at 11 a.m. and went to the house for tailors. There they learnt that John had slept there Thursday night and gone on to Southampton. Arriving at the house for tailors in Southampton at 3 p.m. they were told that he had gone to a friend of his father's at Portsmouth. Going back to the Inn, [probably the Dolphin in the High Street] where they had put the horse and gig, they learnt that the Bath coach was arriving any moment and going straight on to Portsmouth. So they left the horse and gig and took the coach for Portsmouth. John Warburton, now fifty-six, feeling tired and exhausted, travelled inside; it was empty, and John Hayward travelled on the roof.

On that journey the Lord sweetly blessed Warburton with the words, 'Like as a father pitieth his children, so the Lord pitieth them that fear Him.' [Ps. 103. 13.] He describes it as a most profitable journey to his soul, and when the coach stopped in Southsea, [it must have been late in the evening] at his friend's home, [Mr Doudney, the tallow chandler and father of D.A. Doudney, later to be Editor of the *Gospel Magazine*], it was to find young John had arrived there only a couple of hours before. Awaking the next Sunday morning Warburton suddenly realised that he was away from Trowbridge, and they had no minister there. Mr Doudney found him a pulpit for the Sunday evening service and he preached in Portsmouth. This sermon was the means of blessing to a lady, named Mrs Tylford, who [1] had been in great soul trouble and had had a dream in which she had seen a man who had promised her deliverance. When she saw Warburton enter the pulpit that Sunday, she knew this was the man. That evening the sermon was the means of bringing peace to her heart. Warburton preached the following Monday evening again in Portsmouth and then returned by coach to Trowbridge with his son John on the following Tuesday, 13th March.

Now Warburton recalls in his *Mercies*,

> If I recollect right, the week after, which was in the Spring of 1832, I had to go to Abingdon in Berkshire, to preach at the opening of a new chapel, which my much esteemed brother and friend Mr Tiptaft had built. I recollect well I borrowed two pounds to go with, and went pretty comfortably, for I had not entirely lost all the savour of the loving-kindness of God in His goodness towards me in my journey after the lad. I preached in the chapel in the morning, and was to preach again in the evening, so that I did not go out to the afternoon service; and before we retired to bed, Mr Tiptaft told me that they had had a collection for me in the afternoon, which quite struck me up, for I had never heard a hint of such a thing, and as near as I can recollect, he said they had got ten pounds. 'O', says I with astonishment, 'Why, it will pay the ten pounds that I borrowed in all my ramblings after the lad, and a few shillings to spare.' O what a sweet hour I had in my bed to see the tender mercies of God. It was too great for such a worthless worm to look upon. In the morning, before I left, dear Mr Tiptaft put five pounds into my hand. I would gladly not have received it, but he insisted.... I came home as full of the blessings of the Lord as ever my soul could hold. I had money to pay the twelve pound I had borrowed and three pounds to spare. [2]

---

[1] *Memorials of John Warburton of Southill* 1892, p.14.

[2] John Warburton op. cit. p. 203.

Behind this visit to Abingdon, so closely entwined with the wanderings of his son John, lies events of considerable spiritual significance. The date of the opening of Abbey Chapel, Abingdon was Sunday 25th March 1832, two days after the third Reform Bill had passed its third reading in the House of Commons on the previous Friday. The minister who preached the afternoon service that day was Roger Hitchcock, a former Church of England clergyman from Figheldean in Wiltshire, who had seceded from the Church in 1826. William Tiptaft himself was also a former clergyman, who had been Vicar of Sutton Courtney, just outside Abingdon, and had seceded from the Church in November 1831, and built this chapel at his own expense.

The story behind Roger Hitchcock's secession begins with a minister called Henry Huntly, who lived at Enford in the valley of the Wiltshire Avon and preached at Manningford. In the March Supplement of the *Gospel Standard* for 1869 there is the obituary of Huntly who had died in Australia in November 1868, at the age of seventy. This tells of how Huntly was baptised in the River Avon in 1821 at the age of twenty three; had later started to preach in a little chapel, erected for him, in 1825 at Manningford, by John Oram of Rushall; had first heard John Warburton preach in 1825, by which 'he had been greatly established in the truth;' and had become acquainted with Roger Hitchcock, Vicar of Figheldean, who often preached at Fittleton. It explains that, 'It was a good deal through Henry Huntly's conversation with Roger Hitchcock that the latter left the Church of England.' Hitchcock, after he left the Church, preached for a time in a shoemaker's workshop in Figheldean, until he went in 1826, for four years, to Andover. He was baptised at the Old Baptist Chapel at Devizes in January 1827, where he was later Pastor from 1830-1833. The effects of Warburton' ministry are seen stretching out beyond Devizes into the Pewsey Vale and the Valley of the River Avon.

A man who went to hear Hitchcock at Figheldean was Joshua Carby Tuckwell, the son of a former Naval Officer, now farmer, who was born at Netheravon in 1799. [His father had fought with Lord Rodney against the French at the battle of Guadaloupe in the West Indies in April 1782.] Joshua was greatly blessed under Hitchcock's ministry. When Hitchcock left the area another minister, Stephen Offer, preached in a small Baptist Chapel in Netheravon, and Joshua went there with Hitchcock's old congregation, and was eventually baptised in the River Avon in 1828 by Stephen Offer. Shortly afterwards he was forced to leave Netheravon, and moved to Allington, near Devizes where a Baptist Chapel had been built in 1829 by a farmer Joseph Parry. Somewhere in the background, in connections it is now impossible to trace, John Warburton was in touch with all these men, who themselves were in sympathy with his preaching.

How William Tiptaft came to know Roger Hitchcock, is not now possible to trace. Why he invited him to the opening of his new chapel, is hidden. It seems clear that in the four years that Hitchcock preached at Andover in a chapel there, he also travelled widely among the Particular Baptist churches in the area. Tiptaft had come to Sutton Courtney in 1829. He had not been called by grace until January 1827, even though he had been ordained at Wells Cathedral in March 1826. When he started to preach at Sutton Courtney, his ministry filled the Church, it was with such power. He came into contact, at a minister's fraternal in June 1829, with J.C.Philpot, the Curate of Stadhampton, nearby. He was a Fellow of Worcester College Oxford, a first class honours graduate in Greek and Latin. These men were being drawn to the doctrines of election and predestination, and were being shown the hollowness of a form of religion and the need of a saving knowledge of truth with power in their souls. Their ministry was based on what J.C.Philpot used to call, 'the grand doctrines,' the doctrines of grace.

On the evening of Christmas Day 1829, Tiptaft was invited to preach before the Mayor and Corporation of Abingdon, in St Helen's, The Great Church, Abingdon. Although the truths he enunciated that night are embodied in the Thirty-Nine Articles of Faith of the Church of England, they were lost sight of at that time, as they are now. So when Tiptaft, preaching from the text, 'And she shall bring forth a Son, and thou shalt call His Name Jesus; for He shall save His people from their sins,' [Matt. 1.21.] opened his sermon with the words, 'I stand before you this evening, either as a servant of Christ or a servant of the devil,' the several thousand inhabitants of Abingdon, present, were shocked, especially as he went on to outline the grand doctrines of distinguishing grace, supporting them with Scripture, all in accordance with the Church's own Articles. The town was in uproar, and the next Sunday the Church provided another clergyman to preach the opposite to her own Articles. Small wonder that within a brief space of time, Tiptaft felt led to leave the Church and within sight of St Helen's to build, at his own expense, [for he was a man with a small estate in Rutland] a Chapel which would seat four to five hundred people, most of whom would be ex-Anglicans from Sutton Courtney and Abingdon.

Now looking back to that Sunday, 25th March 1832, John Warburton is seen in company with two young, ex-Anglican clergymen, preaching in a new chapel in the heart of the Abbey lands in Abingdon. Looking at Tiptaft's diary for February 1832 in J.C.Philpot's biography [1972, p. 64.] of him, it reads,

> "I preached a month ago at Reading in a large chapel, and it was very crowded; and this week last I have been to see Mr Hitchcock of Devizes, who seceded about six years ago from the Established Church, and is now a minister at a Baptist chapel there. I preached on Tuesday evening, at Trowbridge, in the chapel of an old and faithful servant of the Lord, John Warburton, to some hundreds of persons; and on Wednesday evening at Devizes. On Thursday, I was severely lampooned in the *Devizes Gazette* ; and the *Reading Chronicle* has a copy of it today.

Later in another diary entry, dated Wednesday 4th May 1832, Tiptaft writes,

> The Lord had decidedly blessed my preaching lately, I am rejoiced to say. I am not much of a favourite among the clergy. Philpot has paid me a visit this week, and heard Warburton in my Chapel.

In just over a month since the opening, Warburton was back in Abingdon to preach at the Abbey Chapel, and the Oxford Don, J.C.Philpot had come over from Stadhampton to hear him. On Page 69 of his biography of Tiptaft, in a footnote, J.C. Philpot explains,

> This was the beginning of my acquaintance, and I believe I may add, friendship with Mr Warburton. I met him at my friend's house, and of the interview which we then had Mr Warburton used often to speak. We were, in fact, both of us, before we met, much afraid of one another, - he of my learning, I of his grace. He feared lest I should see his ignorance of human learning, and I lest he should discover my ignorance of divine teaching. But before we parted, our mutual fears were completely dispelled. He would make me pray with him and William Tiptaft, before we parted; and according to his account, my simple petitions, not those of a learned man, but of a poor sinner saved by grace, touched his heart, and created a union of soul which was never broken; for I can truly say we never from that day had the least jar, but walked in peace and union to the day of his death.

J.C.Philpot lingered on, unhappy, in the Established Church for another three years, until he came out in March 1835, and came down to stay at Allington with Farmer Parry and Joshua Carby Tuckwell, who were by then elected deacons at the Baptist Chapel there. William Tiptaft came to Devizes on Sunday, 17th June 1832, and was baptised by Roger Hitchcock. This was an historic occasion for the old Baptist Chapel, which dated its history back to the Seventeenth century, to have men of the Established Church baptised by immersion in her midst. The Articles of the Church of England were generally in line with the Particular Baptist Confession of Faith of 1689, except for Infant Sprinkling, which was a hangover from pre-Reformation days. The presence of godly, able men, coming from the Established Church among the followers of Gadsby and Warburton, a group of Baptists who had broken from the Particular Baptists on the issue of Fuller's errors, caused a considerable stir inside and outside their midst.

It was a remarkable time for John Warburton, as these young men came into his life. J.C.Philpot had been born on 13th September 1802, educated at St Paul's School, London, gained an Open Scholarship to Worcester College, Oxford in 1821, and had taken a First in Classics in 1824, being one of four so placed, eventually to be made a Fellow of his College. When he met Warburton for the first time in May 1832, he was twenty-nine, and still single. William Tiptaft was born on 16th February 1803 of a farming family at Braunston in Rutland. He was educated at Uppingham Public School and entered St John's College, Cambridge in 1821. Both his parents had died before he was fourteen and he had been brought up by his sister, who had married a doctor, William Keal, in 1816. [His sister's daughter, Sarah, was later to marry J.C. Philpot.] He obtained his degree in Mathematics in 1825, and entered the Church as Curate at Treborough in Somerset in 1826. When he first preached for Warburton at Zion in February 1832, he was just twenty-nine, and had not yet been baptised by immersion..

Warburton at this time was a man of fifty-six, still living at Down Gate but on the point of moving nearer the Chapel. His heart must have been filled with wonder to see these young men, well-taught by the Holy Spirit to know their own sinnership, to whom he could at once feel a real union of heart, yet brought from completely outside the Churches among which he was moving. William Gadsby, John Warburton, J.C.Philpot and William Tiptaft were to manifest exactly the same balance as the Seventeenth Century had seen in the balance of John Bunyan, the tinker, and John Owen, the Vice-Chancellor of Oxford University. Owen, godly able divine that he was, had said that he would give anything to be able to preach like John Bunyan. J.C.Philpot with all his ability in the Classical Languages, and all his grace, still looked up to the godly weaver, John Warburton, and was to edit his *Mercies of a Covenant God* for him in 1837.

John Warburton was now entering on another decade of his life in Trowbridge. A letter dated 22nd August 1832 [3] says,

> I should have written to you sooner, to know the reason of your silence, but we have been removing to a new habitation, near the Chapel, and my mind has been so taken up, that I have had little time to write.....We are still going on very comfortably as a Church and people, and I have the pleasure of seeing the work of the Lord going on, and

---

[3] *Gospel Standard* 1842, pp. 327, 328.

giving seals to my ministry. O how it melts my poor soul to see and prove that God honours such a poor worm as His mouth! We shall have an addition to our Church in about a fortnight. It has quite revived my soul to hear them tell how God has brought the truth home to their hearts with power.

Firstly this reveals that John Warburton was moving house again. He had been in his previous house in the area beyond the thatched Turn Pike Cottage on the Down, known as Down Gate, since January 1825. Secondly it shows his ministry was still being blessed at Zion as the Church Book reveals that twelve were baptised in the Chapel on 26th September 1832.

By now two more of Warburton's daughters were married. On 26th March 1823, Leah, at the age of eighteen, had married Isaac Moore, a month older than herself. They had started married life in Castle Street and moved into Timbrell Street about 1831. Later they were to live at Prospect House, in Prospect Place. Isaac Moore developed a successful dyeing business at premises in Bradford-on-Avon and in the Courts, Trowbridge. [His father, Isaac Moore Senior, and Samuel Pitman, [father of Sir Isaac Pitman of Shorthand fame] were the first two Sunday School Superintendents at Zion, when the School was founded in 1828.] By 1832 they had five children, the eldest being eight and the youngest one.

On 13th January 1825 Elizabeth, Warburton's fifth child, [baptised at Ladydown Mill in 1823] had married a widower, John Hayward, ten years older that herself, with three young sons, John aged nine, Edward seven and Samuel three. Their mother, Mary Pourch Hayward had died in 1822, probably following the birth of Samuel, and was buried at Zion Chapel. Originally the family lived in Back Street, but by the time of the 1821 Census they were living in a large house called 'The Laurels' in Hilperton Road. To this home Elizabeth went from Down Gate. The family were prosperous Clothiers with a workshop in Union Street, near Zion Chapel. William Hayward, John's father, was a deacon at Zion, as also was John's brother, James. They had been appointed deacons in 1825. It was William Hayward who had loaned £500 for the building of Zion Chapel in 1816. The first child of Elizabeth was born on 26th

October 1825, and named after her grandmother, Lydia. Another girl was born in May 1828, called, Martha, and a boy in March 1830, named Joseph. Their father, John Hayward became a partner in Salters Cloth Mill. Besides these grandchildren, Warburton's daughter Sarah Earle had two children aged six or seven, called Manoah and Martha, and the boy born our of wedlock, called James who was about fifteen. Warburton's second son, James, had two boys, John aged twelve, and James aged seven. So as the new decade opened up the next generation of young Warburtons was appearing on the scene and Warburton was a grandfather many times over.

Warburton did not now need such a large house. In 1832 there remained at home Rachel [26], Gideon [24], Manoah [21], Ruth [19], and John [17]. As they moved house 'nearer to the chapel' in the year that the great Reform Bill finally became law on 4th June, they were a very different family from what they had been when they arrived in The Halve in 1815. The home they moved into was just over fifteen years old, built about the time they arrived in Trowbridge. It was called Waterloo Terrace and they moved into number 31, the second house from the left in the terrace. Warburton rented it from his old landlord of Yerbury Street days, Thomas Jarvis, and paid £36 a year. The terrace was of a simple design, in Bath stone of Georgian style. There were only five houses in the terrace. They were in Union Street about fifty yards from Zion Chapel, and very close to Brick Plat, where the family had lived from 1817 to 1821.

Here the family stayed for at least sixteen years. The National Census return for 1841 shows them in Waterloo Terrace, as does the Post Office Directory for 1848. The National Census return for 1851 shows that they are again in The Halve. No doubt many young feet crossed the threshold of 31 Waterloo Terrace to see their grandparents, and there was much coming and going to the four families and homes of Sarah [in Prospect Place], James [in Shail's Lane], Elizabeth [in Hilperton Road] and Leah [in Timbrell Street]. Elizabeth's home, 'The Laurels', was a particularly beautiful spot with extensive views to the south over Salisbury Plain and the White Horse Hill, and to the north over the Bath Hills and Sally-in-the

Wood. Also the Haywards had a field besides their home running down to Back Lane, where they probably kept their horses, and in which children could play.

They were near neighbours of John Clark, who owned Bellefield House, to the west of them, a splendid Georgian residence standing in its own grounds with its deer park. This house had been built, above The Halve, on the north side of Hilperton Road, in 1794 and laid out with grounds and a walled paddock. Clark had completed the purchase of it in 1821, about the same time as John Hayward and his family had moved from Back Street to Hilperton Road. John Hayward's first wife Mary had died at 'The Laurels' in 1822 and three years later he had married Elizabeth Warburton. No doubt in this busy home Warburton and his wife spent many happy hours with the family, amidst its relaxing surroundings. Things had changed considerably in the Warburton family since the days of poverty in Narrow Lane at Besses-o'-th'-Barn, and in Brick Plat, when Warburton had tried to escape from his difficulties in his move to Trowle Common. Now his children were grown up and helping to pay towards the costs of the home.

Young John however still enjoyed a ramble, in consequence of which, he must have abandoned his apprenticeship in the tailoring trade, and must have gone from one job to another. He was not at home long in 1832, before he left home again. He says,[4]

> Having secretly joined my old companions in sin, and visited again my former haunts of iniquity, my thirst for rambling came upon me. This time I went to Grittleton, a village in Wiltshire. There I got work, and continued the summer until the dull season, and then returned home. But there was no more rest in me than there is in the sea.

By now he was seventeen, a severe cause of anxiety for his parents, full of adolescent problems and unable to settle to any job. Passing over numerous other 'senseless rambles,' he goes on the describe how, with a friend called Samuel Hurd, he left Trowbridge one night in the Spring of 1835 and went to

---

[4] *Memorials of John Warburton of Southill*, op. cit. p. 15.

London and got work. He says, 'I might have done well, had my mind been as much in business as it was in places of amusement.' Presumably he returned to Trowbridge in a short while. Warburton says in his *Mercies* that he ran away at least four times after 1832. The early years at Waterloo Terrace must have been years of considerable sorrow for the family often for weeks not knowing the whereabouts of young John.

But for Warburton many other things were occupying his mind. His large Church was growing. In 1831 he had baptised eight in April, six in August, and six in September, as well as receiving four more from other Churches in August, making a total of twenty-four new members. In 1832 he had baptised twelve in September. In April 1833, he had baptised eight and received three. In 1834, he had baptised five in July and four in September; and in August 1835 he had baptised ten. In preaching he was not finding his path any easier. In a letter dated July 1834 he says,

> I have hoped and expected that the dear Lord would lead me into some mysterious parts of God's word, that I might come up before the people with some precious new things which they had never heard or seen before. But, alas! when Saturday has come, I have been in the old spot again; instead of having any new things, I have been as dark as a dungeon... Ah! my dear brother this is hard work. But God will bring down high looks... God has brought me down hundreds of times till I could only just whisper out of the dust, and has made me willing to be anything or nothing....Here I have found solid peace... At these times, I have found the Lord to be with me in a precious manner; not giving me, as my flesh has wanted it, a deal of fine flowery things to tickle the ear; but *solid, weighty experimental truth, with divine anointing attending it,* and proving as nails fastened by the Master of assemblies in a sure place; and I have then, proved, by soul experience, that the kingdom of God is not in word, but in power, in the Holy Ghost, and in much assurance.......We have seven added to us last ordinance day, and we are going to have more. We are quite crowded as a congregation. I am quite astonished, and wonder how it is that the people flock from all parts around to hear such simple truth.[5]

---

[5] *Gospel Standard* 1842, pp. 222-224.

On 31st July 1834 Warburton wrote to his friend William Gadsby in Manchester on hearing of the continued mental affliction of his wife. In the letter he speaks of his own nature when under affliction and says that when some trying stroke upsets all his plans, he is like 'a wild bull in a net.' He quotes the text, 'No chastening for the present seemeth to be joyous, but grievous; nevertheless afterward it yieldeth the peaceable fruit of righteousness unto them which are exercised thereby [Heb. 12.11],' and adds, 'You and I have proved this to be the case in every storm we have had to this moment.' He concludes his letter, 'We are going on very comfortably and prosperously as a Church and congregation. The Lord is adding to us many precious souls, that give precious *testimonies* of receiving the truth in the love of it.' [Before baptism and membership, candidates came before the Pastor and Deacons, and then before the assembled members of the Church to give a *testimony* of the work of the Holy Spirit in their hearts. A majority vote of the Church members was necessary to receive them into the Church.] 'I am quite astonished at the multitude of people that come to hear. It appears to me, at times, that the bigger fool I get, the more the people love to hear me preach the Word.'

In December 1834 Warburton wrote to a fellow minister telling him, 'You must go like the rest of God's sent servants with *the things you have tasted, handled, and felt,* so that you may come to the people, not with a, "Lo here and lo there, but, "Thus saith the Lord of Hosts. Ah, what a blessing it is to be at a point in the things which we deliver to the people.' Then he goes on to say,

> You want to know some of the particulars of my journey into Sussex. I left home very low, fearful and helpless... When I arrived there I was informed that there were four to be baptised. The flesh and the devil began to work most vehemently, both in myself and others, and tidings were soon flying about that I was going to split the Church, though God knows I had no desire to do any such thing. I soon learned that if I baptised, it would be grievous to the feelings of many with whom I feel a union, and they with me, for the truth's sake; and besides, it was intended

by some that, if I attended to the ordinance, I was not to preach in their chapel afterwards.[6]

The conflict referred to here was between the Independents led by Mr Vinall at Jireh, Lewes and Church Street Brighton, and the supporters of Gadsby and Warburton at Brighton, who believed in baptism by immersion. Doctrinally and experimentally they were united, but not on the issue of the manner of baptism. Warburton goes on to describe how the Lord spoke into his heart, 'Endure hardness as a good soldier of Jesus Christ,' and that he then proceeded to baptize the four candidates. He says that after the words came into his heart, 'I did not feel any desire after this to desert my colours... I can assure you that poor old John has no stone to throw at the greatest coward in the world.... But the grace of God helped me through; and never did I see and feel the ordinance of baptism more solemn in my life, for the Lord was surely there in a special manner. The chapel was crowded and as still as death... I could bless God in my very soul that He counted me worthy to suffer persecution for His Name's sake..... How they have been at Brighton since I left I have not heard, but I hope, if it be the Lord's will, they may live in peace.' He concludes his letter with the news that at Zion, 'Mrs— has left us as a Church. She gave as her reasons for leaving that we were too carnal and worldly, and that she got no benefit from my preaching. I wonder that anyone is benefited by it.' So Warburton pressed on with his troubles at home and abroad.

1835 was for him a year to be remembered. Not only was it the twentieth anniversary of his Pastorate at Zion Chapel, but in that year on 1st August, William Gadsby published the first edition of a new monthly spiritual magazine called the *Gospel Standard* [7] to represent the group of Particular Baptist

---

[6] *Gospel Standard* 1842, pp. 105-107.

[7] The History of the Gospel Standard Magazine 1835-1985. Edited by B.A. Ramsbottom. 1985.

Churches which had being growing up in the country since he came to Manchester in 1805, through his ministry, and that of his friends John Warburton and John Kershaw. It was in this magazine, eventually in 1840 to come under the Editorship of John M'Kenzie of Preston and J.C.Philpot M.A., that many of Warburton's letters and sermons were to be published. Within six years its circulation had reached 7,400 and by 1847 9,000. It acted as 'a bond of union amongst experimental people throughout England.'[J.C.Philpot] [8] On Sunday 6th September 1835, John M'Kenzie, who had been expelled by the Independents in Preston for preaching the doctrines of grace, was baptized at Blackburn, in Lancashire. On the following Sunday, 13th September, John Warburton baptized J.C.Philpot in the newly built chapel, with its lead lined baptistry, at Allington in Wiltshire, in the presence of the deacons, Joseph Parry and Carby Tuckwell and a large congregation, probably 250 people.[9] Writing to William Gadsby on the following Friday week, 25th September Warburton says,[10] 'I went over and baptised Mr Philpot at Allington, last week, and I have no doubt but that the Lord was there. The more I know of him, the more union I feel to him.' Regarding Zion Chapel he says, 'Three weeks ago we had one added to us, and precious testimonies he gives of the power attending the Word. It is the power, my brother, that we are contending for: what is it all without it? The kingdom is not in word, but in power. We are a crowded congregation: we are obliged, every Lord's Day, to have forms in the aisles. It does not matter whether devils, or empty professors rage and rave, God will have His own way I am sure.' [This was the first letter of Warburton to be published in the *Gospel Standard* for February 1836, when it was just six months old.]

---

[8] *History of G.S. Magazine*. op. cit. p. 13.

[9] *Letters & Memoir of J.C.Philpot* 1871, *p. 50.*

[10] *Gospel Standard* 1836, pp. 41-42.

Writing to James Brookland, a friend in his old Parish of Stadhampton, on 23rd September 1835 J.C.Philpot says, regarding his baptism at Allington, 'Mr Warburton preached, and baptised me with great solemnity, unction and affection.' This was the beginning of a new era among the Churches founded by William Gadsby, John Warburton and John Kershaw. Here was the next generation of leaders being brought by the Lord among them, men of the calibre of J.C.Philpot, William Tiptaft and John M'Kenzie. Roger Hitchcock, although one of the early seceders, left the Devizes area for Devon in 1833, and took no further part in the development of the Churches, which were to centre themselves around the *Gospel Standard.* About 1832, just before he left Wiltshire, Roger Hitchcock baptised Thomas Godwin at a newly formed Baptist Chapel at Uffington in Berkshire. Present at that baptising was James Shorter who was later to be Pastor of the Chapel at Blunsdon Hill, near Swindon from 1834 – 1857. Thomas Godwin, born in 1803, had been brought up in the Church of England at Purton and Shaw outside Swindon. He had heard William Tiptaft and William Gadsby preach at an Independent Chapel in Swindon just after Tiptaft had left the Church of England in November 1831. A shoemaker by trade, he felt led into the work of the ministry and eventually commenced preaching at Swindon on 25th December 1834. He was called to be Pastor of the Baptist Church at Pewsey where he remained from 1836 – 1846.[11]

In the Summer of 1837 Godwin walked over to Allington and met J.C. Philpot, which was the beginning of a life long union of heart together. Later about 1839 he went to Allington to hear John Warburton preach. He says, 'I had never heard but one such preacher before.' This visit resulted in a union between the two men and on 3rd October 1840, Thomas Godwin was invited to preach at Zion Chapel Trowbridge when Warburton was away. So well was his ministry received that he was invited again on 24th October a week or so later. This was

---

[11] *Six Remarkable Ministers,* B.A. Ramsbottom, 1994, p. 7-82.

the start of many preaching visits to Trowbridge during Warburton's lifetime.

Looking down the list of ministers who preached at Zion during Warburton's preaching tours away from Trowbridge, names occur like, William Beard. He first preached at Zion in 1832 and continued regularly on annual engagements until 1846 when he became Pastor at Hankerton near Malmesbury. Another name that appears frequently is Thomas Martin. He was Pastor at Malmesbury from 1812 until 1857. He first preached at Zion on 25th April 1829 and preached each year until 1833. He was given the pastoral charge at Malmesbury in 1812 by Mr Porter, pastor of Somerset Street Chapel, Bath. Somerset Street Chapel was the one which excluded the members who supported William Gadsby, who then formed the York Street Chapel in Bath about 1811. It is of considerable interest to see that in the course of his pastorate, Thomas Martin and his church had moved their position and were now among the group of Churches in Wiltshire centring around Warburton at Zion Chapel, Trowbridge, having turned from the position of John Paul Porter, pastor of Somerset Street Chapel, that the Moral Law is the believer's rule of life. J.P.Porter was instrumental in the formation of the Old Baptist Chapel, in Chapel Lane, the High Street, Chippenham in 1804. John Warburton appears to have had no connection with this Church until Thomas Littleton became Pastor of it in 1846. Then Zion records show that in July and August, Littleton came to preach at Zion. Later William Mortimer, who became pastor at Chippenham after Littleton, in June 1852, also preached at Zion in the last years of Warburton's ministry. This shows that the Old Baptist Chapel at Chippenham did not move into Warburton's circle of Churches until about 1845.

The name of Daniel Smart [12] first appears in Zion records on 3rd November 1833. Born in Devizes in 1808, where his father was deacon at the Old Baptist Chapel, he had gone to school in Warminster, been baptised at Grove Chapel, Wantage on Christmas Day 1829, [the same day that Tiptaft had preached his sermon at St Helen's, Great Church, Abingdon]

---

[12] *Life & Sermons of Daniel Smart,* 1889.

and gone out to preach on 12th August 1832. He preached at Zion for four years until he went to Welwyn in Hertfordshire to be pastor there. When he first preached at Zion on 3rd November 1833 he was only twenty-five.

John Kershaw came from Rochdale to preach at Zion for six consecutive Sundays in October – November 1834. [These sermons were taken down and printed.] He was forty-two at the time. This is recorded in the Rochdale Church books. Kershaw appears to have come to Zion only on rare occasions. Another visiting minister of some note was William Cowper [13] of the Dicker, Sussex. The Dicker Chapel was completed in 1837 and formally opened by William Gadsby on 13th August 1838. Mr Cowper had become their stated minister in 1836. The founder members of this Church had been blessed under William Gadsby's ministry when he preached at Eastbourne in 1816. William Cowper had travelled, preaching and collecting for the building, and had raised £274. Zion Account book for 1831 records a visit of Mr Cowper and states, 'Collection for Mr Cowper £7 13s 1d.' It also states that 'Mr Warburton received £2 10s for entertaining Mr Cowper and that Mr Cowper was paid £10 for supplying. Mr Cowper was again in Wiltshire in 1837 and preached at Zion on 7th October. Previously, that same year, he had stood in for John Warburton when the latter was unable to preach at the opening of Calne Chapel on 17th May.[14] His text in the morning service that day was Psalm 63.2.

Sometime in these years Warburton was writing his book *The Mercies of a Covenant God.* In *The Seceders* Volume I, p. 358, Dr J.H.Philpot, quoting from extracts of the Diary of his father J.C. Philpot for the year 1837, says,

> On April 5th my father is driven into Devizes in a cart to meet John Warburton, who gives him his MS. *Mercies of Covenant God* to look

[13] *Further History of the Gospel Standard Baptists,* Vol. 2, p. 58.

[14] The Seceders, Vol. 1, J.H. Philpot, 1931, p. 358.

over. A month later he meets the old minister again at Mr Robert Dredge's [in Devizes], and strongly advises him to publish. On May 16th he hears to his regret that John Warburton will not be able to come to Calne for the opening of the chapel tomorrow as he had to go to London about his son Gideon's affairs.

A letter of J.C.Philpot, written from Manchester to Joseph Parry at Allington, and dated 13th September 1837 says,[15]

> I find Warburton's MS. will cost me a great deal of labour. Mr J. Gadsby [Manchester printer of the *Gospel Standard* and son of William Gadsby] put it into the hands of a schoolmaster to copy and correct the bad grammar, but he has sewed so much gold fringe upon John's plain cloth, that my present employment is to rip it all off. He has altered John's plain, straightforward language, and made him talk like a schoolmaster, so that my present tedious task is to compare the two copies line by line, and word by word, and restore the original language.

The first part of the *Mercies* [1776 – 1815] was reviewed in the *Gospel Standard* by J.C.Philpot in April 1838. This shows a publication date in the early spring of 1838. It was printed by John Gadsby at Newall's Buildings, in Market Street, Manchester. The second part [1815 – 1838] followed in 1839. Attached to the first part were a series of letters by a lady in Frome, Somerset, to John Warburton, entitled *Letters from Sarah to Barnabas.* In his Review of April 1838, J.C. Philpot suggested the deletion of these letters from any further edition, and this suggestion was followed.

The facts suggest that Warburton probably began to write his *Mercies* about 1835. Knowing how little education he had had, and the length of the complete volume which runs to about two hundred pages; remembering equally, that he was writing with a quill pen, and daylight was probably the limit of his time for writing; also considering his many travels away

---

15 *The Seceders*, Vol. 1, J.H.Philpot, 1931, pp. 321-324.

preaching and his large pastorate and preaching engagements in Trowbridge and the vicinity, it is probable that it was a gradual work over a period of one or two years, which he took up as time permitted. The resignation of Sarah Earle [his daughter] and her husband from Zion Chapel as members, in 1835, possibly indicates the time when the book was first under consideration.

The book was ready on 5th April 1837 and Warburton took it to Robert Dredge's house in Devizes where he met J.C.Philpot, who took it back to Allington, kept it for a month and then met Warburton again in Devizes, handed it back and suggested it be published. In the summer of 1837 it was sent to John Gadsby at Manchester for publication. He gave it to a schoolmaster who marred it, and when J.C.Philpot, who was in Manchester that summer saw it, he stopped the publication, and in September 1837 restored it to John Warburton's simple English, minus the grammatical errors. Thereafter in the autumn and early winter of 1837 Part I was set and printed, to be followed by Part II a year or so later.

Reviewing Part I of the *Mercies* in the *Gospel Standard* in 1838, J.C.Philpot says,

> There are, we believe, but few of our readers who do not know the author of the above work, either by having heard him themselves, or by having heard of him from others. He is indeed a remarkable instance of the discriminating sovereignty of Jehovah, who has raised him from the loom, as he raised Bunyan from the tinker's barrow, and Huntington from the coal barge, to feed His people Israel. In this most interesting and savoury account, of the Lord's transactions with him, he has given a relation of the first work of grace upon his soul, when the Law took him by the throat saying, 'Pay me that thou owest;' of his signal and glorious deliverance by the revelation of Christ; of his clear and manifest call to the ministry, and of many remarkable dealings in providence and grace till the time he was settled as Pastor over the Particular Baptist Church at Trowbridge.
>
> He has written the whole in very simple, sweet and savoury language, and there is a power, unction and reality attending it, which under the blessed Spirit's anointings must drop like the rain and distil like the dew, into believing, circumcised hearts. We are truly glad that he has been led to publish these dealings of the Lord with his spirit, and for this reason. Preaching though a most blessed ordinance of God, is to a certain

extent limited. Local distance, for instance, is an impassable limit, for two congregations cannot hear a man of God at one and the same time. But gracious writings can be in a thousand different places at once. They can penetrate, too, into circles where he may never personally come; and besides that may feed the church of God, when his body is rotting in the grave, and his soul is in the bosom of his Redeemer.

What a blessing have Huntington's writings been to the family of God, and thousands to the end of time will rise up and call him blessed, who would scarcely have known that there had been such a man had not his pen been as much inspired to write as his tongue to preach. May a similar blessing rest upon the work we are now noticing. There is a power in a gracious experience, which can be felt, but not described. It carries with it a divine impress, and bears stamped upon it, a heavenly character. It is a two- edged sword that cuts two ways at once, entering at the same stroke into the conscience of living souls, and cutting to pieces the hypocrisy of rotten hearts. There never was a time when decisive preaching and writing were more needed. The veil of profession has become spread over the Church and under this covering thousands of self-deceived, Satan -deluded wretches are crouching in security. And it is feared that too many of God's children are stretching themselves on this bed too short, and wrapping themselves up in this covering too narrow; and by thus making a confederacy with those, who put bitter for sweet and sweet for bitter, are cutting out terrible work for a death bed.

Now nothing in the hand of the blessed Spirit is so calculated to rend asunder this veil from the top to the bottom, as the insisting on the power of vital godliness by those highly favoured men, who have had the kingdom of God set up with heavenly authority in their own souls. God's quickened children have a conscience. They have felt power. They have heard the voice of the Lord, powerful and full of majesty, and this voice has spoken to their hearts. They can never therefore resist truth as formalists resist it; but there is something in them which hears and recognises the voice of God speaking in one of His ambassadors, and though that voice condemns them, still they must fall under the power of it.

Thus a servant of the Lord, who comes with divine authority, as an eye-witness of the truth that he preaches, must always find an echo in the hearts of God's people. God forbid that any servant of His should keep back a part of the price and for the sake of a large Church, considerable pew-rents, good collections, wealthy deacons, a flourishing cause, and a respectable congregation – these baubles of Mammon, these God dishonouring motives, so widely prevalent, should so pare down experience and the power of vital godliness, as to flood his Church with half and half, soft, undecided, unstript, unhumbled Pharisees, with Calvinistic heads and Arminian hearts.......

Power is the only weapon worth a straw.... Power is a sword that reaches to the very soul. It lays bare the conscience, reveals the secrets of the heart..... and spreads the soul naked and open before the eyes of Him with whom we have to do. Thus those quickened souls who have felt this two-edged sword, piercing even to the dividing asunder of soul and spirit, and of the joints and marrow, and to be a discerner of the thoughts and intents of the heart, never can be satisfied without the blood of sprinkling, and the revelation of Jesus Christ.

The desire of our soul is that the experience of John Warburton may be thus blessed. We can most cordially recommend it to our readers...[16]

The *Mercies* sold well and passed through edition after edition. It has been frequently reprinted in this century both here and in the United States. It was translated into Dutch over fifty years ago, and a revised translation is in preparation in the Netherlands at the present time [1995]. It is a spiritual autobiography of the same character as John Bunyan wrote, when he published his autobiography *Grace Abounding to the Chief of Sinners* in 1666, and followed it with the same spiritual experience in allegorical form in the *Pilgrim's Progress* in 1678. But if John Warburton was influenced by John Bunyan in writing his *Mercies*, it is clear that he was also influenced by two contemporary books, namely *The Kingdom of Heaven Taken by Prayer* and *The Bank of Faith*, both published by William Huntington in 1784. Warburton possessed a leather bound copy of *The Kingdom of Heaven Taken by Prayer.* It was an edition printed in 1813, bound with a second edition of Huntington's book *Light Shining in Darkness,* printed in 1803. In the inside cover he has written, 'John Warburton his book.' Warburton had met Huntington in 1812 and had felt a great union of heart with him spiritually. It is inconceivable that he had not read both these books, which

[16] *Gospel Standard* 1838. pp. 91-93.

were so widely read among the congregations in which he preached, especially at Gower Street Chapel in London, where many of the people were former members of William Huntington's Providence Chapel. *The Kingdom of Heaven* and *The Bank of Faith* would seem to be the prime influences in leading Warburton to write and publish his own spiritual experience. With J.C.Philpot's help, the *Mercies* appeared in plain, simple English, with its grammar and spelling corrected by a sympathetic, loving hand, a scholar who had an affectionate regard for its author.

It was written in an uninhibited way from his heart to the heart of his readers. It speaks of the soul exercises of a man who did constant business with his God in deep waters, and knew what it was to have his 'life given for a prey.'[Jer. 39.18.] It reveals the heart breathings of one whose eyes were constantly heavenwards and knew what it was to feel that his God could only be approached in 'sincerity and truth' and that, 'He that cometh to God must believe that He is, and that He is a rewarder of them that diligently seek Him.' [Heb. 11.6.] It speaks of one who knew 'the Slough of Despond,' and 'the Delectable Mountains,' and could sing the Pilgrim's hymn,

> Thus far did I come laden with my sin;
> Nor could ought ease the grief that I was in,
> Till I came hither: What a place is this!
> Must here be the beginning of my bliss?
> Must here the burden fall from off my back?
> Must here the strings that bound it to me, crack?
> Blest Cross! Blest Sepulchre! Blest rather be
> The Man that there was put to shame for me.
>
> J. Bunyan.

His was an experimental knowledge of truth, of condemnation and pardon and peace. He had entered into the truth, 'The blood of Jesus Christ His Son cleanseth us from all sin.' [1 John 1.7.] As J.C. Philpot pointed out in his Review in 1838, the book strikes a chord in a heart taught by the Holy Spirit, led away from of an intellectual knowledge into a heart knowledge. It was at this level that the Oxford Don and the

Lancashire hand loom weaver found common ground and a life long union of heart in the things of God.

As John Warburton was writing his book in his home in Waterloo Terrace beside Zion Chapel, so other events were unfolding. On 11th September 1835, his deacon of ten years, and loyal supporter in the building of Zion Chapel, William Hayward had died. Warburton had baptised him on 13th August 1815 and he had loaned £500 toward the building of Zion. When he died most of it had been repaid. James Hayward, his son, appointed deacon with his father in 1825 was to remain in office until his death on 12th February 1850. At the time of the death of William Hayward, Thomas Ball, James Porter and Richard Knee were deacons. In the following year [1836] the Church appointed two new deacons, Thomas Tabor, who had been baptised 4th October 1818, and Thomas Hayward who had been received a member at Zion on 23rd September 1821. Richard Knee was to remain in office as deacon until his death in 1864. He was to be deacon for thirty-nine years. He had a bookshop in Church Walk and was the agent for many years for the distribution of the *Gospel Standard* magazines each month in Trowbridge.

In 1835 Mr Philpot and Mr Tiptaft, the young seceders from the Church of England, both preached at Zion, Philpot on 11th October and Tiptaft in November. Philpot did not come again until 25th June 1837. He records in his Diary,

June 23rd	Three days after the accession of Queen Victoria, took the coach from Devonport to Exeter. Preached eve.
Sat 24th	Unable to sleep for ----s [unmentionable bedfellows]; Left Exeter at 8 for Bath; Went outside, 10s, v.fine and warm. Reached Bath 20 p. 6; took fly to Trowbridge; slept at Warburton's.
Sun. 25th	Preached at Trowbridge. Morn. Job 18.9. Evg. Isa. 18. 5,6. v. hoarse both times.

On Monday 26th June he records that he left Trowbridge at 8, he breakfasted with Mr Dredge at Devizes, and reached Allington at 10.30. a.m. It was on this visit that Joseph Parry lent him a horse and he visited Farmer Wild daily on his death bed at Stowell Farm, Wilcot until his death, when he buried him at Allington on 30th July. No doubt John Warburton knew godly old Farmer Wild well. The sermon which Philpot preached at Zion that Sunday evening from Isaiah 18. 5,6, was later to be published as J.C. Philpot's well-known sermon, *Winter Afore Harvest, or The Soul's Growth in Grace.*

While these events were taking place, Warburton was in the throes of another period of trouble with his son John. In the early part of 1837, he had left Trowbridge for London, with the aim of reaching Manchester.[17] Having reached London he walked as far as St Albans, where he stayed the night and then made his way toward Dunstable along the Watling Street, the present A5 road. The weather was cold with snow about. He met with a discharged soldier who was as poor as himself. They begged and stayed at night in barns. One night they spent in the Barracks at Weedon. Eventually he reached Stafford and tried to enlist in the Army, but failed to pass the medical. Outside Stafford, a passing coach driver took pity on him, because he was so lame, and having a half empty coach gave him a free lift to Manchester. There he stayed the night and then made his way to Rochdale to the home of his brother William. He took him to see John Kershaw, who spoke very kindly to him, presumably about the anxiety he was causing his father.

Later he went across to Whitefield to his Uncle William, his father's brother. He gave him a home and got him a job with a tailor, George Barrow, in Radcliffe. His Uncle had only had one son called John, and he had died. So he became very fond of his nephew and did all he could to help him. John stayed with his Uncle in Whitefield for about three months, from the middle of March to the middle of June 1837. Then the wander lust came on him again, and abandoning his job in Radcliffe and his home in Whitefield, he made his way south to Birmingham, Gloucester, Cirencester and eventually to

---

[17] *Memorials of John Warburton of Southill*, 1892. p.15.

Trowbridge, where he arrived about midnight on Sunday 25th June and went to the home of his sister Sarah [Mrs Earle], in Prospect Place.[18] His father was away from home and J.C.Philpot was staying at his home in Waterloo Terrace, having just preached his sermon at Zion that Sunday evening, '*Winter before Harvest.*'

His sister Ruth went up to Prospect Place and wept as she pleaded with him to come home. This he refused to do, and with 5s she had given him, he set off to Bristol on Monday morning, with the purpose of never coming back to Trowbridge again. His father came home to a house full of sorrow. Now he realised that it was useless to follow him. He says in his *Mercies,* [19]

> O how clearly I saw that none but God could ever stop him; that if I were to follow him again, and find him, I could not change his heart; and that *that* was entirely the work of God, and not mine. And O what power and strength did I feel from that text, 'Cast thy burden upon the Lord, and he shall sustain thee, for he shall never suffer the righteous to be moved.' [Ps. 55.22.] O what a lift was this to my poor burdened soul! How easily I could cast the lad into the hands of God, that has angels, men and devils at his beck, that has fixed, 'Hitherto, but no farther.' O what an easement I found in my mind! For I never could freely leave him before this in the hands of God........ I saw it as clear as day that the lad could go no farther than what God had fixed. And O the blessedness of two verses of John Kent's hymns that flowed like honey out of the rock into my soul, and ratified in my heart that the dear lad, notwithstanding all, was one of God's elect.

> There is a period known to God,
> When all His sheep, redeemed by blood,
> Shall leave the hateful ways of sin,
> Turn to the fold and enter in.

---

[18] *Memorials of John Warburton,* op. cit. pp. 21-30.

[19] John Warburton, op. cit. p. 205.

At peace with hell, with God at war,
In sin's dark maze they wander far,
Indulge their lust, and still go on,
As far from God as sheep can run.

Now Warburton had to wait three weeks for any news of him. When it came, it was that the lad had passed through Taunton on his way to Exeter, and had stopped at Taunton one night at a friend's house. They had done all they could to persuade him to return home, but had failed. Warburton describes how he physically shook on receipt of this news. He says, 'I was up in my little shady arbour in the garden, and I thought I could not have crawled into the house.' He describes how at last he got back to his room in the house, shaking like a leaf, trembling from head to foot. Then he opened his Bible on Isaiah 11 and reading the opening verses, his heart was broken down and a sweet peace came into his soul, and when he came to verses six and seven, 'The wolf also shall dwell with the lamb, and the leopard shall lie down with the kid; and the calf, and the young lion, and the fatling together, and a little child shall lead them. And the cow and the bear shall feed; their young ones shall lie down together, and the lion shall eat straw like the ox,' he saw six of God's *shalls,* as firm as the everlasting hills, and felt confident that God would bring the lad home.

John junior was twenty-one at this time. In his *Memorials,* he records how on his journey west, he was tempted to rob a gentleman of his gold watch, but the Lord kept him from doing so. Eventually he reached Exeter and on the evening of 10th July 1837 he entered the city. Next morning he enlisted in the Army in the 37th Regiment of Foot. Some days later he marched with other recruits from Exeter to Plymouth Citadel. He would have been twenty-two on 4th August that year. On arrival here he wrote home to his father,[20] which was

---

[20] *Memorials of John Warburton*, op. cit. p. 28.

about two weeks after they had last heard of him at Taunton. His letter was dated 8th August. In it he explained that he had been forced to join the Army to avoid starvation. Then he wrote,

> You might ask if there was any occasion for my leaving home. No, there was not, and I have no one to thank but myself. Ah, father, I have known some trouble within this last fortnight! The hours of grief and torment I endure night and day, with the stings of a guilty conscience. Who can bear it? Would to God He would take my life and let me know the worst of it! What grief have I cost you, and the hours of sorrow you have had on my account. Why was I born and for what purpose but to fill up my cup and then sink to rise no more? It is like hell to me in the barracks, some swearing, others singing, and of a Sunday no more reverence than if they were beasts...... I expect before this year is out to go out of England to India. I suppose it will be in October.

He concluded by saying he dare not ask his father's forgiveness, for he could not believe he would ever speak to him again. He asked for a letter, a little money, and the address of any friends in Plymouth, where he might go to get away from the Barracks. Sending his love to his brother's and sisters, he sent especial regards to his youngest sister Ruth, saying, 'Poor Ruth, I often think of her.' Strangely, he made no mention of his mother, Lydia. She was the one who so often, in the absence of his father, had had to exercise all the discipline over him for months at a time in his adolescence. A possible reason for leaving home for months at a time [as his stay with his Uncle William at Whitefield for three months in 1837], could have been caused by a strong reaction against his mother.

His father replied to his letter at once, and by the same post sent a letter to Mr Triggs, the minister at Plymouth, whom he says was a 'perfect stranger to him', though in fact Warburton had himself visited Plymouth in 1821, in the year when Triggs first preached there for David Denham. Trigg's reply is given in full in the *Mercies*.[21] Warburton had asked him to go to the Barracks and try and gauge if the lad's sorrow was genuine, and if there was a real spiritual change wrought in

---

[21] John Warburton, op. cit. pp. 210 – 213.

him. John had eventually visited Mr Triggs in his home and Mr Triggs judgement in his letter was, 'There is certainly a great change taken place for the better.' Triggs had asked him whether he was still going on in his old ways of sin and rebellion and John junior's response had been, 'I cannot, for a few weeks ago all my past life and actions were brought before me, with the shortness of time, and the awful circumstances of eternity.' He had tried to stifle these convictions by getting into worldly company, but they were always uppermost in his heart. He was completely miserable and felt there was no mercy for him. Triggs concluded his letter by offering to help to procure his discharge from the Army, by enquiring from the Commanding Officer what the price would be. When this letter reached Trowbridge, Warburton says in his *Mercies*,

> 'Never can I forget the melting I had in reading this letter. I had to put it down three or four times before I could get through it. Never was my heart so broken in reading a letter in all my life; and my dear wife and two daughters that were at home, I do not know which of them wept the most. O the kindness, and love, and feeling that my dear brother Triggs manifested to one so unworthy. [22]

The deep affection and spiritual concern which Warburton had for his children is clearly seen in these circumstances. His temperament moved in extremes, extremes of obstinacy and hastiness, and yet of deep love, affection and the grace of forgiveness. His *Mercies* reveals a gracious willingness to reveal his own faults and failings

John received his father's letter at Plymouth on 14th August, and replying to it by return post told his father, [23] 'Yours this morning I received, and its contents were truly cutting, not for its harshness, but its kindness; such kindness I never expected from you after treating you in the manner I have.' His father had asked whether he was willing to come

---

[22] John Warburton, op. cit. p. 213.

[23] *Memorials of John Warburton,* op. cit. pp. 29,30.

home and his response was, 'Yes, father, I am, and wish to remain at home as long as I live; and I only wish I was within sight of the house [Waterloo Terrace].' He then answered his father's enquiry about his discharge and explained it would cost £20 and suggested that he ask Isaac Moore, [Leah's husband], to go to the Sergeant-Major of the troops in Trowbridge to find out to whom the money should be paid. He concluded by saying that that morning the Regiment had been marched five miles to witness a flogging, when the soldier received 150 lashes.

Warburton says in his *Mercies,* [24]

> As soon as we could we procured his discharge; and the poor prodigal returned home, and a hearty welcome he had; and I soon found the work was of God, and that the lion could lie down with the lamb, and a little child could lead him. Poor thing! He was sorely chastened out of God's law for weeks after he got home; but the Lord in tender mercy broke his bonds asunder in His own time, and brought him to hear and feel the joyful tidings of a free and full forgiveness of all his cursed abominations through the application of the precious blood of Christ to his soul; and he knew what it was to sing with delight and joy, 'Bless the Lord, O my soul, and all that is within me, bless His Holy Name; bless the Lord, O my soul, and forget not all His benefits; who forgiveth all thine iniquities, who healeth all thy diseases, who redeemeth thy life from destruction, who crowneth thee with lovingkindness and tender mercies.' [Ps. 103. 1-4.] O how my soul did rejoice and thank and adore my God when I heard of the glad tidings that God had visited him with peace and pardon.

About eight months later, on 29th April 1838, in the presence of a large congregation, [about nine hundred people] [25] John Warburton baptised his son with five others at Zion Chapel, Trowbridge. Warburton says of the occasion,

---

[24] John Warburton, op. cit. p. 213.

[25] John Warburton, op. cit. p. 214.

Truly I felt it an affecting time, and so did many others...There were few with a dry cheek; and to this day I am fully persuaded the work is of God.... Never, I think, had I a sorer trouble, heavier conflicts with the devil, nor was I ever deeper sunk at times in despair; and never had I more transporting joy, and clearer discovery how God had answered my poor prayers in all my life. O what a wonder- working God is our God! He can turn what we fear will be the greatest curse into the greatest blessing.[26]

John Warburton Junior in his *Memorials* describes the occasion and says,

I was baptised by my father on 29th April 1838, in the presence of a large congregation, and as I stepped forward to go down into the water, my dear father said, 'Come, my brother, take up thy cross and follow a precious Christ.' As he uttered these words, I felt we truly were brothers in Christ. It was indeed a sweet time to my soul, and I had hard work to keep from shouting aloud the praise of God, as I came up out of the water. [27]

Just over eleven weeks later [19th July 1838], John junior married Emma Rudman a domestic servant of Mr Samuel Parfitt on the Bridge, Trowbridge, at St James Parish Church in the presence of his father; Mr William Rudman, her father; and Cornelius Rudman, the bride's brother. [Cornelius later in 1848, was elected a deacon at Zion Chapel.] John junior says,

'The first time I saw my dear wife was at the home of her brother. She had for many years attended my father's ministry, which was much blessed to her soul. What God purposes must come to pass. I said to myself, 'If ever I marry, that is my wife,' and she told me after we were married, that she was similarly impressed.' [28]

---

[26] John Warburton op. cit. p. 214.

[27] *Memorials of John Warburton,* op. cit. pp. 30,31.

[28] *Memorials of John Warburton*, op. cit. p. 31.

Their first home after their marriage was at 13 Timbrell Street, on the left had corner of the entrance to York Buildings. They did not stay here long as there was not much work in the tailoring trade in Trowbridge, and in November 1839 John Junior went to London to find work. He stayed with his brother, Gideon, in Tottenham Court Road and eventually found work with a Mr G. Doudney in Fleet Street. Emma followed him to London and they had rooms, first in Fenchurch Street, then on the third floor of a house in Wells Street, a turning off Oxford Street.[29]

In a letter to William Tiptaft, dated 16th November 1838,[30] John Warburton Senior reveals that he had just returned from Brighton and that 'brother Philpot' had been preaching at Trowbridge. The Church Book of Zion shows supply ministers at Zion for three Sundays in October, one of them being J.C. Philpot, who preached on 7th October. Philpot had been at Zion also on 21st February that year. So in the midst of the resolution of his 'greatest trial' Warburton was still carrying on his extensive travels in preaching.

What he does not reveal or even hint at in this letter of 16th November is that on 19th November 1838 a very large Chartist Meeting was planned in Trowbridge, which was to be of a fairly alarming nature. The Chartists were a political organization with mainly social and economic grievances. The movement had begun in London in 1836, with the formation of the London Working Men's Association. Their formation stemmed from the frustration felt by working people over the failure of the 1832 Reform Act to extend the right to vote far enough. Another major grievance was the effect of the Poor Law Amendment Act of 1834 which had withdrawn the right of 'outdoor' relief and forced needy families into the Workhouses, where husbands, wives and children were frequently separated in different buildings. Other causes were low wages and fluctuating unemployment levels seen to be caused by industrial mechanisation. Chartism flourished in the heartlands of the

---

[29] *Memorials of John Warburton*, op. cit. p. 41.

[30] *Gospel Standard,* 1872. p. 173.

Industrial Revolution and in this period [1838-39] half a million hand-loom weavers formed the backbone of the movement in the North; and in the West, the towns of Bath, Trowbridge, Bradford-on-Avon, Westbury and Frome were deeply involved.

This movement, which sought for political equality and social justice, was divided over its methods to obtain these ends. Many saw the way forward via Parliamentary Reform, a cheap Press, and a national system of education. A minority looked to more revolutionary means and violence. In 1838 the London organization produced a Charter with Six Points. They were:

Universal adult manhood suffrage,
Annual Parliaments,
Vote by Ballot,
Equal Electoral Districts,
Abolition of the Property Qualification for Members of Parliament,
Payment of Members of Parliament,

all of which have now been granted, except for 'Annual Parliaments.' The first Chartist Meeting in Trowbridge, an orderly one, took place in the Market Place on 12th June 1838, when William Carrier, a local man, spoke of the benefits of 'Universal suffrage.' The Trowbridge Working Men's Association was formed in June 1838 and had over 550 members, mostly cloth workers, renting a room at the Barracks.

On the evening of 19th November, a crowd of about 3,000 people assembled at the Barracks in Frome Road, Trowbridge, and by the light of torches, carrying a box [like a coffin] lit with a 'transparency' bearing the word 'Liberty,' marched round the town and halted in Timbrell Street, within a few yards of Zion Chapel, and only an hundred yards from John Warburton's home in Waterloo Terrace, and right outside the home of John junior and Emma. Many wore green ribbons, the colour of Republicanism. There were speeches, a discharge of firearms, and much shouting. The magistrates and a body of troops stood nearby and were abused by the speakers. There were only four constables in Trowbridge and Bradford at the time, and the magistrates had to rely on military aid to keep order. Though this Meeting eventually passed off without a riot, the Chartist Movement carried on throughout the winter and on into the spring of 1839, with various Meetings, some held outside the town on Trowle Common.

Soon the towns and the countryside were in a state of intimidation. Well-dressed citizens were abused in the streets, Church windows were broken and the Government was forced to call in the Hussars and the Yeomanry. On Easter Monday, 1st April 1839, several thousand Chartists converged on Devizes and entered the town marching five or six abreast. The Devizes 'Tories' reacted violently and with stones and bludgeons drove them out of their town. Another Meeting was planned in Trowbridge for 7th May 1839. On orders from the Home Office, the Trowbridge Magistrates moved in and arrested some of the leaders and searched their houses, finding arms and ammunition in at least one house. On Whit-Monday 20th May, the Chartist planned a mass Meeting in North Parade, Bath, but the Mayor would not allow it, and so they met at Midford, three miles to the south. Fifteen to twenty thousand were expected, but in the event about two thousand went. This lack of support emboldened the authorities to act firmly to stop the revolutionary ferment in the area.

On Sunday morning, 26th May 1839, John Warburton addressed his congregation of a thousand people from his pulpit at Zion Chapel, preaching from the text, 'For thou art an holy people unto the Lord thy God, and the Lord hath chosen thee to be a peculiar people unto Himself, above all the nations that are upon the earth.' [Deut. 14.2.] Firstly he showed that the holiness of a believer rested solely and alone in the imputed righteousness of Christ; then he spoke of holiness being implanted in the work of the new birth, which resulted in conviction of sin and a thirst for Christ to be revealed in the sinner's heart as the 'hope of Glory'; finally he spoke of holiness in outward deportment, and went on to condemn all who professed the Lord's name and yet 'joined the men of the world in order to obtain their political freedom.' In the evening sermon of the same Sunday, John Warburton spoke of the Israelites under Egyptian bondage, who instead of rising against the Egyptians to obtain their freedom, 'cried to the Lord.' He used both these sermons to advocate the doctrine of 'political stillness and unlimited obedience to higher powers.' A few weeks previously, he and his church had excommunicated some of his members for attending a Meeting of the Trowbridge Working Men's Association. The Zion Chapel Church Book contains the name of Robert Lucas, baptised by Warburton on 23rd August 1829, and besides his name it says, 'Separated, turned Chartist.'

This sermon resulted in an attack upon John Warburton, both in the local Chartist press and through a printed pamphlet. A disaffected member, Job Rawlings, baptised by Warburton at Ladydown Mill with twenty-five others, on 25th June 1820, had resigned his Church membership on 12th November 1836, because the Church at Zion had disciplined him for ' speaking to my fellow men in the name of the Lord in certain Chapels of which Warburton did not approve.'[31] He now took up his quill to attack Warburton in a letter to the Western Vindicator, accusing him of being a man who had himself risen from the depths of poverty, but now 'opposed poor christians, trying to obtain their just and lawful rights.'

He went on to publish his eighteen page pamphlet in response to Warburton's sermons of 26th May 1839. It is well-written, well- argued and not too vitriolic, considering he had an axe to grind. He has a considerable amount to say about Warburton's salary of £3 a week, to which he adds another £1 a week, taking into account Warburton's visits to London and elsewhere and the generosity of his friends outside Trowbridge. He reminds Warburton that on previous occasions, he [Warburton] has supported various political causes, even to letting his congregation sign various petitions in the chapel vestry. He accuses Warburton of hypocrisy, in that he urges separation from Chartism, but allows women in his Church to wear 'pompous dresses, veils, and carry gaudy parasols, employers in his Church to pay little more that half the wages due, and deacons to open 'needless public houses for selling beer.' He calls Warburton's salary a 'gospel tax' on the labouring poor. As regards the doctrine of political quiescence and non-resistance, he points out the laws of England were not

---

[31] *Animadversions upon a Sermon preached by Mr JohnWarburton, May 26 1839, upon the doctrine of non-resistance to the higher powers,* by J. Rawlings. Printed by S. Gibbs, 5 Union Street, Bath.

consistent with 'moral justice', and Old Testament prophets rebuke evil Kings. 'The rich man's property was protected and the poor man's labour was unprotected.' There was an excess of mechanical power, and many starved because wages were so low. The rich were the consumers, the poor the producers; the labourer was ruined. the poor starved, and crime increased. He advocated practical religion in the spirit and example of Jesus.

Warburton must have been stung by this public attack from a man whom he had baptised. Several of his members, including two sons-in-law, John Hayward and Isaac Moore, either owned their own businesses, and were employers, or were co-directors in large companies employing many people. There was no question that wages were low and the poor were hard hit and under paid. Equally the rights the people claimed were legitimate. Annual Parliaments were not feasible, but otherwise the demands of the Charter were sound.

John Warburton's friend William Gadsby, the Particular Baptist minister of Manchester, was noted for taking part in political matters. In 1821 he had supported Queen Caroline, when George IV had excluded her from the Coronation, and as a result, the Deputy Constable of Manchester had been sent by the Home Secretary, Viscount Sidmouth, to Back Lane Baptist Chapel, Manchester, to see if, on account of his sermon, he could arrest Gadsby for sedition. He failed because Gadsby saw him in the congregation, and pointed out his presence. Equally William Gadsby supported the Anti-Corn Law League, and spoke to large audiences in Manchester Town Hall on its behalf. All his life, Gadsby was noted as a man who collected large sums of money, and quantities of clothes for the poor, unemployed of Manchester. When he died in 1844, a Manchester newspaper in an article, wrote at length about his life long, philanthropic work among the poor. But it does not appear that he supported the Manchester Chartist Movement, though some Non-Conformist ministers did support it in various cities, such as Leicester. The Anti-Corn Law League was a middle class movement, whereas Chartism was a working class movement. The former movement was orderly, while the latter had elements of violence. The violence seems to lie at the root of Gadsby and Warburton's attitude to Chartism.

With this example of his greatest friend before him, it would seem that John Warburton's predicament as regards his failure to support the Chartist movement, consisted solely and alone in its violent tendency, and in the inconsistency between its pacific wing led by William Lovett and the more violent wing led by Feargus O'Connor. The *Western Vindicator* was a seditious weekly newspaper printed by the Chartists for the West of England and Wales. It must be remembered that on 3rd November 1839 a thousand boys and men converged on Newport, Monmouthshire, with a view to going to Monmouth to release imprisoned Chartist leaders. In a confrontation with police and soldiers, fire was drawn and in twenty minutes on the morning of 4th November, in the square in front of the West Gate Hotel, Newport, fourteen lay dead, fifty were wounded, of which a further ten died. John Warburton might well have felt that the scene outside the West Gate Hotel, could have equally taken place in Timbrell Street, Trowbridge. Warburton was not averse to taking part in political affairs, any more than William Gadsby. He had done it before, as Job Rawlings reminded him. He himself had had a Parliamentary vote in Wiltshire since 1819. Nine members of his congregation, including his two deacons, William Eacott and Samuel Hurd had a vote in the same Electoral Register. It was not the Charter with which he disagreed. It would be grossly unfair also, to accuse Warburton of being silenced for fear of his sons-in-law. His son James was a poor weaver living in Shail's Lane, right beside the Trowbridge Chartist headquarters, at the Democratic Chapel, in what later came to be called Chartist Square. To preach as he did on Sunday 26th May 1839 at Zion Chapel, in the heat of the Chartist activity was a very brave act. To advocate non-resistance, clearly suggests that it was at the point of violence that he disagreed with Chartism.

As regards the excessive nature of his salary, he certainly received from Zion Church £156 each year from 1815 to 1857; the Church Accounts show this. What he received over and above that is pure speculation. He alone knew. But equally his friend, William Gadsby, at Back Lane, Manchester, was paid £125 from 1805 to 1819,[32] and from 1820 to 1844 he was paid £230 a year.[33] On Job Rawlings calculation, Warburton at £4 a week was still only paid £208 a year. In comparison with ministers of other denominations it would seem that his salary was not excessive. It was comparable with the average level of the professional classes. What galled many was that he had been a poor weaver. In writing his *Mercies* he had highlighted the extent of his poverty, and therefore the comparison with his present station in 1839. William Gadsby never wrote an autobiography and therefore escaped the comparison.

The next surviving letter from this period, dated 6th September 1839,[34] reveals long journeys and numerous preaching engagements. It is written to a friend in Manchester, almost certainly William Gadsby. In it Warburton says,

> My spare time has been much taken up with scraping together my ins and outs in Trowbridge, for the Second Part of my poor 'Life.' [The *Mercies* published in 1839.] I find a deal up-hill in soul matters, and a deal of infirmities in the old tabernacle. My last journey to Leicester, Oakham, and Stamford shook my frame much. I believe I got a cold, which so fell into my legs that I could scarce walk all the time I was at Leicester, but I hope they are coming round now. I have had a good deal of giddiness in my head, and been nearly deaf in the left ear, but I have had some sweet moments of communion with my God in my last journey...... O how I did sing, when I was at Bedworth, that I had three or four days liberty. I would have gone to Coventry, and, *by the railway*, have proceeded to Manchester, and had a day or two with you, for my very soul longed for it; and when they told me at Bedworth that I might leave there in the morning and arrive at Manchester in the afternoon, I believe I should have done so had I not had to preach at Leicester the following evening. I believe I should have enjoyed it much, but it was not

32 *Works of William Gadsby,* Vol.1, p. 29.

33 *Works of William Gadsby,* op. cit. p. 99.

34 *Gospel Standard* 1840, pp. 30-33.

to be so....... I baptized Mr & Mrs Tryon, Mr de Merveilleux and two more the last Sunday I was at Stamford.

Warburton was putting the finishing touches to the second part of his *Mercies.* He had returned from preaching at Bedworth, Leicester, Oakham and Stamford. At Leicester he had been with Isaac Harrison who on 27th January 1839 had laid the foundation stone of his new Chapel in Alfred Street, which J.C. Philpot was to open on 25th December 1840.[35] At Stamford he had baptised the first members of the Church over which J.C.Philpot had become Pastor that year. Mr de Merveilleux was a surgeon, who had built the chapel at his own expense [at least £1,000.], and was now elected its deacon. Philpot had preached at Zion, Trowbridge for him on 21st and 22nd of July, so it is possible that they had exchanged pulpits.

The reference to railways is of considerable interest. By 1836 the nucleus of the present railway system had been laid down in England. The Liverpool-Manchester line had been opened in 1830, and London-Birmingham, and Birmingham - Liverpool in 1837. By 1838 the trains were entrusted with the Mails. Third class passenger fares were a penny a mile. This was to be followed with the introduction of Penny Post in 1840. Train speeds on the London-Liverpool line averaged about 35 mph, the journey of 200 miles taking between 5-6 hours, including stops. Brunel's Paddington to Bristol line was being built in 1840 and was finally opened on 30th June 1841. Probably on this journey in 1839 Warburton went to London by coach, and then went to Bedworth by train via Birmingham. It is of interest that he contemplated a quick rail trip from Bedworth to Manchester to see William Gadsby. The days were changing from his first journey South in 1814, when he came all the way to Trowbridge from Manchester by Stage Coach, taking several days. It would not be until 1848 before the railway finally reached Trowbridge. Prior to that, from 1841 to 1848 it was possible to take a Stage Coach from Trowbridge,

---

[35] *Further History of Gospel Standard Baptists*, Vol 3, S.F. Paul, 1958, pp. 183,184.

via Bradford-on-Avon to Chippenham and pick up a London train there. The Great Western Line was, of course, broad gauge. It was converted to narrow gauge in Trowbridge in 1874. So Warburton only knew the broad gauge in Trowbridge, and that for the last nine years of his life. For thirty-three years in Trowbridge, he had been dependant on Stage Coaches for all his journeys. Now at the age of sixty-three, when he was beginning to feel his age, complaining of difficulty with walking, hearing and giddiness, 'modern' facilities were arriving on the scene, which would make his constant journeys much easier, quicker and more comfortable.

Having returned from his journey in 1839 to the Midlands, and written to William Gadsby, before the close of the year in which he was to see the final instalment of his *Mercies* published, there awaited him further sorrows. Gideon had already gone to London sometime in 1837. John Warburton had himself been in London preaching at Gower Street in the October 1839. Now through lack of work, in November 1839, young John, whom his father had just baptised, was forced to leave Trowbridge for London in search of work. The boy over whom Warburton had yearned for so long, the prodigal of the family, only just brought home, now married, was to leave Trowbridge for ever. One evening in November, he was to take his place, travelling throughout the night to London in one of the last of the old Stage Coaches.

Then came the crowning sorrow, too late to find a place in the *Mercies,* which almost certainly was already printed. Manaoh, the child born in 1811, just after they arrived in Rochdale to live, the first child to be born in Hope Chapel House, the child of the blessing on the road from Manchester to Rochdale in the days of his poverty, 'The angel of the Lord did wondrously and Manoah and his wife looked on;' *this son* died on 4th November 1839, at the age of twenty-eight and was buried in the family grave, in front of the Chapel, under the footpath, nearest the door, with his sister Rhoda, who had been buried there nearly twenty years before. All Warburton's sons were now gone from the home in Waterloo Terrace, and only Rachel [aged 33], and Ruth [aged 26] were left at home.

The Lord had indeed shown His dear servant the 'balancings of the clouds' in His dealings with him. 'Dost thou know the balancings of the clouds, the wondrous works of Him which is perfect in knowledge?' [Job 37.16] What grace Warburton needed to answer this question on 4th November 1839, for he had called his son, Manoah in response to a blessed visit of the Lord to his soul on 23rd January 1811, and now 'The Lord had given, and the Lord had taken away,' and he needed grace to say, 'Blessed be the name of the Lord.' [Job 1. 21.]

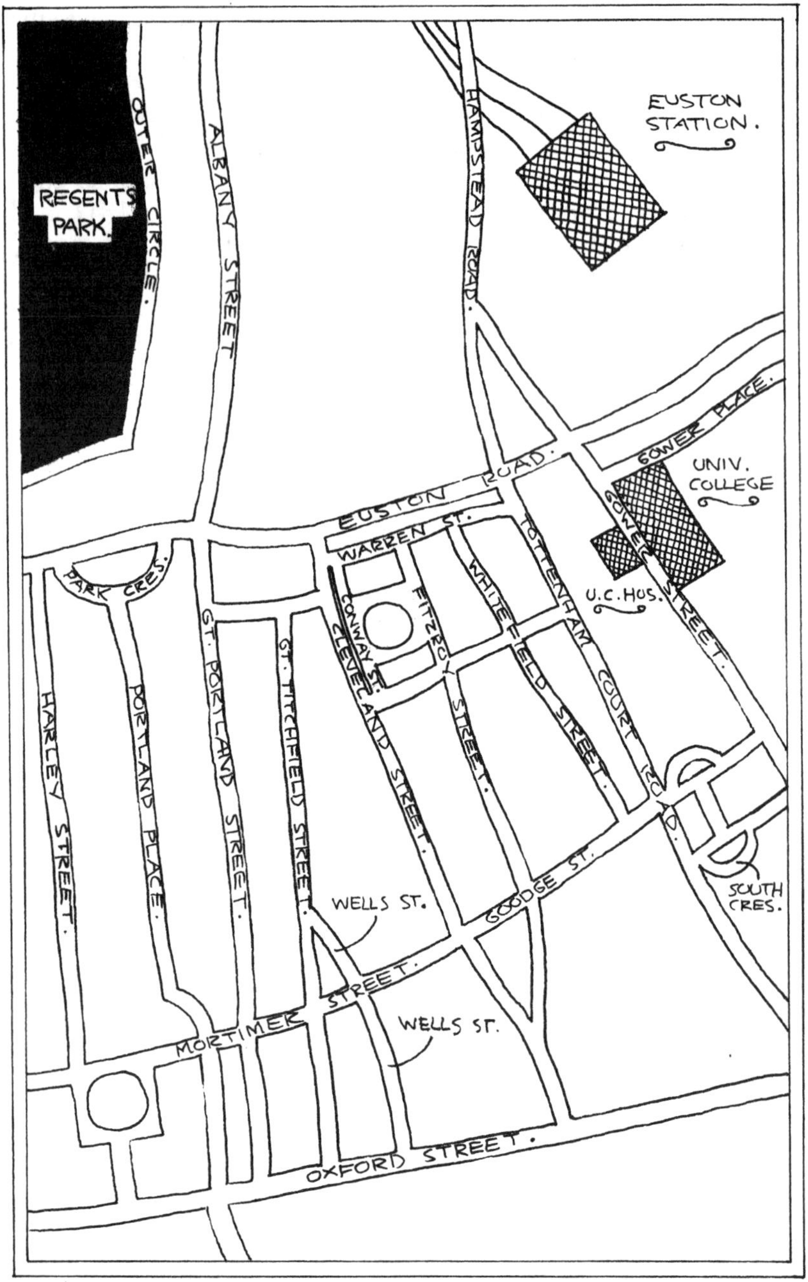

Map of Tottenham Court Road area, London.

Chapter 12

The silver cord loosed

Warburton was now in the last decade of his allotted span. In a letter dated 10th May 1843 [when he was sixty-seven], he wrote to his son John in London, 'How soon our end may come we know not.' In fact, the Lord was to spare his useful life to a ripe old age, and as regards his ministry, there now lay before him, in the sixteen years from 1840 to 1856, one of the most fruitful periods of his life. With the *Mercies* published and concluded in 1839, the sources of information that are available for these years are threefold.

Warburton was a prolific letter writer, and with the establishment of the Penny Post in 1840, his correspondence increased. Also with the monthly publication of the magazine the *Gospel Standard*, many of these letters found their way into print in its pages, sometimes within months of them being written. The letters were largely of a spiritual nature, written to brother ministers and church members all over the country, in churches where Warburton regularly preached. Often, however, they contain useful information as to the writer's whereabouts at any given time. They also contain information regarding his home affairs and Zion Chapel. From 1840 to 1849 the *Gospel Standard* [still published monthly, as it has been without intermission since its first copy in August 1835] was under the Joint-Editorship of Warburton's close friends J.C.Philpot and John M'Kenzie. When M'Kenzie died in 1849, Philpot became sole Editor until his death in 1869. So eventually in the *Gospel Standard* and various other spiritual magazines, in the next fifty years, about seventy of Warburton's letters found their way into print. A list of these letters and their place of publication is given in Appendix A.

Warburton, as will be seen, travelled extensively in these years, taking advantage of the railways, and preached regularly in London, Manchester, Leicester and went as far as Norwich, Brighton, Lakenheath and many other smaller, lesser-known places. At Appendix C is given a list of his preaching engagements in these years, so far as they can be ascertained. Again the *Gospel Standard* has been a useful source of information, because from an early date it became the practice for ministers to send to the publisher, John Gadsby, in Manchester, details of their preaching engagements, which were then published on the cover of the magazine, advertising the date, time and place of services for the following month. On occasions, and often in particular churches, their sermons were taken down, and then published in the *Gospel Standard* and other spiritual magazines. Sometimes they were printed in pamphlet form in various Sermon Series such as *Zoar Chapel Pulpit*, *The Penny Pulpit*, and *The Gospel Pulpit*. In this way, it is believed,[1] between fifty and sixty of Warburton's sermons found their way into print. A list of about thirty, so far traced, is given at Appendix B, with the date and place where they were preached, and also where they were first published.

With these resources it is possible to trace a considerable part of Warburton's preaching activities in these years. One of the churches where he was always welcomed was Gower Street Chapel, London. This was the street in London where the 'University of London' had commenced in 1828 in Gower Street College. It had been 'an undenominational teaching institution' which Matthew Arnold called 'that godless institution in Gower Street.' Later in 1834 a hospital was attached to the College, and in 1836 Gower Street College was renamed London University College. This University set the pattern for secularism in English Universities and opened the door for nonconformists to obtain the highest education in the land, until then reserved for Anglicans. King's College was set up in the Strand in 1831 as a Church of England College, in

---

[1] *The Gospel of a Covenant God*, Zoar Publications,1976. Preface.

opposition to University College. It is of considerable interest that both the sons of J.C.Philpot, Charles and Joseph Henry, were confirmed in the Church of England in order to be trained as doctors at King's College Hospital. One wonders whether William Gadsby, John Warburton or the Gower Street congregation had any inkling of the significance of events taking place around them in these years. It seems highly likely, that J.C.Philpot and William Tiptaft, both University trained men, understood.

Gower Street chapel had been built in 1820 for the congregation which had formerly worshipped in a chapel in Conway Street, Fitzroy Square. They were a substantial part of the congregation of William Huntington but had separated from New Providence Chapel, Grays Inn Lane after his death in 1813. Warburton had preached at Conway Street Chapel in 1818 and had continued preaching at the new Gower Street Chapel during the years from 1821 to 1838, when Henry Fowler had been the Pastor there. One of his earliest surviving sermons, preached on a Sunday in October 1839, was preached at Gower Street Chapel. William Gadsby had opened Gower Street Chapel on Sunday 9th July 1820 and was as welcome there as Warburton. But the congregation were Independents, like William Huntington, and while they stood shoulder to shoulder with Gadsby and Warburton regarding truth as preached by Huntington, they were not Baptists So when in 1821 they called Henry Fowler as their pastor, it was a pastor who was not a Baptist. This blending of the Independents of the Huntington School with the early leaders of the Gospel Standard Baptists was not so strange. They were completely at one in their view of truth and the preaching of the Gospel, only differing on the point of baptism. Another example of this union was at Brighton and Lewes where John Vinall [the Independent] was pastor and for whom Warburton had often preached in his early days in the South.

When Henry Fowler died on 16th December 1838, he was eventually succeeded by Edward Blackstock who vacillated between Open and Strict Communion. When he finally accepted the pastorate at Gower Street on Open Communion principles in November 1842, William Gadsby and John Warburton refused to preach there anymore. Warburton preached at Brighton in January and February 1840 for three Lord's days, and for four Lord's days in July and one in October at Gower Street. In 1841 he was at Norwich in August, at Gower Street in the month of October and at Leicester in November. In 1842 he was at Gower Street on the 9th, 18th and 25th October. This must have been the last time he preached at Gower Street. On 21st December he preached at Gadsby's Yard, Tottenham Court Road and again morning and evening on Lord's day 25th December.

By this time a division had taken place at Gower Street Chapel, and those wishing to maintain strict communion principles had left and formed a new congregation meeting in a large room in Gadsby's Yard, Tottenham Court Road. John Kershaw came from Rochdale to open this new meeting on 13th November 1842. Numbered among them was John Warburton junior, who was living nearby in Wells Street, off of Oxford Street. Later this congregation acquired a chapel in Eden Street, Hampstead Road, which was opened by John Warburton senior on Lord's day 9th April 1843. Warburton stayed on to preach for them on Lord's days 16th, 23rd and 30th April. This marked the establishment of a Gospel Standard Baptist Church on Strict Communion lines in London and proved to be a centralising factor for the group of churches established by William Gadsby, John Warburton and John Kershaw throughout the country. On 25th May 1843 a Church was officially formed, of which John Warburton junior became a member and on 11th June 1843 William Gadsby came to take the first Lord's Supper. Throughout the year the pulpit was filled by John Warburton, William Gadsby, John Kershaw, J.C. Philpot, William Tiptaft, Thomas Godwin, John M'kenzie, Mr Isbell, Mr Francis and William Cowper of the Dicker. This was the culmination of the work of William Gadsby, who rightly must be credited with being the founder of the Gospel Standard group of churches. He returned to Manchester in that summer of 1843 and died there on 27th January 1844, greatly mourned by those who loved his ministry throughout the country. Remarkably, on the very next Sunday, 28th January, John Warburton junior was called to preach his first sermon at

Rochester, so that as one Elijah was taken home another Elisha was raised up in his place.

The senior deacon of Gower Street Chapel, Robert Link, [former valet to Lord Palmerston and Lord Salisbury] [2] writing in July 1898 from his home in 12, Old Quebec Street, Portman Square, London, referring to a letter of John Warburton senior says,

> When I read it, my mind was led back to the good old days of Eden Street, fifty-five years ago [1843], when I used to hear good old John with power, unction and savour; when the voice of the Lord was powerful, and full of majesty, and his doctrine dropped as the rain, and his speech distilled as the dew; as the small rain upon the tender herb, and as the showers upon the grass; - the precious things from the lasting hills! John Warburton used to call himself 'Old John,' and he would say, 'Old John is like an old, empty jug; there is nothing good in him only what the Lord pours in, and when the Lord pours in, he could pour out;' and the golden oil flowed through the golden pipe into the empty vessels not a few, who opened their mouths wide, and God filled them with his hid treasure; – with the bread and water of eternal life, Jesus Christ and Him crucified; and the living ate and drank and carried it away. Your dear father [Joseph Tanner of Cirencester] used to say he 'always found takers-away in Gower Street Chapel'.

Every year, from 1843 to 1854 Warburton preached at Eden Street for a month, mostly the month of April, but from 1849 to 1852 it was changed to May, later reverting to April. Not only did he preach on Lord's days, but also each Tuesday evening. It was here that many of his sermons were taken down and later printed.

The year 1843 was also memorable in the life of Warburton for other reasons. A letter of his dated February 1843 [3] was written in response to one of his friends and a brother minister, William Tiptaft, whose new church he had opened in 1832. For eleven years Tiptaft had formed no church at Abingdon, one suspects because many of his hearers were

---

2 *Memorial of Robert Link,* Oxford, 1898. p. 29.

3 *Gospel Standard* 1843. p. 327.

seceders from the Church of England and had not been shown baptism by immersion clearly. But on Sunday 29th January 1843, Tiptaft had baptised twenty-three people, ten men and thirteen women, and that Sunday night had been favoured with a great blessing in his soul, a spiritual deliverance, greater than he had ever known before. [4] He wrote to tell Warburton of this great blessing in his soul and his church. Warburton was greatly moved by his letter and replying told him how both he and his wife Lydia were touched by his account of what had taken place at Abingdon. Warburton said it reminded him of his deliverance more than forty years ago when the Lord delivered him in Mr Roby's chapel in Manchester.

The covers of the *Gospel Standard* for 1843 reveal an extensive list of preaching engagements. While in London in April at Eden Street, Warburton had also preached at Winchmore Hill chapel on Good Friday morning. Later on 23rd May he had preached at the Calne Anniversary Services, an annual event in Wiltshire, when members of Gospel Standard churches gathered together from all over the County, coming down from Malmesbury, and over from Trowbridge, Devizes, Melksham and Allington. On 23rd and 30th July and 3rd and 13th August he had been in Leicester, where he had stayed for a month and on the final Sunday had formed the Church at Trinity Chapel, Alfred Street, taking the first Lord's Supper there with fifteen baptised members.[5]

In the middle of this Leicester visit, he had returned to Trowbridge for a few days, as the Church Book at Zion shows that, on 1st August 1843, he baptised ten people and received two from other churches, already baptised. Baptisings were now growing less at Zion. With the exception of 1819 Warburton had been favoured with an increase in Church membership every year from 1815 until 1838. In 1839 and 1840 there were no new members, but in 1841 he baptised ten and received four. Again in 1842 and 1844 there were no additions to the Church at Zion. Yet the congregation was maintained.

---

[4] *William Tiptaft,* J.C.Philpot, 1972. p.121.

[5] *History of Zion Chapel, Leicester,* 1923, p. 8.

Writing on 27th January 1841 he says, 'It is Sunday tomorrow and perhaps nearly 1,000 people will be gathered together.'[6] Again, writing on 26th September 1842 he says, 'At Zion we have perhaps 800 hundred people.'[7]

The *Gospel Standard* covers show further engagements in 1843. On Sundays 15th, 22nd and 29th October, Warburton was away preaching at Lakenheath, and on his way home stopped in London to preach for a week evening at Eden Street on 1st November. On 10th October, on his way to Lakenheath, he had preached at Wallingford in Berkshire. Here, no doubt, he stayed at Cholsey, on the farm of his old friend, Thomas Clowes, who had been delivered under his ministry in Zion about 1820.[8] He was not long back in Trowbridge in November before he set out again and this time preached at Abingdon on 5th and 7th November for Tiptaft, and on 8th at Wallingford. So the year ended, a year of much blessing and prosperity in the Gospel Standard Churches. William Gadsby, his godly mentor, was coming to the end of his journey and the mantle of leadership was falling upon Warburton as the elder minister among the churches.

He was now sixty-seven. His health was not good. He records a spell of illness in 1841 when he was 'quite laid up' and could not preach.[9] In August and September 1842 he was laid up for at least six weeks and says he was 'shaken with

[6] *Gospel Standard* 1841. p. 252.

[7] *Gospel Standard* 1843. p.147.

[8] *Seceders,* Vol. 2, J.H. Philpot, 1932, pp. 346-350.

[9] *Gospel Standard* 1843, p. 12.

rheumatism and lumbago,' and could not even sit up to write.[10] In February 1844, he declined to go to Manchester to take the funeral of his greatest friend, William Gadsby, giving as his reason the great distance, 300 miles, and the possibility of lumbago coming on in the cold journey.[11] He waited until the Summer before he travelled up North. He says in a letter dated 20th March 1844 that he had had 'a deal of rheumatism this winter, but had not been laid up with it.'[12] On 10th May he wrote, "I am not free from rheumatism.'[13] The hard work at the loom, the damp living conditions of Park Lane and Narrow Lane, and all the long journeys in which he had walked many miles in his younger days, were now catching up with him. Yet he was still travelling and preaching.

His engagement list for 1844 reveals that he preached for the month of April at Eden Street Chapel in London, and while there at Faversham in Kent and Welwyn in Hertfordshire. Then he was at Manchester on 23rd, and 30th June, and on 7th and 21st July. Sunday 14th July found him in his old pulpit at Hope Chapel, Rochdale. Many of his old friends had died. Thomas Niven had died in 1835, Hannah Lord in 1840, and Jenny Tweedale in 1841. Nichola Pots [the niece of Thomas Niven], Jacob Wolfenden, his old deacon appointed in 1812, and James Butterworth [baptised in 1797], 'the oldest Baptist in Rochdale', were still alive. It must have been a time of many memories for him, and sweet union and communion with his great friend and son in the faith, John Kershaw, as they mourned together the great loss of their beloved brother, William Gadsby. Now they stood together in the forefront of leadership among the Gospel Standard churches and behind

---

10 *Gospel Standard* 1843, pp. 144, 167.

11 *Memorials of John Warburton* 1892. p. 96.

12 *Memorials of John Warburton* 1892, p. 103

13 *Memorials of John Warburton* 1892, p. 107.

them the Lord was raising another generation of leaders in such ministers as J.C.Philpot, William Tiptaft, Thomas Godwin and others.

The foundations had been well laid by 1844 when Gadsby died. The Gospel Standard churches were knit together by the truth, 'as the truth is in Jesus,' and by the strong bonds of love and fellowship that caused their ministers to stand shoulder to shoulder in the confrontation with error. The Gospel Standard under the Editorship of M'Kenzie and Philpot stood in the vanguard, but other than this there were no organisational or denominational ties. Never was the group of Gospel Standard churches stronger than in those days when its union centred around the union of its ministers and the acceptability of their ministry, which was with the power and unction of the Holy Spirit.

Foremost among these ministers, in the savoury nature of his ministry, was John Warburton, loved and respected by ministers, church members and congregations alike. Constantly in these years from 1840 to 1850 his long spiritual letters appeared in the pages of the *Gospel Standard* [often six, a year] and his sermons were in print either in the *Gospel Standard* or in pamphlet form. Year by year his voice was heard in London and throughout the country as well as at Zion, Trowbridge. There was a cohesion among the churches and no mingling of truth and error. The gospel trumpet gave a singularly certain sound. The winnowing of the 18th Century Revival, begun under William Huntington's ministry was effectually carried on by Gadsby, Warburton and Kershaw and their brother ministers, and there was no intermingling with the error of Andrew Fuller, for the Gospel Standard churches had come out from it, and knew from what they had been separated; it was fresh in their memory. The pen of J.C. Philpot was very active in the *Gospel Standard* in the defence of truth.

In his published letters Warburton gives his readers a glimpse of his exercises regarding the ministry. Writing to his son, John, just after he had started preaching in 1844, Warburton says, 'Look to the Lord alone, for gift, ability, knowledge, matter, utterance and power to attend, for a dear, compassionate Jesus has it all to give to the unworthy.'[14] In another letter he tells him,

> It is a poor work, my child, with those preachers *rummaging dead men's brains* to take to the people, instead of going to the people with things they have tasted, and felt in answers from God to their cries and tears. Living souls want living testimonies from the living God.... Oh, my child, may the Lord ever keep thee watching and praying at wisdom's gate. If thou want understanding in the word of God, it is His own gift; if thou want ability to bring the truths before the people, it is His own gift; if thou want to enjoy the liberty of truth, it is His own gift; if thou want to see the sealing testimony of God in the hearts and souls of the people, it is His own gift. Oh, what glory and beauty there is in free gifts to beggars who have nothing to purchase with. What must my poor soul have done for nearly fifty years, if it had not been for these free gifts.[15]

Writing to his son on 21st November 1845 Warburton tells him the substance of his ministry when he says,

> I must speak of the glory of His kingdom, and talk of His power. I want to talk about nothing else but man's emptiness and Christ's fullness; man's nakedness and Christ's righteousness; man's filthiness and Christ's cleansing blood; man's helplessness and Christ's mighty power; man's nothingness and Christ's all in all. So it is all of Him, and to Him, and through Him, are all things, to whom be glory for ever, Amen.[16]

In another letter written in December 1843 he reveals another side of his ministerial preparation when he says,

---

[14] *Memorials of John Warburton* 1892, p. 107.

[15] *Memorials of John Warburton 1892,* pp. 108,109.

[16] *Memorials of John Warburton* 1892, p. 123.

I cannot go to commentators; [17] for I have none to go to; and if I had, I could not go there, and meet with God's disapprobation; for he is against the man that steals his words from his neighbour; and I could not expect the blessing of the Lord if I went into the pulpit with another man's line of things, made ready to my hand. So that I am obliged to go to my old Instructor; and I am confident that there is none who can teach like God; and I am sure of this, that God's people will find those out, sooner or later, who do not go with the Lord's teaching; for they have an unction from the Holy One. [18]

He goes on to speak in another letter of how he has been called a 'corruption preacher' and says,

I fear there are numbers of preachers and hearers too, that can talk wonderfully about a complete salvation of all the elect of God, through the atoning blood of Christ, that know *nothing* about mourning, weeping, and grieving over their wretched departings and wanderings from the God of their affections..... These gentlemen have no better name for God's servants, that have to come before the people of God, at times, with a heart bowed down under a sense of their own vileness, than *'corruption preachers.'* My dear friend, I would a thousand times rather have their frowns than their smiles. If the glorious and holy doctrines of God's grace dwell in the heart as well as in the head, there will be a grieving for sin; there will be a loathing, hating, and abhorring of ourselves for our daily wanderings from our God. [19]

---

17 J.C.Philpot reviewing Dr Gill's *Commentary on the New Testament* in the *Gospel Standard* 1852, pp. 65-71, says, 'Learning, abilities and study are only so far hindrances, and great hindrances too, as they are made substitutes for the teaching and wisdom of the Spirit... A Commentary, therefore, which explains the meaning of the original, where the translation is obscure, may be no more worthy of contempt or disregard than the translation itself.... If kept in its place, if sanctified to the service of God, if used only with a single eye to His glory and the good of His people, human learning is not to be despised.

18 *Gospel Standard* 1844, p. 304.

19 *Gospel Standard* 1846, *p. 137.*

Speaking of the trial of his faith in a letter to his son, dated 22nd August 1845 Warburton says,

> A few of these lessons, my child, will teach us how to preach the everlasting love, and choice, of God the Father; the justifying righteousness, and complete and eternal salvation, through the atoning blood of God the Son; the certainty of the work of grace being begun, carried on, and eternally completed by God the Holy Ghost, in the hearts of all the elect, and the certainty of their bringing forth the fruits of grace in their lives by denying ungodliness and worldly lusts, and living righteously and godly in this present evil world. [20]

This was a far remove from the Antinomianism with which Warburton was often credited. It shows the essence of his ministry. He wrote on one occasion, 'I dread to be left alone, especially in the ministry.'[21] He speaks of reading in the *Gospel Standard* letters which relate blessings received under his preaching, [22] and then says in another letter, '

> I cannot bear that He should leave me alone; for what are all the heads, the divisions, the subdivisions, or the application, if there is no power or unction from the Holy One? What is sound doctrine if it does not drop as the rain? What is a fine sound of words, if there is no distinction in the sound? What is a long string of Scripture texts, if there is no Spirit to send it home to the soul as the bread of God? [23]

It is not surprising that in these years Warburton should express his views on the ministry as his son John had just gone out to preach in January 1844, his friend William Gadsby had

---

[20] *Memorials of John Warburton* 1892, p. 120.

[21] *Gospel Standard* 1843. p. 14.

[22] *Gospel Standard* 1840, p. 279.

[23] *Gospel Standard* 1843, p. 253.

9. Dorset House, The Halve.

12. Warburton's Grave – the Moore grave in front – Sarah beyond – James to the right.

13. Various panels on the Warburton grave.

14. The Hayward Family grave, The Laurels, Hilperton Rd. [below]

hn Warburton[Jnr] & wife, Elizabeth, Phinehas, Ruth, Lydia & R. G. Hitchcock.

15. Southill Chapel

16. Graves of John Warburton[Jnr], and his sister Ruth.

died in the same month, and he himself in these latter days of his ministry had been brought into much self- examination. He says in a letter dated 7th June 1844,[24]

> I have had *much searching of heart* since the Lord took our dear brother and friend, Mr Gadsby, home to himself, and have experienced some blessed testimonies that his God is my God. My soul feels for the loss the church of God at large has sustained by his removal, and especially that portion of it with whom he laboured so long and faithfully. I feel for them in their destitute situation.

He could see the balancing of the clouds. Not only had young John commenced preaching, but he was soon well received by the churches, and within a matter of months had a call to a pastorate. In *The Memorials of John Warburton [Jnr]* published after his death in 1892, there is included a series of fifteen letters written by Warburton to his son in the years 1843 to 1846. They include much advice for young John, regarding his ministry and the circumstances relating to his call to the pastorate at Southill. But when young John wrote from Southill to Trowbridge in the spring of 1846, asking for specific advice because the church at Southill practised Open Communion, his father replied from Trowbridge,[25]

> You have a Bible at Southill and so have I at Trowbridge. You have a throne of grace at Southill, and so have I at Trowbridge. There is a God at Southill, the same at Trowbridge; that is the only place I have to go to for directions for my family, for my soul, and for all church matters; there I counsel you to go. The Lord give you wisdom in all things. Your affectionate Father.

This is interesting, because in an earlier letter of 18th October 1844, written just over a fortnight after young John had commenced, on 29th September, a six week probation at

---

[24] *Gospel Standard* 1845, pp. 118, 119.

[25] *Memorials of John Warburton* 1892, p. 54.

Southill, with a view to the pastorate, his father had written to him,

> I just write to say that it impresses my mind, as far as I can judge, that you would do right in accepting the invitation at Southill. It appears to me to be the hand of Providence; and as regards your not being able to be with the people for three months to keep them together, for want of matter; my dear child, if matter is to come out of your own corrupt mind you would not do two Lord's days for the living souls of God's dear children; but as there is plenty of matter, plenty of gift, abundance of knowledge, treasured up in the fountain-head Jesus, the Lord of life and glory, free from all expense, to be given to the unworthy, there you must go, and beg and cry, groan and sigh, and have no denial, for He has promised, 'Open thy mouth wide, and I will fill it.'

John junior had gone to Hitchin several times to preach in the early part of 1844. It was a place where his father had preached, so that he was following in his father's steps. People had come to Hitchin from other churches to hear him and as a result he was asked to go in June to preach at Barton. The chapel was crowded with people from several miles distance, which included some from Southill, nine miles away. Mr Joseph Lockey, from Stanford, Southill, approached him on behalf of the Sunday School Superintendents at Southill to come and preach for their Anniversary at the end of July. He had already met a Mr Fane, a grocer from Southill chapel, who lived at Shefford, when he had come over to Hitchin to hear him.

Now at the end of July he went on Saturday by the 'Times' Coach to Shefford and stayed with Mr Fane. On Sunday morning, greatly exercised in his heart, he went into the pulpit at Southill, the chapel ' crowded in every part' and gave out his text, 'Upon this rock I will build my church, and the gates of hell shall not prevail against it.' [Matt. 16.18.] He says in the *Memorials* [p.47],

> There stood a young man [28 years old], tall and slender, with a sallow countenance, full of fears, not knowing for the moment what to say; when all at once such a light shone upon the words, that both words and ideas came rolling into my mind just as fast as I could utter them. I felt

it to be a solemn time, to many it was a soul reviving time; indeed to this day many of our old friends remember my first coming amongst them...To me the chapel was a Bethel, for I felt it was the house of God.

Here is a glimpse of the stature of the Warburton family, 'tall and slender;' the lad who had wandered the country on foot from Manchester to Plymouth, now on a different errand for His Master, being used like his father had been for so many years in His Master's service. The members of the church at Southill were called together in the afternoon of that Lord's day, and after the evening service the deacons came to tell John that they had voted to ask him to supply their pulpit for six Sabbaths from Michaelmas [i.e. 29th September]. To this he agreed and on the Thursday before Michaelmas 1844, he came from his home in Wells Street, London with his wife and two children [John aged four and Lydia just over a year old] to Mr Fane's at Shefford and on Friday went over to Southill to stay in the chapel house.

He eventually stayed for eighteen months, until by majority votes in the church he was able to establish the church as a Gospel Standard church on, Strict Communion lines, using Gadsby's hymnbook in its services. Then on 11th October 1846 he accepted the pastorate. Shortly afterwards on 6th December 1846 he baptised his wife Emma and having put the house and chapel in a thorough state of repair, on Thursday 6th May 1847, his father, now over seventy years old, came to Southill to preach the Opening Services. His text that day was, 'The Lord hath done great things for us; whereof we are glad.' [Ps. 126.3]. It must have been a remarkable day for the old man, to be with the son, who had been his father's greatest sorrow and now was his greatest blessing.

When he died on 19th January 1892, Dr D.A. Doudney, [Editor of the *Gospel Magazine* (1840-1893), to whose home John Junior had gone when he ran away in 1832], wrote an article for the *Christian's Monthly Record* (1892. pp 101,102) in which he says,

It was our privilege to hear the late Mr Warburton [Jnr] preach his first sermon in Eden Street, London. It was a week evening. His aged father was present, seated in the extreme corner at the entrance of the chapel. As the son's manner was so exactly that of the father, at that time, namely, commencing his sermon in so low a voice as scarcely to be heard, and then, warming to his subject, bursting forth with a loudness and an animation, as we retired from the service, and shook hands with the dear old man, whom we had long well-known, we could not help remarking, 'They'll say it's a chip off the old block.'

This service was almost certainly in April 1844 when Warburton senior was preaching his usual monthly engagements in London. This gives a rare first hand description, from a close friend, of the manner of preaching of both father and son.

In 1845 as John junior settled in at Southill, Warburton was fulfilling his engagement at Eden Street, London in April and in July at Trinity Chapel, Alfred Street, Leicester, where Mr G. Isbell had become pastor in 1843. While in London he had preached at Southill on 30th March and 2nd April, and at Hitchin on 3rd April. In Wiltshire, on 23rd March 1845, Warburton had baptised nine at Zion and received thirteen [already baptised] from Bradford-on-Avon. What was behind the transfer of these thirteen in unclear. Then on 12th August he preached at Hankerton Anniversary services, together with William Beard, who became their pastor in the next year.

In 1846 he was entering on his seventieth year, but his travelling did not abate. In April he was a month at Eden Street and travelled out to Southill on the 14th and Hitchin on the 16th. For five Sundays in August he preached at Leicester.This was the year, on 25th June 1846, when the hated Corn Laws were finally repealed in the face of the failure of the Irish potato crop in 1845. Sir Robert Peel, Prime Minister from 1841-1846 had been introducing Free Trade policies in the country in his Budgets of 1842 and 1844, and this was the culmination of his policy. William Gadsby had spoken to large audiences in the Town Hall in Manchester against the Corn Laws, and the Parliamentary lobby, known as the Anti-Corn Law League, had finally obtained their object, of removing these hated restrictions on the price of corn which had such an effect on the price of bread for the poor.

In this year Warburton had been the subject of an attack in the pulpit and through pamphlets by Mr Tryon of Market

Deeping, Lincolnshire. Philpot and M'Kenzie also came under his ire. Warburton knew Frederick Tryon when Tryon was Vicar of Deeping St James in 1838 and 1839. He seceded from the Church of England in 1839 and continued his ministry in a chapel called Cave Adullam, built for him at Deeping St James. Warburton baptised him and his wife with Mr de Merveilleux and one or two others the last Sunday he preached at Stamford in 1839, just after he seceded from the Church of England. But for some reason, Tryon, rather than becoming his friend, as Philpot and Tiptaft, the other seceders had done, became his enemy, and the enemy of his friends in the Gospel Standard churches. In a letter dated 21st May 1846, [26] Warburton says,

> Mr Tryon opened the chapel for the people separated from Zoar, while I was in London; all about which I suppose you have heard. Mr Philpot, Mr M'Kenzie, and old John Warburton came under his mighty arm. How Mr Philpot and Mr M'Kenzie have felt it, I do not know, but old John has not lost one wink of sleep through it. Mr Tryon could not make it out how a man could have a clear conscience and live a consistent life, and run into debt with three pounds a week coming in. He could not understand it! Poor man, I do not think he could. But if ever he ploughs with the same heifer, yoked up with eleven in a family, he will understand the riddle better. But I have no occasion to be angry with him, or bitter against him for it; for I had a very sweet blessing after I heard how he had gone on. I could not help smiling, when a person told me that he hoped the Lord would support me under it. I told him I felt no burden at all..... But the blessing I had from the Lord brought to my remembrance all the way he had led me; and how he had brought me through it all, and had enabled me to pay every debt clean off in hard cash; and there is no creditor that I ever had, but what was paid twenty shillings in the pound.

It is clear that Frederick Tryon had read the *Mercies of a Covenant God* published in 1838 and 1839 and now seven years later was expressing his views in public. It must have been hard for Warburton to be abused regarding his finances, from a London pulpit, by a fellow minister, especially one

[26] *Gospel Standard* 1846, p. 275.

whom he had baptised, but such are the wounds the Lord's servants are commonly called to endure. Tryon set about J.C.Philpot on the grounds that when he married Sarah Keal in 1838, he had no evidence that she had a work of grace in her heart, and eventually forced Philpot into an admission that this was the case. He further attacked Warburton with the accusation that his writings showed a lack of assurance as to his spiritual state before God, and that at one time he felt that he was in the Covenant, and at another time he doubted it.

Tryon lived to be pastor at Deeping St James until 1903, and proved himself to be a constant 'troubler of Israel', often attacking his fellow ministers from the pulpit and causing constant friction in the churches. He was a sad man and caused much sadness. A report in the *Christian's Monthly Record* for 1886, [p.8], says, 'Some there are still living who painfully remember the thrill of indignation which rolled through the churches, when in 1846, Mr Tryon denounced Mr Philpot in Zoar Pulpit, London, and then commenced a series of virulent pamphlets against Mr Warburton, Mr Philpot and Mr M'Kenzie. It seems the accusations did little lasting damage to the reputations of those concerned. The year closed for Warburton with the Lord's blessing at Zion when he baptised thirteen and received five into membership on 6th December.

In June 1846 John Grace, the pastor of Church Street Chapel, Brighton had preached for Warburton at Zion Trowbridge.[27] In the following April 1847, he was forced to leave his chapel in Church street and move to the Tabernacle in West Street. He wrote to Warburton to come to Brighton to preach for him at the Tabernacle and Warburton who was in London beginning his usual month of preaching at Eden Street wrote back, [28]

> I have only time to say that I would have complied with your request to preach for you one Lord's day when I have done in London; but

---

[27] *Recollections of John Grace* 1893, p.128.

[28] John Grace, op. cit. p. 138.

I am engaged to preach one Lord's day for my son John, at Southill [Sun 2nd May]. But if you and the friends would like me to come to Brighton for one evening I have no objection, if the Lord will, to do so on Wednesday fortnight; if that suits you, drop me a line direct at Mr Clowes, 3 South Crescent, Tottenham Court Road, London.

So Warburton preached at Eden Street Sundays, the 4th, 11th, 18th and 25th April, went to Brighton on Wednesday 14th and went on to Southill for Sunday 2nd May and stayed to preach the opening services after the renovation on Thursday 6th May. This was quite a load for a man in his seventy-first year, but the railways made his travelling easier than when he went to Brighton in the early years after he started at Trowbridge.

This letter shows that while in London he was staying at 3 South Crescent, with his old friend Thomas Clowes, [29] who had farmed at Cholsey, near Wallingford since 1834, but had moved to London in 1847. He was living just off Tottenham Court Road, was attending Eden Street Chapel, and was entertaining the ministers whilst they were in London. Thomas Clowes had first come into the Wallingford area from Norfolk in 1818. He had taken a farm at Park Corner, near Nettlebed and afterwards at Long Wittenham, Berks, a village situated between Wallingford and Abingdon. At that time he had been under a deep law work in his soul. He had determined to go to Trowbridge to hear John Warburton, who, as well as William Gadsby, used to stay at his house when he came to Wallingford to preach. Warburton took for his text that Sunday morning, 'Call upon me in the day of trouble; I will deliver thee, and thou shalt glorify me.' [Ps. 50.15.] Under that sermon Thomas Clowes's was blessedly delivered, pardon sealed in his heart and the love of God shed abroad in his soul. Later about 1833, he had met Tiptaft, who had introduced him to Philpot. In 1855 Philpot stayed with him at South Crescent, Tottenham Court Road, when preaching at Gower Street and continued to do so every year until Philpot's death in 1869.

Now it seems when Warburton left Southill in 1847, after the Opening Services, it was to return to Trowbridge and

---

[29] *The Seceders,* Vol 2, J.H. Philpot, pp. 346-350.

not have any more long journeys that year. He was beginning gradually to cut down on his engagements and his travelling. His journeys to London, Leicester, Lakenheath, Stamford, Brighton and Manchester, preaching in each place for a month at a time had been unusual for a man of his age, but had he been asked about it, he would have revealed the inner strength of his God that had supported him. Now in 1847 for the first time for many years he had a quieter time, and limited himself to one preaching tour that year.

He was still writing his letters and they were appearing in the *Gospel Standard.* In 1847 five were published and one of them was written to a friend in America. Dated 30th September 1847, [30] he wrote,

> Having received a part of a letter addressed to poor worthless me, saying that the Lord had blessed a few of my scribbling letters to some of his tried children in your part of the world, I feel it in my heart to drop you a line, to say that I felt thankful and humbled before God to think that ever he should own and bless his truth through such a worthless pipe. My soul has proved some thousands of times during these fifty years, that by the grace of God I am what I am..... I have been above fifty years learning two parts of the word of God, and am still learning, and believe I shall never get beyond it; one is, that without Christ I can do nothing; the other is, that with Christ strengthening me I can do all things.

There is no question that his writing towards the end of his days became very shaky. Equally while he had done very well, writing was not his forte. He was much more made in a practical mould, and was far more at ease preaching than writing. While he had a clear mind, and was gifted with an ability to express himself, he did not find it easy to commit his thoughts to paper. As some of his congregation and church members had gone to America, it is possible that it was to one of these that the *Gospel Standard* magazine had gone out, and that they had read his letters in its pages. The reference to the 'worthless pipe' is of interest. John Warburton and his wife smoked clay pipes. A photograph exists showing them sitting

---

[30] *Gospel Standard* 1849, pp. 309-311.

either side of their fireplace. J.H. Philpot in the *Seceders*, Vol 2, p. 33, relates that when Warburton went to Stamford to stay with his father J.C.Philpot, he was never allowed to smoke his long churchwarden pipe in the parlour, but had to go to the servants quarters in the basement, for the simple reason that J.C.Philpot had been a victim of tuberculosis in his youth and suffered from a very weak chest. There was nothing more worthless, as Warburton well knew, than a broken clay pipe. [They were, in fact, manufactured in Trowbridge.] J.C. Philpot, writing to Joseph Parry at Allington on 1st December 1836 [*Seceders* Vol. 1. pp 313-316] says, 'I am glad that friend Warburton has paid you a visit, and that his word was blessed. John *with all his faults*, has the right stuff in him, and will outlive a thousand May-flies, who flutter their hour in the religious world.' Possibly, the clay pipe was one of his faults, another was his hasty spirit, yet underneath he had loving heart.

In 1848 the railway finally reached Trowbridge. The broad gauge line was extended from Chippenham, via Melksham to Trowbridge and Westbury. The London to Bristol line had been opened on 30th June 1841, now the Trowbridge line was opened on 5th September 1848. No longer did Warburton have to travel by horse drawn coach to Chippenham, but could walk down to the new elegant Trowbridge Station, simply designed in Bath stone. The Westbury to Warminster line was opened in September 1851, but the line to the terminus at Salisbury was not completed until June 1856. So Warburton was never able to go via Salisbury and Southampton on his Brighton journeys. Other lines which affected his travels were the Oxford branch from Didcot, which was opened on 12th June 1844, with two halts at Appleford and Abingdon Road. The Abingdon branch line was not opened into the town until 1856. The Wallingford branch at Cholsey was not opened until post 1866. So in his visits to Abingdon after 1844, he had to alight on the A 415 road out of Abingdon beyond Culham, at Abingdon Road Station, and have transport to bring him into Abingdon.

Two letters written in February 1848 and published in the *Gospel Standard* in 1849 reveal a number of events in his life. The first written on 2nd February [31] [probably to John Kershaw in Rochdale] says,

> It has been a very sickly time here this winter, and many of our old members have ended their pilgrimage and gone home, where there is no sickness, but all tears are for ever wiped from their eyes. Last May, after I got home from my London journey, I had a fall and broke my shin bone; for two months I was unable to stir out at the front door, but now and then hobbled to chapel. It is not well yet, but is so that I can walk pretty well; it is, however, very weak, and I cannot stand much exertion. It is gradually getting better, but is still very weak....... How good it is to have a humbling sight of His glory....
>
> His worth, if all the nations knew,
> Sure the whole earth would love Him too.
>
> But I am sorry to say that I have some sad moments at times, arising from the cursed old man that I used to talk about at Hope Chapel...... We are still as a church and people kept in love and peace one with another, which I feel a great mercy in this day of confusion.

The next day, 3rd February, [32] he wrote to his old friend Thomas Clowes, at South Crescent, London,

> I just drop you a line to say that if the Lord will, I hope to be in London on the first four Lord's days in April. Is there room in the house and in the heart of Mr & Mrs Clowes, to receive the poor, old, worthless worm once again? If there is any straitness in either place, in the house or the heart, be so kind as to let me know as soon as you can. It will be a pleasure if you say there is room in both places, but if otherwise it will be no offence, for I am so feelingly sensible of my unworthiness that I wonder many times that any of God's jewels will ever receive me into their house...... My dear friend, my soul has moments when I want to be gone to be with His dear Majesty, to see Him as he is, to be with Him and to be like Him, where there is no sin to torment... I know that there are

---

[31] *Gospel Standard* 1849, pp. 167-170.

[32] *Gospel Standard* 1849, p. 230.

crowds of professors in the present day that have no castings down from the devilish workings of an ungodly heart, no mournings from the hidings of a Father's countenance, no faint-heartedness for fear the Lord has forsaken them.........I am still a poor pauper after charity; not one grain of faith, not one spark of love...not one breath of real prayer... but what comes from above.

The first of these letters shows why his journeys had been curtailed in 1847. Like William Gadsby, who broke his leg in 1840, Warburton had suffered a broken leg in May 1847 and was still suffering from the effects in February 1848, but as the second letter reveals, he was intent [with his usual perseverance] on continuing with his annual engagements at Eden Street, London in April 1848. He carried out his engagements on Sundays 2nd, 9th, 16th and 23th at Eden Street and on Good Friday 21st he preached at 11am at the Opening Services at a new Chapel at Cheshunt and his son John preached at 3pm. Back home in May he preached at Calne Anniversary on 23rd May at 10.30am and Thomas Godwin preached at 2.30pm. On June 14th he came over to preach at Studley Chapel, near Chippenham on Wednesday evening at 7pm. But it is clear that his engagements are curtailed and that he will never be able, after his fall, to do the constant long journeys he had managed before. It appears that the rest of the year, 1848, was spent preaching at Zion or in the locality, not going much further than such places as Allington. Quite remarkably he was well enough to baptize eleven new member at Zion on 3rd December and receive another ten, previously baptised, into membership.

The year 1849 opened with a letter, dated 1st February, written to his friends at the chapel at Wallingford, in which he confirmed the transfer to their church of one of his members, Anne Rogers, whom he had baptised on 7th September 1834. In May he undertook his usual monthly engagement at Eden Street Chapel in London, and while there went to Cheshunt on Sunday 3rd June and on the following Monday evening. On Thursday 5th July, he was at Hadlow Down in Sussex [where Mr Hallett was pastor from 1824-1874], to preach morning and evening, with his friend John Grace of Brighton preaching in the afternoon, at the Opening Services for a new chapel there.[33] Such was the congregation in the afternoon, there being about a thousand present, that John Grace was requested to preach out of doors. In his *Recollections* [p.151], John Grace reveals that on the following Sunday, 8th July he preached at Zion Chapel, Trowbridge, and Warburton preached for his people at the Tabernacle, West Street, Brighton.

In October Warburton preached at Eden Street for another month of Sundays, closed the year's travels with a visit to Abingdon on Sunday 2nd December, and preached at Uffington in Berkshire on the following Tuesday evening, 4th December. In July and August his friend, John Grace had had a serious, life threatening illness and Warburton had written to him, 'Now I feel a hope that this affliction is not unto death, but for the glory of God; and hope to have the pleasure of hearing of the kindness of God in raising you up again, and bringing you forth like gold seven times purified.' [*Recollections* p. 156.] It is possible that John Grace had had cholera. This was the year in England when between 25th June and 26th September, 13,685 people died from cholera. On Friday 28th September John Grace preached morning and evening at West Street chapel, a day set apart as a day of humiliation on account of the scourge of cholera.

In 1850 Warburton was again very active. He preached at Eden Street London on Sundays 5th, 12,& 26th May and 2nd June. On Sunday 19th he went out to Cheshunt and preached there, also on Tuesday evening, 21st May. On 30th June he preached morning and evening at Providence Chapel, Lower Bristol Road, Bath. On 7th July he baptised eleven people at Zion and received a further seven into the Church A letter he wrote on 31st July that year was published in the *Gospel Standard* a few weeks later in the November issue. In it he says,

> I have had a very sharp trial, both in body and mind for the last fortnight. So much so that I despaired of life for both body and soul..... I was *racked with pain day and night*; the precious Bible a sealed book; not

---

[33] *Recollections of John Grace* 1893, p. 154.

the least appearance of a grain of faith, love, patience, hope, humility, or resignation to the will of God..... O my dear friend, I was sunk very, very low. I sat in my chair and I wept like a child and cried out from my very soul, 'Dear Lord, I have been a poor pauper upon Thee for near sixty years, and Thou hast never failed me yet; hast Thou left me at last? Is Thy mercy clean gone for ever? Wilt Thou be favourable no more...... And I can bear witness that he is a God that heareth and answereth the cry of the poor and needy; for he spoke these words into my soul with such light, power and sweetness that all was well and right in a moment: '*Charity never faileth.*' O blessed words! How they caused my soul to look back for about fifty-five years, when charity picked me up out of the devil's kingdom; and how surprisingly charity has helped, defended, supplied and delivered me out of all distresses to the present moment.

This acute pain must have come on within a week of the baptising service at Zion on 7th July. Warburton would have been seventy-four on 28th October that year. It would have been quite an effort for a man of his age to baptize eleven people at one time. This was the last time he baptised at Zion, and it would appear that possibly the effort had brought on a very severe attack of his old back trouble. On 23rd September,[34] he was well enough to write to Mr Lawrence at Welwyn to tell him that he hoped, God willing, to preach there on Thursday 17th October. He said in his letter,

O what a comfort it is in my old age that we are living in union, peace and love as a church and people.... I have now wintered and summered with the people, I think, going on for thirty-six years, and I believe our hearts are closer knit together in one heart that at first; and I am proving the blessed word of God to be true that fixed me at Trowbridge: 'Abide in this city; for I have much people here.' And here I abide and, notwithstanding all the hatred, opposition and persecution that I have met with from professors and profane, am still proclaiming a full, free, complete, unalterable, finished salvation, through the blood and righteousness of the Lord Jesus Christ.

34 *Christian's Monthly Record* 1893, p. 188.

Little did he know the trouble that was to break out in his church at Zion in a year or two and was to blight the last few years of his ministry and life there. But that was hidden when he wrote to Mr Lawrence in Welwyn in September 1850. On 30th September he wrote to a friend, [35]

> It is my greatest grief and sorrow in my latter days, to find such opposition in my heart against my best Friend, who has ever stood with me, through all my troubles, to this present day.....O how good it is, now and then, to have a few moments of sitting at His feet and hearing His gracious words, learning of Him that is meek and lowly of heart. Here is rest and peace, and no where else.

Warburton went on to preach throughout October at Eden Street, London for a second month of Sundays, and Tuesday evenings. Three of these London sermons of 1850 were taken down and published. [See list of published sermons at Appendix B.] In the *Gospel Standard* for 1851, p. 273, was printed the first sermon of his taken down at Zion, Trowbridge, preached on Tuesday evening 24th September 1850. Nearly all his printed sermons had been taken down in London at Gower Street, and Eden Street chapels. While Sir Isaac Pitman, the inventor of Pitman's Shorthand, had attended his chapel,and Pitman's father had been a Superintendent of the Sunday School with Isaac Moore as early as 1828, yet there had never been any effort made to take down Warburton's sermons until 1850. Then in 1850 and 1851, right at the end of his life, three sermons preached at Zion, were recorded and published.

In 1851 Warburton managed to get to London again and preached at Eden Street throughout May and also the first Sunday in June. No doubt he stayed with Thomas Clowes and his wife. When he returned home trouble was stirring in his Church. In his letters of recent years he had often spoken of how much he valued the harmony in his church. Now it was to be shattered and not fully restored before his death in April 1857. The cause of the trouble is not clear. On 24th September 1851 four members, Uriah Batchlor, Thomas Martin, Henry

---

[35] *Gospel Standard* 1863, p. 163.

Tucker [Deacon] and William Chamberlain were 'set aside by a majority of the Church.' This meant they were banned from partaking of the Lord's Supper. They felt that they had been treated unjustly and defended their case in a pamphlet published by Houlston and Stoneman of Paternoster Row entitled, *'A Series of Letters by several members of the Church of Christ meeting for worship at Zion Chapel under the Pastoral care of Mr John Warburton Senior, showing the cause of the unhappy divisions now ruling amongst them.'*

The Church Book reveals that Thomas Martin was *the first* to be 'set aside by the majority of the Church for saying that he would sit down and take the bread and wine at the ordinance of the Lord's Supper whether the Pastor of the Church was reconciled to him or not.' The cause of the disagreement between Warburton and Thomas Martin is not stated. Then the Church Book reveals that 'Henry Tucker [elected deacon in 1848], William Chamberlain and Uriah Bachelor were set aside [a temporary excommunication] for sanctioning Thomas Martin at a Public Church Meeting on 24th September 1851. There the matter rested until a Church Meeting held on 4th June 1852 when, 'Henry Tucker, Thomas Martin, William Chamberlain and Uriah Bachelor were separated [excommunicated] by the *unanimous* voice of the Church for keeping up a spirit of strife and contention for nine or ten months. At the same meeting another fourteen members were set aside by the *unanimous* voice of the Church for 'sanctioning Henry Tucker and Thomas Martin.' One of these fourteen was Jacob Hawkins elected deacon in February 1851.

It seemed that the centre of the trouble was criticism by a group of members of Warburton's preaching, an antagonism to what they described as 'experience preaching.' It may have been that there was a move to remove him from his pastorate in his old age and get a younger man. The majority of the members had reacted to this criticism of their pastor by removing the members who constantly criticised him. As two of them were deacons, it suggests there was also a split in the diaconate. It seems that sadly in his old age, [Warburton was now seventy-five], some of his church members had grown tired of his ministry; but equally the majority had not. Each of the four separated from the Church had been baptised by Warburton in the period 1835-1843. Eight of the fourteen set aside in June 1852 had been baptised by him. Six of them were eventually restored to church membership, including the deacon, Jacob Hawkins.

Reports of the troubles at Zion became common knowledge among the churches and various religious magazines contained reports and letters about the trouble, some for, some against. One reporter sympathetic to Warburton wrote, 'There is a people in Trowbridge, who will not, or cannot settle down comfortably under parson John... They are like children who have been spoiled and nobody can manage them.' The trouble must have caused Warburton great sadness. At first the excommunicated members continued to attend the services and tried to sit down to the Lord's table, going so far as to disrupt the service. But as the Pastor and Church stood firm and time went on, the matter simmered. The ill-feeling continued right to the end of Warburton's life, and was undoubtedly a means of loosening the cords of affection that drew him to Zion, preparing him to lay down the mantle of office as Pastor.

In 1852 Warburton preached at Eden Street on the 2nd, 9th, 16th and 23rd May and also Tuesday evenings. On Sunday 30th May he went on to preach for his son at Southill. He came home to take Calne Anniversary on 8th June together with his great friend and brother, J.C. Philpot, Warburton preaching at 11am and Philpot at 3pm. No doubt, they listened to each other's sermons. In October, John Kershaw came from Rochdale to preach at Zion for four Sundays for Warburton and on Sunday October 24th baptised eight and received one into the Church at Zion for Warburton. It seems that Warburton was now unable to baptize, though he was almost certainly present at the services. Whether he stayed at Trowbridge in the month of October is not clear. There is no indication that he was elsewhere and it seems possible that he may have been unwell.

Little is known of his whereabouts in 1853, though he preached at Eden Street chapel London on Monday Evening 25th April that year, which suggests he probably preached at Eden Street throughout the month of April The Church accounts show £2 payed out for supply ministers in April and

£4.13s paid out for the same reason in November, which suggests he was either away preaching or else ill. The Church Book lists twenty new members for that year but does not state the date of the service nor who took the baptising.

There is no information about Warburton's movements in 1854, which suggests he remained in Trowbridge, though the Church accounts again show a payment of £4 5s for supply ministers in June and £3 in October, which again could mean he was away preaching. On 24th September John Warburton Junior came from Southill and baptised for his father. On this occasion twelve were baptised and two received from other churches.

In Europe there had been great changes in the last years of Warburton's life. A Revolution in France in February 1848 had seen the removal of the French Monarchy and the King, Louis Philippe, leading to his abdication and flight for refuge to England. In England, 1848 had witnessed the last outbreak of the Chartist movement. At the time it caused great consternation. A crowd of thirty thousand tried to march on the Houses of Parliament and present a Petition with two million signatures. The Government enlisted 170,000 special constables and London was occupied by a military force under the Duke of Wellington. The date of the event was 10th April 1848. Warburton, in fact, was in London at the time for his usual month and had preached the previous Sunday, 9th April at Eden Street Chapel. He makes no reference to these events in any of his letters. He would have been staying with Thomas Clowes at 3 South Crescent, off Tottenham Court Road, so he was not in the immediate vicinity of Westminster, though near enough to get first hand information about events. No violence took place. The crowd which had gathered on Kennington Common, south of the Thames, was banned by the police from crossing Westminster Bridge, and when eventually the Petition was examined it was found to include forged signatures of Queen Victoria, the Prince Consort and the Duke of Wellington which greatly damaged its public image. Chartism eventually passed out of existence, though that day in April 1848 must have brought back to Warburton's mind memories of an unpleasant night on 19th November 1838 in Timbrell Street, Trowbridge.

On 1st May 1851 the Great Exhibition had been opened by Queen Victoria and Prince Albert in Hyde Park. Warburton was in London throughout the whole of May that year, preaching at Eden Street Chapel. It seems highly likely that he would have gone the short distance from Mr Clowes home at 3 South Crescent, down Oxford Street, to see it. Paxton's 'Crystal Palace' was 1,848 feet long and 408 feet wide, a gigantic greenhouse of cast-iron columns and girders and walls and roof of glass, even housing some of the elms of Hyde Park in situ beneath its roof. Joseph Paxton, its designer was the chief gardener of the Duke of Devonshire at his estate at Chatsworth. One half of the exhibition came from Britain and her Colonies, and there were exhibits from most of the countries of Europe, as well as from the United States. It demonstrated the great achievement of Victorian Britain in Manufacturing, the Fine Arts, Civil, Mechanical, Industrial and Railway Engineering; the Ross telescope was there and photographic apparatus, textiles, precious metals and Wedgwood pottery. Warburton knew well some of these achievements, as in the last ten years he had been a constant user of Brunel's Great Western Line, and had many times passed through Box Tunnel. Fine cloths, such as doeskins and moleskins were exhibited by Trowbridge firms and medals were won at the Exhibition by Trowbridge cloth firms, such as Clarks, Stancombs and Salters.[36] Salters was the company in which Warburton's son-in-law John Hayward was a partner, together with the two son's of John Hayward's first marriage, John E. Hayward, and Edward P. Hayward. The Exhibition was very successful. Between May and October 1851 more that six million visitors came to see it. Fourteen thousand exhibitors showed their wares.

In the first few days of December 1851 there had been a *Coup d'Etat* in Paris, when the President, Louis Napoleon had overthrown the democratically elected Government and within twelve months, after a plebiscite, had declared himself Emperor Napoleon III of France. This must have brought back to Warburton many memories, and perhaps some of the fears, of

---

36 *Warp & Weft,* K.H. Rogers 1986, p.113.

his early married life, during the years of the Napoleonic Wars, which had ended just as he reached Trowbridge in 1815.

On the 27th March 1854, another European War broke out, the first for forty years, when Britain and France declared war on Russia in defence of Turkey. The Russians had designs to split up the Turkish Empire with possible consequences of expanding into the Mediterranean. The Crimean War, which followed, lasted until March 1856 when the Treaty of Paris was signed, and had its highlights in the Battle of the River Alma [20th September 1854], the Charge of the Light Brigade [25th October 1854], and the siege of Sebastopol [finally surrendered on 9th September 1855]. The cost was £76 million and 25,000 dead. In Trowbridge a street was named, Alma Road, after the battle, and no doubt Warburton heard of the work of Florence Nightingale, the Hampshire nurse, who, in the Crimea, tended the wounded with her helpers.

In 1854, John Warburton Junior came again to Zion Chapel, Trowbridge from Southill to baptize for his father. On 24th September, he baptised twelve and received two others into membership. In the same year in London, the congregation meeting at Eden Street Chapel bought the Chapel which they had left in 1843, and so returned to their old home in Gower Street. The old Gower Street Chapel was re-opened with services on Sunday 7th January 1855, when John Kershaw came from Rochdale to preach in the morning and evening, and William Cowper of the Dicker preached in the afternoon. John Kershaw had a prayerful interest in this return of the Gospel Standard congregation of Eden Street to old Gower Street Chapel, and describes how he stood outside Gower Street chapel one day when in London and prayed that the people who built it might one day return.[37]

John Warburton had often preached there in the old days of the original Gower Street Church in the pastorate of Henry Fowler. Now in the last years of his life he came back to preach to the original congregation in their old building. On Sundays 8th, 15th, 22nd & 29th April he preached in old Gower Street pulpit and stayed with Thomas Clowes at South Crescent. The

[37] *John Kershaw Autobiography* 1968, pp. 310-311.

sermon he preached on Sunday evening 6th April was published. Returning home he preached at Calne Anniversary with his friend J.C. Philpot. On 30th September he was again back in London preaching at Gower Street. This was to be the last occasion that he preached in Gower Street pulpit. These visits of 1855 were to be the farewell sermons of a lifetime of preaching in London, since the days when he first came down to London from the North and met William Huntington in 1813.

In the following year, 1856, as he was in his eightieth year, he preached for the last time on 3rd June at Calne Anniversary Services with J.C.Philpot, and as usual, he preached at 11am and Philpot at 3pm. It was to be the last time they would be in harness together. Later in that month he preached one Sunday at Abingdon to two large and overflowing congregations. William Tiptaft says of the occasion, 'Many were very much blessed in hearing him, and although he did not think he could preach the second time, yet he was enabled to speak about an hour, and loudly too, and enjoyed much in his own soul of the glorious gospel, which was heard with much savour and dew by many of the Lord's people. Such a blessed time of hearing will not soon be forgotten.'[38] In August Warburton went to Hurstpierpoint, near Brighton and preached on Sundays 17th and 24th. Then he went on to Brighton to preach at West Street for John Grace on Sunday 31st. This was to be his last visit to Sussex. In January, on Sunday 20th, John Grace had preached twice at West Street, and had had a collection for John Warburton's poor.[39] Warburton had engaged to preach at Gower Street on 12th, 19th and 26 October, but an announcement in the October issue of the Gospel Standard said, 'We regret to state that Mr Warburton is unable, from his increasing infirmities, to fulfil his engagements for Oct. 12, 19, & 26 as announced in the September issue.' John Warburton Junior, writing in a small booklet entitled, *Mr Warburton's Last Days,* says, 'It was some time in October 1856 that my dear

[38] John Warburton, op. cit. p. 225.

[39] *Recollections of John Grace, p. 222.*

father was first taken seriously ill, his complaint being, as I understand, a disease of the heart.' So gradually the silver cord was loosed.

A Sermon preached at the Opening of Providence Chapel, Eden Street, Hampstead Road, London, on Lord's Day Evening, April 9th 1843, by John Warburton.

'Jesus saith unto him, I am the way, the truth and the life, no man cometh unto the Father but by Me.' John 14, 6.

Such of you as were here, recollect that we read these words as a text in the morning. We then took up the time in noticing Christ Jesus the I Am, equal with the Father, one with Him. We made a few remarks to show that I Am is the name of the mighty Jehovah, who stood by Israel through all their trials and difficulties, and we noticed that Christ as I Am is with His people in every sorrow and distress and always a present help in trouble. We noticed that Christ said, 'I am the way.' We remarked that He is a way, *the way of access* unto a Holy God for sinners.

There is no other way. There is no way for sinners to a just God by works of righteousness that they can do. But Christ has made an open way of access through the rent vail of His flesh, justice is honoured, the law is magnified, the iniquities of the church are blotted out; and here in Him mercy and truth have met together, and righteousness and peace have kissed each other; and here in Him the vilest wretch out of hell, who is brought by the good Spirit to the blessed exercise of faith in Jesus' name, meets with acceptance.

We may, once more, notice that Christ is *the way of peace* to the child of God in all his troubles, griefs and sorrows. The Lord's dear church and family, God has told them that, 'In the world they shall have tribulation,' but, 'Be of good cheer, I have overcome the world.' He has told us that, 'Many are the afflictions of the righteous but the Lord delivereth him out of them all.' He has said to us, 'In the day of prosperity be joyful, but in the day of adversity, consider. God also hath set the one over against the other, to the end that man should find nothing after him.' And the Lord tells us by the mouth of David that, 'He that hath no changes fears not God.'

But what a consolation it is when God favours the soul with a blessed sight that all his troubles come from the appointment of a Father; that his crosses of flesh and blood are all the appointments of a dear and lovely Brother and Head and portion, Christ. When he comes to have a sweet sight of this, there is strength, support under it. But what a scene it is when he comes into various exercises and the Lord withdraws the light of His countenance, and he is left to flesh and blood and carnal reason. How many times the child of God is thus like a wild bull in a net, and like a bullock unaccustomed to the yoke. Nature never can submit to be cut off. Human wisdom never can bear to be completely upset and overcome. How many times the child of God, like Job in this respect, is ready to cry out in the pangs of his crosses, burdens afflictions and griefs, 'My soul chooseth strangling and death rather than life.' How many times does the child, when left to himself, and flesh and blood and carnal reason, say, 'Has the Lord forsaken me, is His mercy clean gone for ever, and will He be favourable no more?'

Now, God overrules all these things to strip His people of their own wisdom and there own strength, and to bring them to see what they are in themselves. For what end? That they may come to praise Christ, come to exalt Christ, come to crown Christ, come to love Christ and to esteem Him as the chief of ten thousand and the altogether lovely. 'Well but then,' say you, 'You do not mean to preach contentedness with fleshly troubles and trials and to say that this is an evidence of christianity?' Let me tell you that such trumpery nonsense does not require an answer. What when the child of God is drawn to his wits end by his trials such trumpery as this does not require an answer. I should think it beneath such a poor ignorant fool as myself, to answer such a trumpery question as this. God's purpose in exercising His people and trying them to their wits end is to strip them of all comfort but Christ; it is to bring them to magnify the exceeding riches of His grace, of His wisdom, of

His mighty compassion; and it is to bring them to praise Him as the chief of ten thousand and the altogether lovely.

And what does the Lord do to bring the soul to such a position as this? Perhaps there are some of you now in the presence of God who have got crosses in your family and crosses and trials in your circumstances; everything appearing to be cutting you off and going against you on the right hand and on the left hand. Perhaps you have been to a throne of grace, and you have been restless, and crying, and weeping, and begging of God to open the way here; to open the way there; to incline such a heart there; to open such and such ways and such and such places. Ah! You may pray, and you may cry, and you may pull a long face, and you may make a great ado, telling God what to do in this place and in that place. What have you to do with all that? Is that any business of yours? Are you to come to infinite wisdom and to dictate the plan, and the place where, and the time when? God has said, 'Take no thought for the morrow; for the morrow shall take thought for itself. Sufficient unto the day is the evil thereof.'

But flesh and blood can go no further than flesh and blood; and to go beyond flesh and blood we must have omnipotent grace, power, unction, and life dropped into the heart, to direct us and to lead us up above flesh and blood. It is thus when the soul has tugged and toiled, and his strength is all gone, his wisdom all proved to be nothing but folly and foolishness, and all his plans are completely upset; he is brought to God at last as a poor helpless worm, pressed down with trouble and having neither life nor strength, and his soul lays at God's feet, and his language is, 'Lord help me! Lord appear for me!' How sweet and what a strengthening thing it is when Christ makes His way into the heart, when He whispers with His still small voice, 'Fear not, for I am with thee.' O, what strength, what sweet strength, is communicated into his heart, – yes, and into his body too; for when the soul feels strong and courageous the body also feels animated; there is a very near relation between them. 'Fear not, for I am with thee; be not dismayed, for I am thy God.'

No, though the soul could not find the way by flesh and blood to get strength and knowledge, Christ saith to all such that He is the 'strength of the needy in their distress.' And when

His blessed and sweet power is communicated to the soul he feels the enlivened vigour of this is his heart: 'For I am thy God, I will uphold thee; yea, I will strengthen thee; yea, I will uphold thee with the right hand of My righteousness.' Here the soul is led out of flesh and blood, and out of his own plans, out of his own schemes; from every arm of flesh, from every human source of strength; from human nature the soul is led up unto his dear and blessed Jesus, who has all in His hands, and the cattle upon a thousand hills are His, and the earth is His and the fulness thereof. O what strength he feels in this way! When he comes there, his burden is easy enough, his circumstances are right enough, his troubles have all come well enough, and everything in this way, when he comes here into Christ, and Christ is the way in his heart, it is the highway of holiness, and here the redeemed walk. When the soul is brought into Christ, and has a blessed sight of His mighty power, His glory, and His beauty, O, how strong he is in the Lord: 'Strong in the Lord and the power of His might.' Then his troubles and his burdens he sees are all right, and all straight, and God will bring him out of them. Now it is right and just at the very appointed time. Aye, and the poor soul, when he is walking in Christ by faith, sees that his Jesus is head over all; aye, and not only that, but he sees that all is his because Jesus Christ is his; he sees that whether it is Paul, or Apollos, or Cephas, or the world, or life, or death, or things present or things to come, that all is his, for he is Christ's and Christ is God's. He finds that every treasure is in his dear Lord. O how sweetly he can walk here. Why, bless you, my soul has been here many times. I have had many blessed seasons of walking here, when I have not had a loaf of bread in the house; I have been over head and ears in debt; the rent-day coming on, and nothing apparently to pay with; but when Christ was brought into my heart by faith as the way of strength and the way of power, and I looked up to Him, I saw that the cattle upon a thousand hills and the earth was His, and that He had nothing to do but to touch the heart of whom he would, and a supply would be given. Sweet place to walk!

'Ah!' says some child of God, 'O, that my soul could but come into this way and look to Jesus, and see Him as mine, and receive His blessed strength to support my mind. What am

I to do, to get there?' I have nothing to do with answering the question, what thou hast to do; but I will tell thee what must be done before. Before you can get out of your troubles, this way must get into thee. Christ must make way into the heart; it is He who increaseth strength. When the soul is blessedly and preciously here, what sweet walking it is, through trouble and through storm. But it is only at times and seasons that God favours His dear children with this walking. I am not going to bind infinite wisdom and say that all God's people, who are His own jewels, are favoured with such measures of these things. God may communicate to some of His dear people more of the sweetness of leading them in this way than to others. But those who have the most of it, have still sufficient to prove that in this world they have tribulation. In their hearts there is nothing but sorrow and misery; they have enough to prove that this world is not their rest, and that their strength is in the Lord as a sovereign, and a blessed gift from Him as the way of strength. And I find to this day, that He is the way of strength to my soul.

I hear of some people who say that they have nothing to do but look back at past deliverances and past helps, and to trust the word of God that it will abide firm for ever. But I do really think and believe in my very heart that I get a poorer, weaker, blinder fool than ever I was in all my life. I have had my soul in this way, Christ be praised, hundreds of times, in deliverances temporal and spiritual; and it has always left me with a solid standing upon the mighty power of the Holy God. But, I find now, if the Lord is not there I cannot think on Him; if the Lord is not there I cannot meditate blessedly upon Him; if the Lord is not there I cannot wait on Him. If the Lord is not there, and I am left to myself, I am carnal, careless, dead, lukewarm, wandering upon every fleshly object; and yet my very soul feels abhorrence of it. Look back! Why, I do look back; but, what can I see without the light of God? It is the prerogative of the Spirit to bring to remembrance. What can I look back and see? I am a sinner and am obliged to come as I ever did, a poor, ignorant, weak, forlorn, dejected, backsliding, vile wretch and beg of Christ that He will reveal Himself again to my heart and set it all right. And, bless you, when the dear Lord comes again, and whispers into my heart, 'Fear not, it is I,' I know His voice. 'Why,' say you, 'by what?' By the power that attends it, the strength that comes with it; it is such a way of strength, such a way of courage, such a way of sweetness, such a way of blessedness, my heart drops down at His feet. I blush at my base ingratitude and my accursed unbelief, and I tell the Lord that I am not worthy of His notice, and that I wonder that ever he can give me another token of the light of His countenance, and that ever He can bless me with another token for good; and then when He comes in such a sweet way as this, He says, 'My dove, my undefiled; the sight of thee has refreshed my very heart.' How does that break my soul; what love does it bring into it. What grief it produces to think that I should dishonour such a blessed covenant God, when His way is so precious and delightful. Nay, my very soul, feels more than my tongue can ever tell. When my soul comes here, it is a way of strength, a way of courage, and a way of life.

We may, again, notice Christ as the way, and *the only way, or victory over the corruptions of the heart*, over the fiery darts of the devil, and over all the devilishness of human nature. O, we little know the depths of our own ungodly hearts. I thought I had seen the depth of mine forty years ago; but I am now brought to see, that it is a depth without a bottom; that noone can know it, nor search it, nor come to the bottom of it, but God. O the filth of it, the enmity of it against God! Have you ever wondered child of God, to think what feelings you have had in your hearts against God? Have you never felt enmity against the Bible, enmity against prayer, enmity or hatred against the Being of a God, enmity against everything like God? Ah, and sometimes some soul says, 'I believed and feared that God has given me up to desperation; that I was given up to a horrid and an awful presumption, that I could no more be a child of God than the Devil was one; such enmity was there in my heart, such diabolical things pointing against Christ, and pointing against a Father, against the Holy Ghost, against the Trinity, and also against everything that is secret and revealed.' Ah poor soul! This was the Devil and the old man. Thou poor soul, didst not love these things; they were no consolation to thee.

'Ah,' some will say, 'But what a foolish thing in the child of God to take notice of them.' Yes. When the man is down and you see things from a distance, it is easy to talk, it is easy to say that these things are nothing; but when the child of God is in this condition, when the Enemy comes in like a flood – and you know the flood drives everything before it - he sometimes thinks that God has given him over; and the Devil will come to the poor child of God and tempt him to blaspheme the Holy Ghost, pouring into his heart such blasphemies against the Spirit as make his very hair to stand on end. 'Ah,' says the Devil, 'Now you have it ; it is all over. Though you have not done it with your words, you have done it with your thoughts ; it is in your heart, and God looks at the heart.' And the soul thinks that this is all true and that he has really done as the Devil says. Why poor soul, it is all the Devil doing it in thee. Didst thou not hate and abhor it and didst thou not pray to God to keep thee from presumptuous sins, and didst thou not ask that He would bless thee with deliverance, and bring thee to set thy foot upon these cursed things in thy heart? By and by the Lord speaks; He it is who conquers these things. O yes! Thy prayers cannot do it, nor thy tears cannot do it, nor thy groans cannot do it, nor all the prayers of all the people of God cannot do it; it is Christ, the great Captain of our salvation, He it is to whom Satan will bend to. Satan will fly at His command, when He comes with His mighty power and His great loving-kindness, and sweetly proclaims into their heart, 'Shall not God avenge His own elect which cry day and night? Yea, He will avenge them speedily.' 'When the enemy cometh in like a flood, the good Spirit of the Lord will lift up a standard against him.' Where His bloody standard is, victory is lifted up in the soul. O! These devilish enemies will flee, - they all flee at the blessed and glorious appearance of the Captain of our salvation. The soul rises up, like a giant refreshed with new wine, and he says, 'Rejoice not against me, O mine enemy, for when I fall I shall arise, when I sit in darkness the Lord will be a light unto me.' Yes. He comes now to perceive that no weapon formed against him shall prosper, and that every tongue that riseth up in judgment against him, he shall condemn; for this is the heritage of the servants of the Lord. Now, when by the Spirit this is blessedly revealed to the heart, he sees that Christ is the way of conquering. What a sweet and glorious way is it now, when he can see that His blessed Captain has caused every devil to flee, lifted him up out of his captivity, and brought him into the way of holiness. Thus he walks in joy and peace until the Lord is again pleased to hide His face.

Christ is *the way of humility to the soul*. When the child of God is sweetly blessed with precious faith, and when he has found what a little creature he is in his own eyes, how humiliating to see the loving-kindness of his God. What base views of himself does it produce. How it fills his soul with gratitude and thankfulness to his God, with contentedness and resignation to His sovereign will and pleasure. He is the way of peace, the way of love, the way of contentedness, the way of fruitfulness in everything that is God-like and full of glory.

People may have a knowledge in their judgment and head, of Christ being the way, and they may talk about it with such lightness, with such emptiness, that the very sound of their talking does not produce any effect; but where there is the love of God in the soul, where the soul has seen the humiliating nature of the way and how it has been helped to walk here; when the poor soul feels its own littleness, and the sovereignty of God, and how God blessed him when he little thought of it and little expected it, he says, 'Come hither,' my brethren and my sisters, 'all ye that fear God, and I will tell you what He has done for my soul;' and he will exalt God in such a manner, so put the crown upon His head and speak of Him with such tenderness and godly feeling, that it produces the same feeling in those who have been blessed with the same spirit, and been blessed in the same way. What a sweet knitting together it thus produces. Christ produces a blessed fruitfulness in every good work, that He is the way of all glory.

But He tells us again that *He is the truth.* He is the substance of all the blessed truths which are revealed in the glorious Gospel. What part and branch of it without Him is worth having? He is the substance, the very substance of the word. What would all the shadows and types have been but for Him, the Antitype? He is the truth, the substance of the whole. Christ seen by faith was the grand substance. And when the substance came, and there was a clearing up of all the types and the shadows, what became of all the offerings? Where do the Jews now offer up sacrifice? The substance is come, they have rejected the substance, and here they are banished up and down the earth to the present day, without a territory, without offerings, without priests to come and offer up. With all the money that may be collected and all the money that may be made in London or in the country to convert the Jews, what will they do? God may pick up here and there one – I am not going to say that we shall not find here and there one; for we have one in our church[1] who I believe feels and loves the truth and knows and rejoices in the truth when the truth appears in its glory – but the Jews as a body will never be converted to God until the fulness of the Gentiles shall come. God has fixed it, and all the workings of men will not overturn the purposes of God. He Himself shall accomplish it. A nation shall be born in a day; they shall believe in Christ the Lamb of God, who was set forth in the types and shadows, who was rejected by their forefathers; and they shall be brought to see in Him the substance of them all.

He is *the truth of all the prophecies* concerning Himself; and how pointedly did He fulfil them, relating as they did to the very time of His birth, the very manner of His life, the very miracles that He wrought, the very death that He must die, the treatment He should receive, Judas betraying Him, nay, the very parting of His garments. All was fulfilled in Him. He was the truth of it all, the grand substance of it all; and the Jews never spoke a greater truth, though not out of love to Him, than when, as He hung upon the cross, and heaven and earth and hell seemed to be combined together, the very sun hid his face, the very dead were moved in their graves, devils roared and men laughed; they cried out, 'He saved others, Himself He cannot save.' They never spoke a greater truth. But I would mention

---

[1] Either a Jew was in church membership at Zion Chapel, Trowbridge, or Warburton is referring to the Gospel Standard churches and had Edward Samuel [a converted Polish Jew] in mind, who was baptised by David Denham at Hartley Row Chapel in the early 1840s and became Pastor at Farnham in 1845. *Six Remarkable Ministers.* B.A. Ramsbottom. 1994. p.181.

this with solemnity. He had engaged to suffer, He had volunteered for that purpose. Thus He says to His disciples, 'Ought not Christ to have suffered these things, and to enter into His glory?' So that He could not save Himself. He saved others, He saved His church and family, He saved all His elect; but Himself He could not save from this suffering, this agony, and this death, because He had engaged to come and pay the debts of His people. Thus everything was done according to what had been prophesied, so as to prove that Christ was the truth and the substance of prophecy.

He is *the truth of all the promises*. What are the promises without Him? They all centre in Him, they are all yea and amen in Him; He is the grand immortal substance of the whole of them. What promises are there which do not centre in Him and of which He is not the substance?

He is *the substance of the glorious ordinances*. If we look at baptism, there He is the substance, for there is His death, His burial, His resurrection. And if we look at the Lord's Supper, there He is the substance; the breaking of the bread and the drinking of the wine, these show forth His sufferings and His death.

If we come to look at *the precepts, He is the truth of these*; they all centre in Him and end with Him. The invitations and all the blessings of gospel truth are summed up in Him, the ever blessed and grand truth.

And *He is the life*. He is *the life of preaching*. I believe there are hundreds and thousands whom the devil deceives in preaching as much as in anything else. It is not an uncommon thing for a number of empty, light professors of religion to be wonderfully melted, and what they call humbled, at hearing a clever sermon. If a man who has got a little talent, a ready expression, a clear judgment, and a good memory, speaks of the sufferings of Christ, he may work up the passions of natural men in such a way that they will be melted to tears at hearing him. But after all there is nothing but the working upon the natural passions; there is no life of God in the soul! The child of God, who really has the life of God in his heart, comes to chapel, and he thinks and feels that he has neither part or lot in the matter. He actually has hard work to get along; he is tempted to turn back again; he fears that he shall be an Achan in the camp, and that God perhaps will not visit His people on his account. At last he staggers in, not knowing what to do; he reels into the place, fearing that there will be nothing but condemnation, and feeling that it is what he deserves. The preaching is not without effect; life comes down with power to that man, life and power enter into his heart, peace and love enter into his soul, liberty sweetly lifts up his heart and he sings for joy.[2] This man has now proved that Christ is the life.

Yes, He is *the life of prayer*, He is *the life of meditation*, He is *the life of conversation*, He is the life of everything the soul has to do with. If there is no Christ, there is no life. 'I am,' says Christ, 'the resurrection and the life.' I have known what it is to feel this thousands of times. O Lord quicken my soul; keep my soul alive, I pray Thee! Let Thy tender mercy come unto me, that I may live, for Thou art my life. An empty religion will not do for my soul. I want Christ to come in His sweetness and preciousness and to fill my heart.

Perhaps there are some dear children in the presence of God who are ready to say, 'Ah! I have had nothing today. I thought I should have been picked up today, but I have had nothing all day.' You know the Lord says to Peter, 'Feed my lambs,' and we must try to bring something forth that God has provided. You know it is the prerogative of God to bring comfort into the heart; but, bless His dear and precious name, He says that the smoking flax shall not be quenched, nor the bruised reed be broken. He says that He will not despise the sighing of the needy. He says that when the poor and the needy seek water, and there is none, and their tongue faileth for thirst, He, the Lord, will hear them, and He, the God of Israel, will not forsake them. Nay, He says, 'I love them that love me, and they that seek me early shall find me.' And hast thou never had a little sweet word dropped into thy heart which hath encouraged thee for a moment and given thee strength by the way? Why this is life! This is the way, Christ! These are the very tokens of His dear loving-kindness, and a manifestation that He has

---

[2] An accurate description of his own deliverance under Mr Roby, in the chapel in Cannon Street, Manchester in 1796/7.

begun a good work in thee; and He that has begun a good work in thee will perform it until the day of Jesus Christ. *He is the way, the truth and the life*; and no man cometh unto the Father but by him. It is not by your prayers or anything that you can do.

'But,' say you, 'do you condemn prayers?' My poor dear soul, no. God knows I cannot do that, for prayer is the greatest thing in my religion. I can safely say this. If prayer were taken away from my soul, I do not know what I should do. My soul is by the hour in prayer. I cannot study, or what people call such, – go to the Scriptures and be dividing and subdividing them. I have tried it hundreds of times, and have prayed to God to give me the knowledge and the gifts to enable me to do it, telling Him that he could give them to me if he pleased. Then I have to look at four of five texts, and my soul has been led to exclaim, 'Why, what is all this, if there is not the power of God? What is all this to the souls of the people? What is this to the hungry, what is it to the faint, what is it to the weak?' My soul then goes again to God, beseeching Him that He will be with me, and direct me, and keep me. So that I cannot speak against prayer. But what I mean is that it is not your prayers that will do you any good, but God's answers to your prayers. When God puts the spirit of prayer into the hearts of His people, it is that He may answer their prayers; not that they may look into their hearts and worship their prayers, but that He may bring forth His sweet presence. None can approach the Father but the Son; and when the Lord leads us by Jesus to have faith in Him, the holy Trinity smiles and looks down with love and delight.

May God bless the few hints which have been thrown out, and He Himself shall have the glory. Amen.

Chapter 13

Man goeth to his long home

Between 1848 and 1851 Warburton moved house for the last time in Trowbridge. It is not clear why he should leave his little Georgian house in Waterloo Terrace, Union Street, in which he had lived since 1832. The *Post Office Directory for Wiltshire* [1848], records his name as still there in 1848, but the National Census Records for 1851 show he had moved by then to Dorset House in The Halve. This was a far larger house with three storeys, built in the early years of the 19th century, of a late Georgian style. Here Warburton spent the last years of his life with his wife and his two daughters, Rachel and Ruth.

According to an account of his last days and death, edited by Job Rawlings, and published in the *Earthen Vessel* magazine for May 1857, p.98,

> John Warburton began to feel his strength to decline in March 1856, and the Church agreed to get a supply for Sabbath-day mornings, so that from that time he preached but once, and that was in the evening; his sermons from that time were solemn and weighty. He continued thus until October, just finishing his eighty years, and then his strength began to fail; and being afflicted with disease of the heart, he gave up altogether, and was confined to his room.

A month after his death, in May 1857, John Warburton Junior published an account of his father's last days, with a Preface by his father's friend J.C.Philpot. This provides a fairly detailed account of the period of his life from October 1856 to 2nd April 1857, when he died. In the Preface to this twenty-nine page booklet, which sold at the time for four pence, J.C.Philpot says,

My great esteem and affection for my departed friend, as well as my deep respect for him as so eminent a servant of God made me at once accept the labour of love [of editing this work for the press]. When I learnt that the little work would be published for the benefit of his bereaved widow and family, I felt a more additional willingness to render aid that lay in my power had it even demanded ten times as much of my time and attention.... Light indeed has been my labour, for I have scarcely altered a word from beginning to end......

In September 1835, Mr Warburton baptised me, and I shall never forget the power with which he preached that morning. Soon afterwards I went down to Trowbridge to supply his pulpit, and found there a gracious people, most of whom were his spiritual children. He several times supplied for me at Stamford and Oakham, after my lot was cast in those places; and there are those still there, who can bear testimony to the power and savour with which he spoke. We have for many years generally met annually at the Calne Anniversary, a well-known and remarkable gathering of the saints of God in that district of North Wilts, where we have been in the habit of preaching together, and I hope ever met and parted with renewed affection.

I have heard Mr Gadsby preach as great, perhaps greater sermons; but I never met a minister whose prayer in the pulpit, or whose conversation out of it, was so weighty and savoury. Indeed, I never heard a man ever ask a blessing at the breakfast or dinner table like him. There was such a simplicity, such a reverence, and yet childlike approach unto God; such a savour in his few words, that it seemed to sanctify the meal in a peculiar way. Hundreds, perhaps thousands, have borne witness to the power and savour which rested on his ministry; but the blessing he has been made to the church of God will never be fully known until that day when the secrets of all hearts shall be revealed.

The crowning testimony is given in the following pages, wherein we see the aged servant of God supported amidst all the languishing of disease, blessed with what he had always contended for – a *feeling religion*, enjoying the presence and power of his dear Lord, and favoured with a glorious and triumphant departure.

In life he stuck by a feeling religion, and in death a feeling religion stuck by him. His desire was, as a Christian, to experience the sweet inflowings of the love of God to his soul; and, as a minister, to debase the sinner, exalt the Saviour, and trace out the work of the Holy Ghost in the heart, from a feeling, living and daily experience of it in his own conscience.

As he lived, so he died, never wavering from the truth, never carried about with divers and strange doctrines, never venturing beyond his depth, never speculating or reasoning beyond what he knew and felt for himself; ever seeing more and more in himself to loathe and abhor, and ever more and more in the Lord Jesus to admire and to love.

He has run his race; has fought a good fight, and finished his course with joy, and left us still to sigh, and groan in the wilderness, but looking to the same Lord, and hoping in the same rich, sovereign and super-abounding grace. Dated 5th May 1857. J.C.P.

Philpot in the June issue of the *Gospel Standard* for 1857 reviewed this booklet at considerable length. The larger part of this review constitutes the Preface to this biography. These two analyses [The Preface and the Review] of John Warburton and his work provide a clear view of him from an able minister and scholar, who knew him and loved him; one who was not unaware of his faults, but was equally conscious of what the Lord had done in him and what He had made him to the churches in his day. It is a first hand assessment from a contemporary. The title of John Warburton Junior's booklet was, *A Testimony to the Loving Kindness and Faithfulness of a Covenant God, as displayed in the last illness and blessed death of the late John Warburton, Minister of the Gospel, and for 42 years Pastor of the Church of Christ assembling at Zion Chapel Trowbridge.* Southill, Beds. 23rd April 1857.

John junior says in it, that when he was preaching at Hurstpierpoint in November 1856, he was sent for urgently by the family. When he reached Trowbridge he found his father in a very weak state. His father told him how before he was taken ill, the Lord had favoured him in his soul. He went on to say,

Go where I would, there was the Lord with me. If I went into the garden, there He was; if into my summer-house, He went with me; if into the wood-house, sawing and chopping wood, He was with me too. He led me back through all the footsteps He had brought me, both in providence and grace. O how my soul was broken down with His lovingkindness. I tell thee what, John, I could hardly walk about; for the smiles of my God seemed too much for the body to bear. At last, I said to him, 'My dear Lord, what art thou about to do with Thy poor worm?' O, I wanted Him to take me home.....

Not long since I thought upon my book. Some people have said that it has been blessed to them. It being many years since I read it, I thought I would read it again; but O John, my soul was broken within me to see the poverty and distress, the fears and despair, the misery and sorrow that he had brought me through. O how I sat at His feet and washed them with tears of gratitude..... I do hope, John, when I am gone nobody will say anything about me. Let my name sink into dust; but let the name of Jesus be exalted for ever.....

It is astonishing that I feel no more anxiety about the chapel. And see how anxious I have at all times been for the cause. O the prayers that have gone up from my heart, the tears that have rolled down my poor cheeks, for that place, that God would bless it with prosperity both in spirituals and providentials! *But now* it is entirely taken from me. I can leave them all in the Lord's hands.....

Going once, many years ago, from Manchester to Stand, I was then up to the neck in poverty, over head and ears in debt. As I walked, I wondered what would become of me. I could not see it possible that ever I could get through with honour. O how I pitied my hard fate! But my dear Lord soon silenced all my complaints, and stopped my mouth of every murmuring devil in my carnal mind, by speaking the words of the poet in my heart,

> When through fiery trials thy pathway shall lie,
> My grace all-sufficient shall be thy supply;
> The flame shall not hurt thee; I only design,
> Thy dross to consume, and thy gold to refine.

> E'en down to old age all My people shall prove
> My sovereign, eternal, unchangeable love;
> And when hoary hairs shall their temples adorn,
> Like lambs they shall still in My bosom be borne

The Lord then told me, 'I will be with thee, and bring thee through all thy troubles honourably, and bring thee to a good old age; hoary hairs shall thy temples adorn; and like a lamb thou shalt still be borne.' And see how all has come to pass! Bless His precious Name.

William Tiptaft came to Trowbridge in November to preach at Zion Chapel on Sunday 23rd and Tuesday evening 25th. He called to see Warburton twice while there, once on Saturday evening 22nd and again after the evening service on the Tuesday. Warburton had last preached for him at Abingdon on a Sunday in June that year, when, though weak, and hardly expected to preach twice, he had preached both morning and evening to two large and overflowing congregations for about an hour, with great power and savour.[1] William Tiptaft writing of his Saturday evening visit says,[2]

> He was sitting by the fire in his bedroom, and appeared to be in a very happy frame of mind, and under the influence of the blessed enjoyments he had had the previous night... He said his enjoyments were as great during the night as his soul could contain, and that the words of David were applicable to his state of mind, "Thou anointest my head with oil; my cup runneth over.... The following Tuesday I found him in a very different frame of soul. Instead of praising and blessing God, he was begging and praying for the enjoyment of Divine blessings. He did not take a high place, but honestly said, "I am now in the poor publican's place, begging for mercy."

In November, John Gadsby of Manchester came to Trowbridge to see him. Asking Warburton about his concern for his church, he replied, [3]

---

1 *Warburton's Last Days,* J.W. Jnr. 1857, p.15.

2 *Warburton's Last Days.,* op. cit. p. 14.

3 *Mercies of a Covenant God,* Reiner, 1974, pp. 226,227.

Have I no care about the church [i.e. Zion Chapel]? I feel sometimes as if I never had had a church or a chapel at all. I have to think before I can find the way to the chapel in my mind, and sometimes I get to the corner [i.e. of The Halve and Union Street] of the street and can't get any further.

Then turning the conversation Warburton said,

O to think of that Park Lane, near the Dove House! I remember going with the two children [William and Sarah] and finding all my things marked to be sold for rent. And now look at me! Here I am, surrounded with feather pillows. [He was resting upon a sofa, supported by feather pillows.] I once walked round my garden here [Dorset House], and I saw a hamper that had had some fruit and things in that a friend had sent me, and another that had had some wine in. Then I went into the kitchen, and there was plenty of everything. And I said, 'Is this old Warburton, the pauper?' Eh! Bless the Lord.... Isn't it wonderful that such an old irritable fool as I have been should be made to lie so quiet? I assure thee, lad, I hardly ever have a single anxious thought about any one thing....

This shortness of breath is quite new to me. When it first came I thought it was all nonsense, and I was determined I would break through it; so I went and preached, and made as much noise as ever I did in my life, and felt so much better after it that I was *sure* it was all nonsense, but that was my last sermon. The doctor said he wondered I had not died in the pulpit. I remember once, when thy father [William Gadsby] was here, going with him to Mr Hayward's and he walked along well enough till we came to a little bit of a rise, only about half a yard, and then he stopped to take a breath, and I said to him, 'Why man, there's no hill here! it's only fancy!' And then we came to level ground again, and off he went again as well as ever. So I said to him, 'It's only nervousness, I'm sure.' 'No,' he said, 'that's all, it's only nervousness. And now, John, as you know the disease, tell me the remedy.' 'Poor dear man, I've found it out now! How he did suffer with his breath for years, while mine's only just now.'

In January he was gradually sinking with heart failure and dropsy. He suffered greatly with fluid in his legs and was given at times 'a composing draught,' presumably to induce sleep and relieve pain. His mind was back in his days up North and he referred from time to time to his own sinful youth, the

Lord's great mercy in calling him out of nature's darkness, and his deliverance under Mr Roby in Manchester. He was not able for nearly a month to lie down and had to be propped up with pillows. His children continually were with him, especially his two daughters Rachel and Ruth who were living at home, his son James who lived in Trowbridge, and his daughter Elizabeth, Mrs Hayward, who lived nearby at The Laurels [now Ethendune] in Hilperton Road. Leah was also close, living in Prospect House, Prospect Place.

From time to time his deacons came to see him. There were six deacons at this time. Richard Knee, who ran a bookshop in Church Walk and was the Trowbridge agent for the *Gospel Standard*, had been a deacon since 1825 and lived on until 1864. Jacob Hawkins, appointed deacon in 1851, was a baker and shopkeeper in Hilperton Road and lived until 1876. The other four deacons were all appointed in 1853. Samuel Moore [who lies buried at the foot of Warburton's grave], was a grocer and draper in Castle Street and lived until 1868. John Phillips was a Tailor in Roundstone Street. He did not die until 1895. Isaac Waite died in 1870 and William Applegate, who lived in Roundstone Street, outlived them all, dying in 1907. He had originally attended Back Street Baptist Chapel, from which the Zion Church had come in 1813, and had been baptised there. Brought to attend Zion, he had been in bondage under the law for ten years until he was brought into liberty under Warburton's ministry in 1850. His wife, Mary Ann Applegate was one of the last group that Warburton baptised on 7th July 1850, and both she and William were received into the Church at the same time.[4]

While on occasions Warburton felt a desire to go down to the Chapel and preach again and tell his congregation what the Lord had done and was doing for him, at other times he felt he must resign as Pastor and relieve the Church from the double burden of paying him and Supplies to fill the pulpit in his long illness. So in January he resigned his office and salary as Pastor. But the Church met and refused to accept it and voted him his full salary for six weeks. At the end of this time they

---

[4] *Gospel Standard* 1888, pp. 499, 500.

met again and agreed to continue the arrangement for another six weeks. At this time his dropsy in his legs became easier and it appeared he might rally and live another year. But within the second six week period he began to fail rapidly, losing his appetite, and eventually for the last two weeks of March confined to his bed with attendants day and night. [5]

His wife coming in the room one day, he lifted up both his hands and said, 'Here are two rebels saved by grace! all of grace. We have had many trials together! We have lived with each other more that sixty years; but it will not be long before we shall meet again. Then what an eternity we shall spend together; but it is too much to think of the glory. Jesus, Jesus, Jesus, when shall I be with Thee?'[6] On the last Sunday of his life, 29th March, a letter was received from a friend. When told the contents, he said, 'It has been my desire once more to go round and see my old friends, and tell them how good the Lord is, and how precious He is to me.' In the evening of that Sunday he remarked to friends what a comfortable day he had spent in body and soul, and how happy he was with the blessed testimony within that the Lord was his God. He continued in this peaceful state until the next Wednesday, when it became apparent that his end was near.

On Thursday 2nd April all his children living in Trowbridge were called to his bedside. As they gathered there, Sarah [Mrs Earle] was the eldest aged fifty-nine, James was fifty-six, Elizabeth [Mrs Hayward] was fifty-five, Leah [Mrs Moore] was fifty-two, Rachel fifty and Ruth forty-four. There is no mention of either Gideon or John being present and it seems that William, who had stayed up North must have died previously. When one of his daughters asked him, 'Father, you feel Christ precious, and want to praise Him in glory?' He lifted up both hands and pointing with one finger said distinctly, 'I haven't room, I haven't room.' Between four and five in the afternoon, it became very difficult to understand him. Then

---

[5] *The Earthen Vessel,* 1857, p. 98.

[6] *Warburton's Mercies,* Reiner, 1974, p. 238.

about seven he said, 'Pen, ink.' It was brought to him and he grasped the pen but could not write. When asked by Rachel what he wanted to write, 'Was it about the Church? was it about the family?' he shook his head. When asked if it was to tell them how good the Lord was to him, he responded, 'Yes! Yes!' But still not making himself fully clear, he lifted up both his hands and pointing with his finger, tried to speak. At last he said, 'Hal---, Hal---,' and then with a firm voice without a waver, 'Hallelujah!' and immediately passed into the presence of his God. It was 7.15, on Thursday, 2nd April 1857.

The week evening service had just commenced at Zion Chapel, when the news came from Dorset House, in The Halve that their pastor had died. Mr William Hatton of Wolverhampton was in process of giving out a hymn in the service. [This shows, that in the order of service at Zion, it was the practice for the minister to announce his own hymns.] At the announcement a silence followed, then many members burst into tears. Eventually a Prayer Meeting was held at Zion that night. An era had ended in the history of the Church. Exactly forty-two years had passed since John Warburton began his Pastorate in Trowbridge in the Room on Wicker Hill, on the first Sunday in April 1815. The following Monday evening [6th] a Church Meeting took place at Zion Chapel when John Warburton Junior spoke to the Church members and thanked them for their great kindness in supporting his father to his end.[7] A letter[8] of John Grace, written from Brighton on Thursday 9th April says,

> My old and beloved friend Warburton, died in peace on 2nd inst., in his 81st year. He has done with the fight. He is to be buried on Friday; his people wanted me to go to Trowbridge to bury him, but my engagements will not allow of my going. I dare say a funeral sermon will be preached for him at Gower Street Chapel on Sunday.

---

[7] Earthen Vessel 1857, p. 99.

[8] *Recollections of John Grace* 1893, p. 243.

Warburton was a close friend of John Grace, but the latter was unable to take his funeral. It is of interest that others of his closest friends, such as J.C.Philpot, John Kershaw, William Tiptaft and Thomas Godwin were all unable to get to Trowbridge on that Friday, almost certainly for the same reason as John Grace.

The Funeral took place on Good Friday 10th April. The coffin left Dorset House in The Halve, shortly before eleven o' clock. It was a beautifully clear, calm, warm, and sunny day.[9] It was carried by six members of the Church at Zion, preceded by two of the eldest deacons, one of which would have been Richard Knee, baptised by Warburton on 25th June 1820 at Ladydown Mill. The pall was borne by the remaining deacons. The family followed on foot the short distance to Zion Chapel. As the coffin was borne into the Chapel the choir in the gallery, led by William Keates, struck up a mournful piece of sacred music. [Clearly, singing at Zion, during the forty-two years of Warburton's Pastorate, had been without any musical accompaniment]. The coffin was placed in the Communion Pew [or Table Seat]. The Chapel being then full, the outer gates were shut to prevent overcrowding. The Chapel was clad in deep mourning. The pulpit would have been in black. The gallery had hangings of black cloth in folds all round on three sides. The service commenced with hymn 467 of Gadsby's Selection, led by the precentor, William Keates [baptised by Warburton, 3rd December 1848], and the choir,

Why should we shrink at Jordan's flood.
  Or dread the unknown way?
See, yonder rolls a stream of blood,
  That bears the curse away.

Death lost his sting when Jesus bled;
  When Jesus left the ground,
Disarmed, the King of terrors fled,
  And felt a mortal wound.

---

[9] Zion Chapel Trowbridge, 1813-1913. p. 15.

And now his office is to wait
Between the saints and sin;
A porter at the heavenly gate,
To let the pilgrims in.

And though his pale and ghastly face
May seem to frown the while;
We soon shall see the King of grace,
And he'll for ever smile.

[Joseph Swain. 1761-96]

Mr William Hatton, Pastor of Wolverhampton, himself a Lancashire man from Warrington and Accrington, [father of Joseph Hatton[10] (1821-1884), who was Pastor of Smallfield and Shaw's Corner, Redhill, Surrey] addressed the congregation. Mr Robert Roff of Stow-on-the-Wold [Pastor there from 1842-1862] took part, as also did Mr William Mortimer [Pastor of Chippenham from 1852-1869].

After the service the coffin was placed in a horse-drawn hearse and with the procession of mourners proceeded to the New Cemetery via Timbrell Street, Islington and the Down. The hearse was preceded by Mr Spragg [Surgeon] and William Fowler Esq. [Doctor], and also by the following ministers, viz., Mr George Gorton, Pastor of Milton-under-Wychwood, Oxon., Mr Pocock of Seend, Mr Nightingale of Southwick, Mr Hatton, Mr Roff, Mr Mortimer and other friends, the pall being borne by the deacons of the Church. The chief mourners who followed were: Three sons of John Warburton, James, Gideon and John; two sons-in-law, John Hayward and Isaac Moore; eight grandsons, all young men, John (37) and James (32) Warburton [sons of James], Joseph (27) and Benjamin(22) Hayward [sons of Elizabeth], William(33), Reuben(26), Frederick(24) and Edward(30) Moore [sons of Leah]; John Price, husband of a granddaughter, and John Gadsby, son of William Gadsby and

---

[10] *Memoir Joseph Hatton* 1884, pp. 11, 23.

publisher of the *Gospel Standard* Magazine. Then followed in pairs, an hundred male members of the Church or Congregation and an hundred and thirty lady members, all in deep mourning, the men wearing crape hatbands and gloves. The route was lined with people and at the cemetery the congregation was estimated to be between two and three thousand. Mr Foley, Superintendent of Police, kept order and prevented obstructions to the procession.

On arrival at the cemetery, [which had at the time only recently been opened, Warburton's being one of the early burials], Mr George Gorton gave 'an affecting and powerful address.' Hymn 468, Gadsby's Selection, was then sung, led by William Keates and the choir, of which the first verse is,

> Death is no more a frightful foe;
>   Since I with Christ shall reign,
> With joy I leave this world of woe;
>   For me to die is gain.
>
> W.W. Horne.[1773-1826]

The vast congregation of several thousand sang the six verses of this hymn, with its refrain at the end of each verse, 'For me to die is gain', and it must have been a remarkable scene as they sang in their broad Wiltshire dialect. Mr Roff concluded the service with prayer.

So the service was over and the great congregation melted away on that beautiful April day in the spring of 1857. A life had ended, but a precious memory and a gracious influence remained. The brick tomb with its large stone monument was to be re-opened in five years time when his wife, Lydia, died on 21st May 1862, at the age of eighty-five, and was buried with her husband. She had lived for the remainder of her days with Rachel and Ruth in the house next door to the Moore's home in Prospect Place, just off Timbrell Street. It was to be opened once more in 1870, when Rachel, who died 19th August 1870, was buried there. The Church Accounts for 1858 show that the Church paid £11 10s as part of the expenses of John Warburton's funeral, and went on, at their own expense, to erect the large stone monument over his grave, and a marble tablet over the pulpit at Zion Chapel.

The second of the three founders of the Gospel Standard Baptist churches had been taken to his eternal rest. A work, begun by the ministry of William Huntington and his contemporaries, taken up after his death in 1813 by William Gadsby, John Warburton and John Kershaw, was now continued by the next generation of leaders, numbering J.C. Philpot, William Tiptaft, Thomas Godwin, William Cowper and many other ministers, preaching throughout the country in about one hundred churches at the time of Warburton's death in 1857. The *Gospel Standard* since its commencement in August 1835, now the principal organ of the churches, had first reached a circulation of 7,400 in 1841,[11] then had reached 9,000 in 1847,[12] and eventually in England and abroad, exceeded 17,000.[13] The bond, which bound this group of churches together, was the strong spiritual cohesion among their ministers, centring on a revelation of truth to the heart by the Holy Spirit.

John Warburton had been a man, endowed by God with evident abilities as a leader. He had, not without difficulties, held together a church of several hundred members and a congregation of a thousand, at Trowbridge, for over forty years. Throughout the country, especially in the North and in London, his ministry had commanded large congregations of those who valued his preaching and whose hearts were touched by it. J.C.Philpot said of him, 'No minister in these last fifty years [1807 - 1857], except William Huntington and William Gadsby, has been so blessed to the Church of God or had so many seals to his ministry.' Many owed their conversion under God to his ministry.

---

[11] *Gospel Standard* 1841, p. 89.

[12] *Gospel Standard* 1847, p. 7.

[13] *The Seceders*, Vol. 2, J.H. Philpot, 1932, p. 35.

His *Mercies*, like the *Pilgrim's Progress* was, when first published, read in 'the weaver's cottage and the servant's hall,' or in the families of the industrial workers and the middle class homes of early Victorian England. Republished many times since 1839 in this country, The Netherlands and the United States, it is like the *Pilgrim's Progress* a timeless piece of spiritual experience. J.H. Philpot, writing in 1932 about his family's memories of John Warburton, [*The Seceders* Vol. 2, p. 31] says that Warburton had 'an undoubted air of distinction,' and speculates from which side of his family it was derived.

After researching his life for over twenty years, there still remain many unanswered questions, such as the absence of any information regarding the life and death of Manoah, many letters and sermons to be discovered, and a family tree extending down to the present day, which still has many gaps in it. But much is quite clear. With William Gadsby and John Kershaw, he was an eminent successor of William Huntington, whose mantle fell on the shoulders of this triumvirate, and was later taken up by J.C.Philpot and his contemporaries. After the death of Huntington, his work fed the roots of the newly rising group of Baptist Churches which were to take the name of 'Gospel Standard.' This 'Banner of Truth' [Ps. 60, 4.] is still maintained today in the Gospel Standard Churches and from the pages of its magazine *The Gospel Standard*, the longest continuously surviving, spiritual, monthly magazine in this country at the present time. The 'Banner' may appear small, but it remains. The same truths are contended for today, as were contended for by John Warburton, and as J.C. Philpot so succinctly put it at the time of his death, 'In life he stuck by a feeling religion, and in death a feeling religion stuck by him.... As he lived, so he died, never wavering from *the truth.'*

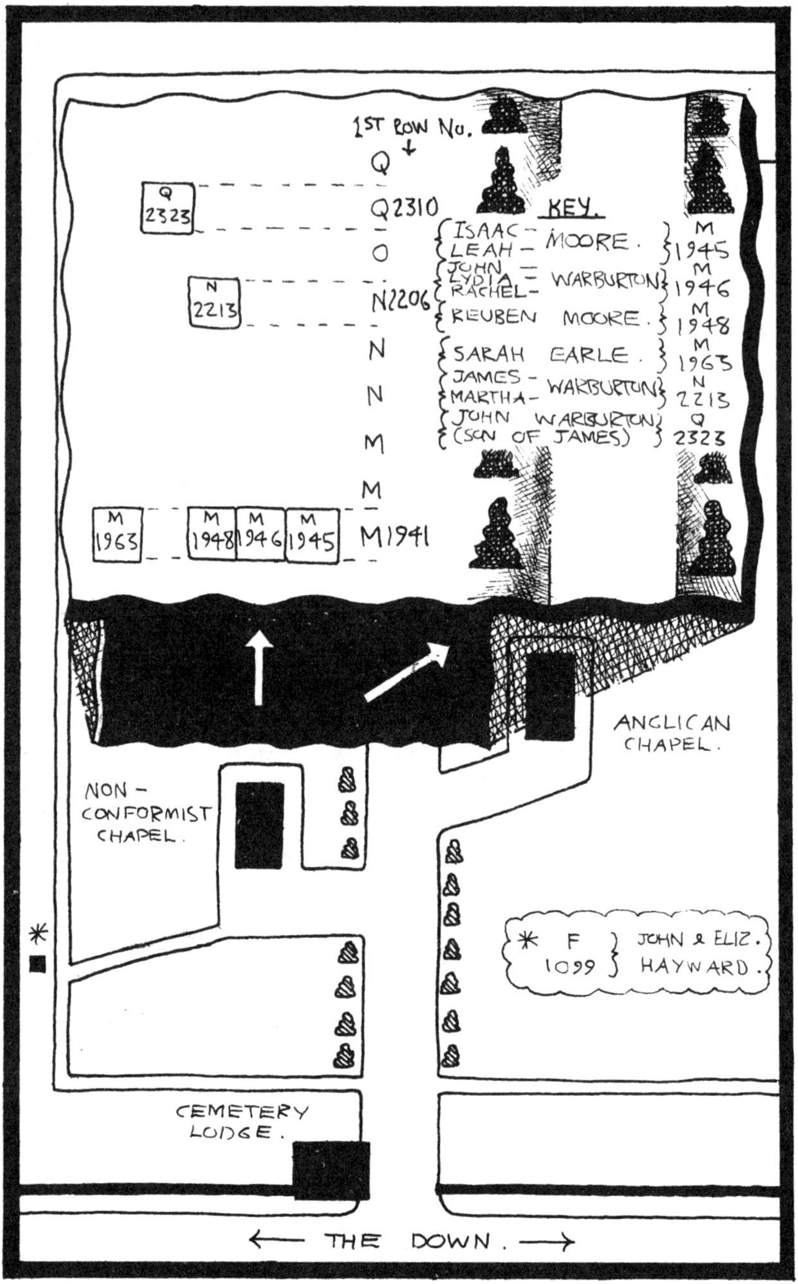

Plan of Trowbridge Cemetery

Appendices

Appendix A

John Warburton Letters

GS – Gospel Standard.
GB – Gospel Banner.
GA – Gospel Ambassador
CMR – Christian's Monthly Record.

		1815	
14 May	GS 1878. p. 207.	**27 July**	GS 78. p. 33.
		1816	
6 Feb.	GA 1847. p. 127.		
		1818	
8 Apr.	GS 73. p. 313.	**2 Oct.**	GS 74. p. 232.
		1819	
12 May	GS 81. p. 321.	**20 Aug.**	GS 75. p. 120.
		1820	
29 Apr.	GS 76. p. 482.		
		1821	
4 May	GS 51. p. 403.		
		1822	
4 June	GS 52. p. 216.	**5 Nov.**	GS 53. p. 207.
		1823	
14 May	GS 54. p. 44.		
		1825	
15 June	GS 48. p. 77.		
		1826	
7 Dec.	GS 71. p. 155.		

		1832	
? April	GS 41. p. 341	**22 Aug.**	GS 42. pp. 327.
		1833	
16 Dec.	GS 42. p. 280.		
		1834	
? July	GS 42. p. 222.	**31 July**	CMR 85. pp.44.
? Dec.	GS 42. p. 105.		
		1835	
25 Sept.	GS 36. p. 41.	**18 Dec.**	GS 77. pp. 348.
		1836	
26 Feb	GS 66. p. 368.	**16 June**	GB 80. p. 307.
		1837	
16 Mar.	GS 92. p. 377.	**? Sept.**	GS 42. p. 49.
		1838	
16 Nov.	GS 72. p. 173.		
		1839	
6 Sept.	GS 40. p. 30.		
		1840	
10 Jan.	GS 40. p. 162.	**? June**	GS 41. pp. 121.
18 June	GS 40. p. 279.	**6 Nov.**	GS 44. pp. 358.
		1841	
27 Jan.	GS 41. p. 250.	**5 Aug.**	GS 44. pp. 105.
20 Aug.	GS 42. p. 153.	**18 Nov.**	GS 43. pp. 12.
No date	GS 41. p. 225.		
		1842	
16 Feb.	GS 65. p. 81.	**18 Apr.**	GS 46. pp. 85.
5 May	GS 44. p. 14.	**21 Sept.**	GS 43. pp. 167.
13 Dec.	GS 43. pp. 198.		

		1843	
? Feb.	GS 43. pp. 327.	**29 June**	GS 67. pp.366.
7 Sept.	GS 44. pp. 166.	**22 Sept.**	GS 44. pp. 240.
1 Dec.	GS 44. pp. 303.	**15 Dec.**	GS 46. pp. 136.
		1844	
16 Feb.	GS 46. pp. 247.	**24 May**	GS 45. pp. 247.
25 May	GS 45. pp. 170.	**7 June**	GS 45. pp. 117.
14 June	GS 45 pp. 52.	**25 Oct.**	GS 46. pp. 21.
		1846	
9 Jan.	GS 46. pp. 316.	**6 Mar.**	GS 48. pp. 113.
7 May	GS 46. pp.366	**21 May**	GS 46. pp. 275.
3 Sept.	GS 47. pp. 268.	**19 Dec.**	GS 69. pp. 165.
		1847	
21 Jan.	GS 47. pp.146.	**5 Apr.**	Recol. J. Grace.pp.138.
28 Sept.	GS 49. pp. 313.	**30 Sept.**	GS 48. pp. 309.
5 Oct.	GS 48. pp. 174.		
		1848	
5 Jan.	GS 48. pp. 58.	**2 Feb.**	GS 49. pp. 167.
3 Feb.	GS 49. pp. 49.		
		1849	
1 Feb.	GS 83. pp. 36.	**27 July**	GS 49. pp. 421.
16 Sept.	GS 50. pp.278.		
		1850	
13 May	GS 55. pp.111.	**31 July**	GS 50. pp. 373.
23 Sept.	CMR.93.pp.188.	**30 Sept.**	GS 63. pp. 183.
		1851.	
15 Aug.	GB 91. pp.364.	**23 Sept.**	GB 87. pp. 239.
		1852	
18 Nov.	GB 86. pp.169.	**No date**	GS 52. pp. 29.

		1853	
6 Jan.	GB 93. pp.302.	**29 July**	GB 91. pp. 114.
		1856	
6 June	GS 70. pp.346.	**9 June**	Original in private hands.
30 June	GB 95. pp.44.		

Appendix B

Sermons of John Warburton

Date	Place	Text	Publication
27 July 1810 Mon. Eve	Conway Street	Isa. 3.10	GCG. pp.83.
31 Oct. 1812 Mon. Eve	Conway Street	Matt. 5.4.	GCG. pp.95.
Oct. 1839 Sun.	Gower Street	Deut. 31.6	GS.57. pp.325.
12 July 1840 Sun. M	Gower Street	S of S 2.16.	GS 41.pp.17.
13 Oct. 1840	Gower Street	Ps. 2. 10-12	GS 94. pp.51.
22 Aug. 1841 Sun.M&A	Norwich	Judges 4.14	G.C.G. pp.19.
17 Oct. 1841	Gower Street	Prov. 12.25.	GS 81. pp. 53.
9 Oct. 1842 Sun. M	Gower Street	Isa. 55. 10-11	pamphlet.
18 Oct. 1842	Gower Street	Ps. 40.17	GS 87. pp.333
25 Oct. 1842	Gower Street	2 Cor. 1.7	GS 90. pp.108,156.
25 Dec. 1842 Sun. M&E	London	Romans 8.3	GCG. GS 80.101.
9 Apr. 1843 Sun M&E	Eden Street	John.14.6	CMR 93. 229.257.
9 Apr. 1844 Tues. E	Founders Hall Lond.	Num. 11.23	GCG. ZP.62.
21 Apr. 1844 Sun.	Eden Street	Ps 64. 10	GCG. ZP 63.
2 Apr. 1848 Sun. E	Eden Street	Ps. 94.14.	ZP 132.
4 Apr. 1848 Tues. E	Eden Street	Isa 30.18	ZP 133.
11 Apr. 1848 Tues. E	Eden Street	Nahum 1.7.	ZP 134.
15 Apr. 1848 Tues. E	Eden Street	John 16.22	ZP 135.
1849	Eden Street	Prov. 29.6.	GS 96.pp. 275.
1849	Eden Street	Ps. 68.10.	ZP 158.
15 May 1849	Eden Street	Eph. 1. 1-4.	ZP 151.
27 May 1849	Eden Street	Isa. 43 18-19.	ZP 159.
May 1850	Eden Street	1 John 4, 7-8.	GS 62.165,192.
28 May 1850 Tues. E	Eden Street	Ps. 23.6.	GCG pp.41.
4 June 1850 Tues. E	Eden Street	Heb. 10.23.	ZP. 157.
24 Sept 1850 Tues. E	Trowbridge	Matt. 18.14.	GCG GS 51 273.
18 Feb. 1851 Tues. E	Trowbridge	2 Cor. 6.10	GS 52 387.
21 Oct. 1851 Tues. E	Trowbridge	Acts 21. 5	GS 60 165,197.
25 Apr. 1853 Mon. E	Eden Street	1 Cor. 13.8	GCG. pp. 143.
8 Apr. 1855 Sun. E	Gower Street	Ps. 36.10	GCG. pp. 53.
No date	No place	Matt. 10.31	GS 58 pp. 229.

GS Gospel Standard. **GCG** Gospel of a Covenant God. **ZP** Zoar Pulpit.

Appendix C

John Warburton Ministerial Engagements

1843
Good Friday [morning] Winchmore Hill, London.
April 9 16 23 30 Eden Street, London.
May 23 Calne Anniversary.
July 23 30 & August 3 13 Alfred Street, Leicester.
October 15 22 29 Lakenheath; 10 Wallingford.
November 1 Eden Street, London; 5 7 Abingdon; 8 Wallingford.
1844
June 23 30 & July 7 21 Manchester; July 14 Rochdale.
October 8 Bedworth.
December 15 Wallingford.
1845
March 30 Southill.
April 2 [Wed] Southill; 3 [Thur] Hitchin; 6 13 20 27 Eden Street, London.
July 6 Alfred Street, Leicester.
August 12 Hankerton Anniversary. [M] JW; [A] Mr Beard; [E] Mr Matthews.
1846
April all Sundays, Eden Street, London; 14 Southill; 16 Hitchin.
August 2 9 16 23 30 Alfred Street, Leicester.
1847
April 4 11 18 25 Eden Street London; 14 West Street, Brighton.
May Sun 2 Southill; Thurs 6 Southill [Opening Services after renovations.]
1848
April 2 9 16 23 Eden Street, London;
April 21 [Good Friday] Cheshunt Opening Services 11am, JW Jnr 3pm.
May 23 Calne Anniversary JW. 10.30am, T. Godwin 2.30pm.
June 14 Studley 7pm [Wed. Eve.]
1849
May all Sundays in month & Tuesday evenings, Eden Street, London.
June 3 [Sun] 4 [Mon Eve 7pm] Cheshunt.
July 5 [Thurs] Hadlow Down. Opening New Chapel JW. M & E. John Grace Aft.
July 8 [Sun] West Street, Brighton. [John Grace 8 Zion Chapel, Trowbridge.]
October All Sundays & Tuesday evenings, Eden Street, London.
December 2 {Sun] Abingdon; 4 [Tues Eve] Uffington.

1850
May 5 12 26 June 2 Eden Street, London; 19 May [Sun] 21[Tue] Cheshunt.
June 30 Providence Chapel, Bath . 11am & 6pm.
October All Sundays in month & Tues. eves Eden Street, London; 17 Welwyn.
1851
May All Sundays in month & Tues eves, also 1 June, Eden Street, London.
1852
May 2 9 16 23 & Tues eves Eden Street, London; 30 Southill.
June 8 Calne Anniversary JW. 11am. J.C. Philpot 3pm.
1853
1854
1855
April 8 15 22 29 Gower Street Chapel, London.
June 5 Calne Anniversary JW. 11am. J.C. Philpot 3pm.
September 30 Gower Street Chapel, London.
1856
June 3 Calne Anniversary 11am. J.C.Philpot 3pm.
August 17 24 Hurstpierpoint, near Brighton.
August 31 [Sun] West Street Chapel, Brighton for the last time, for John Grace.
October 12 19 26 engaged to preach at Gower Street Chapel, London, but an announcement in the October 1856 issue of the *Gospel Standard* said , 'We regret to state that Mr Warburton is unable, from his increasing infirmities, to fulfil his engagements for Oct. 12, 19 & 26 as announced in the September issue. In *Recollections of John Grace* 1893 pp. 222, it says, '20th January 1856, I [John Grace] preached twice at West Street, and had a collection for Mr Warburton's poor.'

This list of engagements is far from a complete record of all his engagements in the last fourteen years of his life [from the ages of sixty-six to eighty], but it gives some indication of the nature and extent of journeys among the Gospel Standard churches. In these latter years of his life, the Railways allowed him to travel further with greater comfort and greater speed.

Appendix D

Trustees at Zion Chapel 1816.

Church Book Number.	Name	Remarks.
369	William Hayward	
325	Samuel Hurd	
330	Thomas Ball	
331	William Eacott	
338	John Paskall	Separated 1841.
345	Joshua Loxley	
371	Isaac Long [x His mark]	Excluded 1824.
337	William Avens [x His mark]	Died 1825.
384	John Shipway	Excluded 1823.
324	William Chapman	
326	George Usher	
361	James Hayward	
332	James Porter	

Witnessed: John Warburton.

Appendix E

Deacons 1813 - 1857

1813		
327	William Marvin	Excluded 1816.
325	Samuel Hurd	Excluded 1826.
324	William Chapman	Excluded 1826.
331	William Eacott	Dismissed 1825 Chapmanslade.
323	Benjamin Marshman	Dismissed 1813 Broughton.
1825		
361	James Hayward	Died 12 Feb. 1850.
369	William Hayward	Died 11 Sept. 1835.
330	Thomas Ball	Excluded 1839.
332	James Porter	Died 1848.
424	Richard Knee	Died 1864.
1836		
412	Thomas Tabor	Died 1839.
454	Thomas Hayward	Died 1841.
1839		
563	David Simons	Left 1848.
1848		
645	Cornelius Rudman	Died 1851.
701	Henry Tucker	Set aside 24 Sept. 1851.
1851		
54	Jacob Hawkins	Died 1876.
670	John Millard	Left 1853.
700	Thomas Land	Left 1852.
1853		
60	Samuel Moore	Died 1868.
66	John Philipps	Died 1895.
73	Isaac Waite	Died 1870.
102	William Applegate	Died 1907.

Appendix F

Zion Church Rules.

First

Any debate or any difference that may arise in the Church, to be settled by the majority; that is the greatest number shall decide.

Second

No member of any Church in this Town to be a transient member, or receive the Ordinance of the Lord's Supper with this Church without the consent of this Church.

Third

Any member or transient member of this Church receiving the Ordinance of the Lord's Supper with any other Church in this Town cannot again receive it with us without the consent of this Church.

Fourth

No transient member to be at our Church Meetings.

Fifth

Any member knowing another to act disorderly shall go to the offending brother or sister and tell them their fault alone or acquaint their minister or deacons of the Church of the same, and any member neglecting to do so and found reporting it to others, such members to be visited as acting contrary to the rule laid down on the Scriptures.

Sixth

Any member suspended for immoral conduct or in any manner bringing an open reproach shall make a public asknowledgement of the same to the Church before again being admitted to enjoy the Ordinance and privileges thereof.

Seventh

That when any question has been decided by the vote of the Church, if any member shall attempt to set aside or oppose the same afterwards, such member shall be accounted as acting disorderly and contrary to the First Rule of this Church.

Eighth

Any member relating to any other person, not a member, what has been said or done at the Church Meeting, such member shall be set aside for Six Months and acknowledge their fault before they are received again.

Appendix G

Articles of Faith Zion Church 1813

We the Church of Christ of the Particular Baptist Persuasion, maintaining the following Divine and Important Doctrines and Truths,

First

We believe in the being of one God, who is infinite in wisdom, power, and glory.

Second

We believe in the divine inspiration of the Scriptures and receive them as a gracious revalation of the mind and will of God wherein are recorded all these doctrines and truths we here state.

Third

We believe in a Trinity of persons in the Godhead, Father, Son and Holy Ghost, who are of one substance and equal in power and glory.

Fourth

We believe in the everlasting and unchangeable love of God, and that it is fixed on a certain number of the human race which he purposed to create, and that those were predestinated and elected by God unto eternal bliss and glory.

Fifth

We believe in the Fall of man and that by it the whole human race became original and [as they are born into the world] actual transgressors against God, and that by the Fall they were rendered both unable and unwilling to deliver themselves.

Sixth

We believe in a full and free Redemption, Salvation and Justification of the elect by Jesus Christ alone.

Seventh

We believe in Effectual Calling [and efficacious grace] by God the Spirit of all the Redeemed.

Eighth

We believe there are two Ordinances appointed by our Lord, viz., Baptism and the Lord's Supper. The one to be administered by way of admission into the Church, and the other as a Standing Ordinance of God's House with respect to Baptism. We believe it should be administered to none but believers and that this Ordinance is only rightly performed by inmmersion or dipping the whole body under water. We believe persons thus Baptized have a right to the Supper of the Lord and to enjoy all the privileges of God's House.

Ninth

We believe in the Final Perseverance of the Saints.

Tenth

We believe in the Resurrection of the dead and Final Judgment.

Eleventh

We believe in the Eternal and unalterable state of the Wicked.

Twelfth

We believe in the Complete and Eternal happiness of the Righteous

Appendix H

The Warburton Family

John Warburton, born at Stand, Pilkington, 28 Oct 1776, married at Prestwich Parish Church, 28th December 1795,

Lydia Sandiford, born at Ratcliffe, 4 May 1777, had the following children.

William born at Pilkington, in Parish of Prestwich 1796.

Sarah born at Pilkington, in Parish of Prestwich 16 Apr. 1797.

Child born at Pilkington 1798? Died 1800.

James born at Pilkington in Parish of Prestwich 10 Aug. 1800.

Elizabeth born at Whitefield, in Par. Prestwich 20 Nov. 1801.

Leah born at Whitefield in Parish of Prestwich 16 Apr. 1804.

Rachel born at Whitefield in Parish of Prestwich 16 June 1806.

Gideon born at Whitefield in Par. of Prestwich 14 Sept. 1808.

Manoah born in Parish of Rochdale 23 Jan. 1811.

Ruth born in Parish of Rochdale 27 Oct. 1813.

John born in The Halve, Parish of Trowbridge 4 Aug. 1815.

Rhoda born in Brick Plat in Parish of Trowbridge July 1817.

William Warburton.

William was John Warburton's first child. Born in the first family home in Park Lane near the Dove Cottage at Stand; he probably was apprenticed as a weaver, like his father. At the age of about fourteen, he appears to have left home, possibly to live with his uncle, John Warburton's only brother, in Whitefield. When his father left the North and came to Trowbridge in 1815, William was about nineteen. He stayed in the North. The only mention of him occurs when his yougest brother John, went North in in 1837[1] and stayed with him, and also with John Warburton's brother, William. In 1837 he was about forty, and young John about twenty-two. He took young John to meet John Kershaw. When he died is not known

There is no mention of him at the time of his father's death in 1857, so presumeably he had died by then. Records show a family of Warburtons, living in Hope Street, Rochdale with three children; John born 2nd May 1818; Hannah born 11th Jan. 1824; and Samuel born 13th Dec. 1830. Their mother's maiden name was Hannah Tweedale, and their father was *William Warburton.* This is of interest as there was a family of Tweedales among the early founders of Hope Chapel, Rochdale; a deacon from 1815-1832 was James Tweedale, and his mother, Jenney Tweedale, was one of the nine founder members. As William took young John to see John Kershaw in 1837, it would appear that he was attending Hope Chapel, or at

[1] *Memorials of John Warburton Jnr* 1893. p. 19.

least knew Kershaw. As *William* was born in 1796, there is a distinct possibility that this could have been *him* and his family.

Sarah Warburton.

Sarah was Warburton's first girl. She had a child before her marriage, born about 1816, when she was about nineteen. She married **John Earle** on 22 March 1819 at St James, the Parish Church of Trowbridge. Her husband was baptised by John Warburton on 21st July 1822 and she herself was baptised by her father on 13th July 1823. She lived in Prospect Place, Trowbridge, according to the National Census for 1841, which reveals that she then had two children, **Manoah** [an apprentice blacksmith] and **Martha,** both aged over fifteen. The Census return shows that Martha Earl was staying at Waterloo Terrace, the home of her grandfather. The Zion Baptist Chapel, Birth Register, show that a **John and Ann Earl** had children born; Mary Ann Earl, 11th October 1835; and John Earl, 17th June 1836. It is *possible* that this father, **John Earl,** was Sarah's child, born out of wedlock in 1816, and married when eighteen.

Sarah's husband, John Earl, died in 1853 and was buried at Zion Chapel. She, herself lived on until her death on 13th November 1877 at the age of eighty. She was buried by Edwin Porter, the Pastor of Allington Baptist Chapel, in Trowbridge Cemetery in grave M1963, which is in the same row as her parents grave [M1946] and exactly seventeen graves beyond their's. Her grave is unmarked. She was a widow for twenty-four years. It would appear from the fact that Edwin Porter took her funeral, that she probably attended Zion Chapel until her death. Hers was a sad life in many ways.

The Third Child

Of the third child, Warburton says nothing. Whether it was a boy or girl is unknown. It was born sometime in the early part of 1798 in the basement dwelling where they were living in

Park Lane, Stand. His wife was crippled with cramp from the dampness of the place, at the time it was born, and it finally succumbed to its pitiful environment, and died in March 1800, aged about two.

James Warburton

James was born in the basement in Park Lane six months after the death of the little two year old. He grew up in Narrow Lane, Besses-o-the- Barn, and at Hope Chapel House Rochdale. He married **Martha Edwards** at Trowbridge Parish Church on 28th March 1819. He was a weaver like his father. They lived for the first part of their married life in Shail's Lane Trowbridge and had five children, of which three girls died in infancy.

John was born 27th Nov. 1819.
James was born 1st Jan 1825.
John was a weaver. He had four sons and a daughter.
Manoah was born in 1851
Alma was born in 1855
George was born in 1857
Frederick was born in 1859
Frank was born in 1861

He died on 9th Dec. 1899 and is buried in grave Q2323 in Trowbridge Cemetery. Through his line it is possible to trace the Warburton family in Trowbridge, down to the present day.

James married Elizabeth Webb on 28th Sept. 1845 He was a dyer. He died on 20th Jan 1892 and is buried in Trowbridge Cemetery in grave H3762. His wife died in 1899 and is buried in grave P2485.

Elizabeth Warburton

Elizabeth married **John Hayward** [1791-1870], a widower, at Trowbridge Parish Church on 13th January 1825. She had been baptised by her father at Ladydown Mill, on 13th July 1823. Her husband was a director of Salters Cloth Mill. He had three sons by his first marriage to Mary Pourch, who died in 1822 and was buried at Zion Chapel:

John Edward Hayward born 5 Jan 1816 - died 14 Feb 1903.
Edward Pourch Hayward born 7th Oct 1817.
Samuel Hayward born 8th Jan 1822

Elizabeth had eight children by John Hayward:

Lydia born 26th October 1825.
Martha born 5th May 1828.
Joseph born 11th March 1830.
Benjamin born 17th July 1835

James, Jesse, Mary and Alice, who are mentioned in their father's will, proved 2nd June 1870, but whose dates of birth are not known.

She was a member at Zion Chapel for sixty-one years. She died on 21st October 1884 at the age of eighty-two, and was buried in Trowbridge Cemetery in grave F1099 with her husband, who had died on 19th January 1870.

A beautiful granite monument marks the spot, which is also a family grave, and the tomb of John Edward Hayward, who was a co-director of Salters Cloth Mill with his father, until 1863, when the family moved to Upper Mills, near Cradle Bridge, and established their own Cloth Business. They sadly, went bankrupt in 1879, an event which Elizabeth lived to see, though her husband, ten years her senior, was spared the sorrow.

Prior to 1860 John Hayward, Samuel Salter and Jesse Gouldsmith were in partnership at Salters Cloth Mill. In 1860 the partners were Jesse Gouldsmith, Jesse Gouldsmith Junior, William Gouldsmith, John Hayward, John E. Hayward and Edward Pourch Hayward. About 1858, Jesse Gouldsmith built himself an beautiful house in Victoria Road, named Rodwell Hall. When John Hayward died in 1870 his estate was worth £4,000. The Hayward family lived at The Laurels in Hilperton Road. Edward Pourch Hayward lived in a large house at Cockhill, on the road to Bradford-on-Avon.

[2] The family owned two houses in Frog Lane, thirteen houses in The Halve, nineteen houses in Shail's Lane, five houses in Islington, two houses in Brickplat, and one house in Hilperton Road. It appears that much of this property came to John Hayward through his first wife, Mary, who was the daughter of Edward Pourch, a pawnbroker, who lived on the Conigre. John Hayward's father, William Hayward, was also a man of property. He built a house and workshop in Union Street in 1817 and was able to loan Zion Church £500 at 5% interest in 1816, towards the cost of building their new Chapel. He was a deacon at Zion from 1825-1835. John Hayward's brother James was also a deacon at Zion from 1825-1850. He loaned £100 at 5% interest towards building Zion. They were a prosperous family, typical of several Particular Baptist families in Trowbridge, such as the Houlton's in the Eighteenth Century, who were Particular Baptists and prospered though the Cloth Trade, and used their finances liberally, to support their Baptist churches.

Leah Warburton.

Leah married Isaac Moore at Trowbridge Parish Church on 26th March 1823. He owned a Dyeworks in the Courts Trowbridge, and leased another Dyeworks in Bradford-on-Avon. The family lived in Castle Street in 1824, when first married. They moved to Timbrell Street about 1831, and later to Prospect House, in Prospect Place. Born in March 1804, Isaac Moore died in January 1868 at the age of sixty-three. He was buried immediately in front of John Warburton's grave [M1945]; but today the inscription on the tomb is worn beyond recognition. Leah outlived him by twenty-one years, dying on 2nd October 1889.

Leah had twelve children by him:

---

2 Rate Assessment Book for Trowbridge. 1878.

William born 27th Jan. 1824
Rhoda born 28th Sept. 1825
Edward born 2nd Dec. 1829
Ebenezer born 4th Nov. 1829
Reuben born 17th Nov. 1831
Frederick born 17th Nov. 1833
Henry born June 1835 died 16th Mar. 1836.
Henry born early 1838 died 2nd Nov. 1841
Charles born 7th Sept. 1838 died 7th Dec. 1840
Ellen born 1841
Julia born 1844
Georgiana born May 1848 died 15th June 1848.

Zion Baptist Church's Register of Births provides most of these dates of birth, and Register of Burials tells of the deaths. The four little ones, who died, are all buried 'in the front of Zion Chapel, under the footpath, about the middle,' just in front of the graves of little Rhoda, buried in 1820, and Manoah buried in 1839. The others were alive at the time their father made his will, and signed it on 3rd May 1862, in the presence of John Forster, Minister of the Gospel, Witham in Essex, and John Gadsby of Cowley Hall, Middlesex.

Prospect House, now demolished, was in Prospect Place, on the South side, between Charlotte Street and Thomas Street. Isaac Moore moved to Bradford-on-Avon just before his death on 16th January 1868. His funeral recorded in the *Trowbridge Advertiser* for 22nd January 1868, describes how the funeral procession had to pass through floods in Trowbridge town centre in order to reach the Cemetery where he was buried by Rev. Isaac Spencer, Pastor of the Old Baptist Chapel, Bradford-on-Avon [1863-1879].

If the position of the Moore family grave is anything to go by, the Moores were very close to John Warburton and his wife. It was they who took Mrs Warburton, Rachel and Ruth under their wing in 1857, and provided a home for them next door to Prospect House. When Leah died on 2nd October 1889, she was living at Bradford-on-Avon and was buried with her husband by the then Pastor of the Old Baptist Chapel, Bradford, James Clark [1886-1891]. It would seem that she spent her widowhood with her sons in Bradford, where they had their Dyeworks by the River Avon.

Rachel

Rachel was the daughter, who never married, and stayed at home and looked after her parents. Of her, nothing has emerged. She must have kept her mother company in her many lonely hours, when her father was away for months at a time on his preaching tours. She lived to care for her aged mother in her widowhood, and outlived her by about eight years, dying on 19th August 1870 at the comparitively early age of sixty-four. Like Sarah, there seems to be a tinge of sadness about her life, yet that may be a very wrong judgment, and she may well have been a very happy person, finding complete fulfillment in her single pathway in life, and her care for her godly father and mother. Spiritually nothing is known about her. She was never baptised, but attended Zion Chapel all her days, so far as is known. She was born in Narrow Lane, Besses-o-the Barn, and followed her parents to all the various family homes. No doubt, she could have told much about the family, especially her innumerable neices and nephews. Certainly Martha Earle stayed at Waterloo Terrace with her, as of course did Rachel's own sister Ruth, who did not marry until late in life. Had she kept a Diary, it would have been of great interest.

Gideon Warburton

Gideon was born in Narrow Lane, Besses-o-the -Barn on 14th September 1808, and spent his childhood days at Hope Chapel House Rochdale from 1811 to 1815. He was six when the family travelled south to Trowbridge in April 1815. Nothing is known of his childhood days in Trowbridge. He would have been twelve when his father took the family out to the thatched cottage at Trowle Common and no doubt, would have enjoyed the facilities of the Common and countryside together with his younger brother Manoah, who was just ten at the time. He would have been old enough to appreciate the sorrows of the death of Rhoda in 1820. When John Junior started his wanderings in 1832, Gideon was twenty-four and showed none of the propensities of his brother. What his trade in life was is not known. He was in London in 1837, because his father was unable to preach at the opening of the new Calne Chapel on 17th May because he was called to London to deal with 'the affairs of Gideon.'

Gideon was at this time living in the area of Tottenham Court Road, because when John Junior went to London looking for work in 1839, he called on Gideon who told him how difficult it was to find work in London. Later Gideon married and lived at 33 Russell Road, Seven Sisters, Middlesex. He was present in Trowbridge at his father's funeral in 1857 He had one son, **Henry Gideon**, who was a piano teacher. Henry married Anne Jane Grey on 7th April 1860 at St Pancras Old Church and they had four children, Edith, Alice, Herbert and William Henry. Gideon died on 5th March 1879. No information survives as to whether he attended any of the Particular Baptist Churches in London in which his father preached. It seems that he may have reverted to the Anglicanism from which his father came out, seeing that his son was married in the Church of England.

Manoah Warburton.

Even less is known about Manoah than about Gideon. What his trade was is unknown. He was born at Hope Chapel House, Rochdale, within weeks of the family's arrival there in January 1811. The date of his birth was 23rd January. His father had a great blessing at his birth and through it called his name Manoah. But after that, he lived the first four years of his life at Rochdale, and then the next twenty-four years in Trowbridge, until his premature death. He appears to have caused his parents no undue worry and like his other brothers, William, James and Gideon, he has hardly any mention in the *Mercies*. But what mention he does have, leads to a hope that he may have been the subject of the answers of his father's fervent prayers for him at his birth; and the sweet blessing, which his father had, taking him up in his arms and saying, 'His name is Manoah, and may the Angel of the Lord do wondrously for him, and his poor soul look on, which God grant may be the case in His own time,' may well have been answered in his soul. He died on 4th November 1839 and was buried at Zion Chapel in the same grave as Rhoda beneath the path at the entrance to the Chapel. There is no stone to mark his grave, nor does any letter of his father's survive which could tell anymore about his end. He was twenty-eight when he died and unmarried. Knowing the way in which John Warburton was 'wrapped up' in his children, and remembering the blessing he had had for Manoah, his death must have been a cause of great sorrow to his parents. It seems certain, that, had the *Mercies* not been in print already, something would have appeared in Warburton's book about Manoah's death.

Ruth Warburton

Ruth stayed at home like Rachel, and did not marry till late in life, possibly after the death of Rachel in 1870. Little is known about her, whether she *ever* worked in the Cloth Factories, or whether she was dependant financially on her family until she married. She was close to her brother John, who was two years younger then her. She pleaded with him to stay at home in 1837, and her affection for him, and the tears she shed over him, give, all the impression that they grew up in their youth like twins.

It is not therefore surprising to find that she must have been a regular visitor to Southill, where her brother was Pastor, and that eventually she married a farmer there, Joseph Gudgin, who farmed at Hill Farm, Warden. The place and date of this wedding is so far not known. Her husband, Joseph, died on 11th April 1894, aged seventy-eight, and she died the following year on 4th September 1895 aged eighty-one, having outlived all the rest of her brothers and sisters. She lies buried in Southill Chapel graveyard side by side with her brother John, and to the right of his grave.

John Warburton

John Warburton Junior grew up in Trowbridge and trained to be a tailor. After an unsettled adolescence, he married Emma Rudman at Trowbridge Parish Church on 19th July 1838, in the presence his father and her father, William Rudman, a shearman. Also a witness to the ceremony was her brother, Cornelius Rudman, who became a deacon at Zion Chapel in 1848 and died in 1851. Their first home was at 13 Timbrell Street, but they were soon forced in 1839 to go to London for John to find work. There they lived first in Fenn Street in the City, and later in the third floor of a house in Wells Street, off Oxford Street. They attended Gower Street Chapel, then the Meeting in Gadsby's Yard, Tottenham Court Road, and finally settled at Eden Street Chapel in 1843. In 1844 John commenced preaching and accepted the call to the Pastorate at Southill on 11th October 1846, where he remained until his death on Tuesday 19th January 1892. His funeral service was taken by Charles Hemington, Pastor of St Mary-le-Port Baptist Chapel, Devizes on Monday 24th January. He baptised his wife Emma, at Southill on 6th December 1846.

They had eight children:

John born 5th May 1840 in Fenn Street, London.
Lydia born 22nd Aug. 1843 Wells Str, London.
Ebenezer born 21st Dec. 1845 at Southill.
William born 27th Jan. 1848 at Southill.
Manoah born 14th Jan. 1849 at Southill.
Phinehas born 5th Aug. 1852 at Southill.
Ruth born 31st Dec. 1854 at Southill.
Elizabeth born 21st Nov. 1859 at Southill.

John died 8th Feb.1899 and was buried at Henlow Churchyard

Lydia married Richard G. Hitchcock. She lived all her life in Croydon and attended West Street Chapel, where J.C. Philpot had attended in his last days. She died 5th Dec. 1924, and her husband in 1935 at the age of ninety. They are buried at Queens Road Cemetery, Croydon, the same cemetery in which J.C.Philpot rests.

Ebenezer married Harriett Heaver on 10th Sept. 1870 and lived at Buxted Mill, near Uckfield, Sussex. Many of his father's letters were written while staying there.[3] They had eleven children. His wife, Harriet, died on 8th March 1933 aged 84 and he on 14th April 1929 aged 83. They are buried at Five Ashdown Independent Chapel, Buxted, where presumeably they worshipped. Through their fifth child, **Ebenezer,** born 10th Sept. 1879, who married Helen R. Newnham in 1903,the family line is traceable through three generations [Eric John Newnham Warburton born 22 Nov.1904; Richard John Warburton born 30 May 1935; Charles Martin Francis Warburton born 24 July 1970.] to the present day. [One of Charles Warburton's sisters, Fiona M.L. Benham, has researched an extensive Warburton family tree, which has proved of great value in tracing the various branches of John Warburton Senior's family.

William died in infancy on 5th March 1848.

Manoah died at Clifton on 1st October 1838, when nearly ninety, and is buried in Henlow Churchyard

Phinehas, the youngest boy, proved to be a wanderer like his father. At the very end of the life of his mother and father, in April 1890, when thirty-eight, he went to America. It was a great grief to them in their last days. But he found a good home in Brooklyn, New York, in the Axford family, who had often come to England, Mrs Axford in her early days, having heard John Warburton Senior preach at Zion Chapel, Trowbridge.[4]

Phinehas eventually married Carrie Axford, an adopted[5] daughter of the Axford family, on 15th April 1891. An interesting series of eight letters of his father's appear in his

---

[3] *Memorial of John Warburton Jnr,* 1892. p. 240.

[4] Memorials John Warburton Jnr, 1892. p. 265.

[5] *Memorials John Warburton Jnr,* 1892. p 234.

Memorials [1892] between pp 233-236,directed to New York, two to Mr Axford, two to his son Phinehas, and four to Mrs Axford. Mr Axford eventually died in August 1891, a few weeks after the death of Phinehas' mother, Emma, on 17th July. Phinehas and Carrie Warburton returned to England and settled at Stanford-le-Hope in Essex. Carrie died on 10th February 1931, and Phinehas on 7th March 1933. Both lie buried in Stanford-le-Hope Churchyard.

Ruth married William Fane, a Grocer whose business was at Shefford, near Southill. Her daughter Rhoda died on 10th November 1896 at the age of eighteen, which must have been a bitter sorrow. Her husband died on 26th October 1918 and she lived on in a long widowhood until her death on 31st March 1942 at the age of eighty-seven.

Elizabeth was born just two and a half years after the death of her grandfather, [the subject of this biography] on 21st November 1859. She stayed in the Southill area of Bedfordshire all her life, remained single, and used to cycle to Clifton Strict Baptist Chapel on her tricycle, until near the end of her life. She lived at 19a Park Lane, Henlow. She died at the great age of one hundred and one, on 27th February 1961. Her funeral took place at Bedford Cemetery Chapel, at 3.15 pm., on Friday 3rd March 1961, bringing to a close a remarkable time span of three generations, stretching from the birth of her grandfather, 'Old John Warburton' on 28th October 1776, to the birth of her father John Warburton Junior on 4th August 1815, to her own death on 27th February 1961; a span of one hundred and eighty-five years. Our great regret has been that we visited Southill Chapel in August 1959 and never knew Elizabeth was still alive at Henlow. What a mine of information she must have carried about her family ! The Pulpit Bible at Southill Baptist Chapel contains the family tree, including of births and deaths of John Warburton Junior's children.

Appendix I

Homes of John Warburton & his Family

Address	Date	Reference
1. Park Lane, Near The Dove House, PILKINGTON.	1795 – Aug. 1800	*Mercies p.226.*
2. Narrow Lane, Besses o' th' Barn, WHITEFIELD.	1800 – Jan. 1811	*Mercies p.40.*
3. Hope Chapel House, ROCHDALE.	1811 – Apr.1815	*Mercies p.98.*
4. The Halve, TROWBRIDGE.	1815 -1817	Zion Birth Register. [Birth John 4 Aug 1815.]
5. Brick Plat, TROWBRIDGE.	1817 – May 1821 Nat. Census 1821.	Zion Birth Register. [Birth Rhoda July 1817.]
6. Trowle Common, TROWBRIDGE.	1821- Feb.1822	*Mercies pp. 152,158.*
7. Yerbury Street, TROWBRIDGE.	1822 -1824	Trowbridge Poor Rate Books, 1822, 1823, 1824.
8. Down Gate, TROWBRIDGE.	1825 – Aug. 1832	Trowbridge Poor Rate Book, Jan 1825.
9. Waterloo Terrace, TROWBRIDGE.	1832 – 1850 ? Post Office Directory 1848.	*Gospel Standard* 1842, [pp. 327, 328.

10. Dorset House, The Halve TROWBRIDGE.	1850 ?-1857	National Census 1851.
11. Prospect Place, TROWBRIDGE.	1857 – 1870	National Census 1861. Lydia Warburton, Rachel & Ruth.

Appendix J

Obituaries of Zion Church members

CMR. Christian Monthly Record. **GS**. Gospel Standard.
FHGSB. Further History of Gospel Standard Baptists. Vol. 6. S.F Paul. 1969.

Church Bk No.	**Name**	**Baptism**	**Reference**
498	Richard Eacott	1 Aug.1824	CMR 1889. P.76. FHGSBVol.6 p.57-9.
460	Edward Oram [Deacon]	21 Jul.1822	GS 1865 Jan.Splt. p.17. FHGSB Vol 6. p.60-1.
495	Anne Oram	13 Jul.1823	GS 1864 Jun Splt. p.16. FHGSB Vol 6.p.59-60.
30	John Alderwick [Chapel Cleaner 1842 – 1854]	30 Dec 1827	FHGSB Vol 6. p.61-2.
54	Jacob Hawkins [Deacon; son Esther Hawkins 329]	9 Aug.1835	GS 1876 p. 410- 413. FGHSB Vol 6 p.62-5.
55	Elizabeth Hawkins	9 Aug.35	GS 1876 p. 410 – 413.
58	George Norris [Deacon]	1 Oct. 1837	GS 1877 p.231 FHGSB Vol. 6 p. 65-6.
102	Wm. Applegate [Deacon]		(GS 1880 P.500 (
99	Mary Applegate	7 Jul.1850	(FHGSB Vol 6 p. 68-9.
86	Benjamin Porter [Son James Porter 332]	3 Dec.1848	GS 1913 p. 237-40. FHGSB Vol. p. 74-5.
81	Jacob England	6 Dec.1846	GS 1927. pp, 300-302, pp, 324-331, pp, 357-362.

Index of Names and Topics.

Index of Places

Bibliography

Primary Sources

Zion Church Books, 1813 onwards,
2 Vols.
Zion Birth & Burial Registers
Rochdale Church Books 4 Vols.

National Census Returns

Post Office Directories of Wiltshire
Pigott's Directories

Wiltshire County Council Archives.
Parish Poor Relief Records, Rate Books, Poll Books, Wills.
Trowbridge Cemetery Records

Mercies of a Covenant God, by John Warburton, Reiner Publications, 1974.

The Gospel of a Covenant God Zoar Publications, 1976

Memorials of John Warburton Jnr 1893

Booklets & Pamphlets

Brief Memoir of Richard Davis, by John Davis 1833

Brief Memoir of William Eacott by Joseph Rudman.

Secondary Sources

Works of William Gadsby, 2 Vols 1851.

Gospel Standard Vols, 1835-1900

Biography of Wm Tiptaft, by J.C.Philpot. 1972 Edition.

Twenty Golden Candlesticks by W. Doel. 1890

Further History of the Gospel Standard Baptists, Vols 1-6, by S.F. Paul, 1951-1969.

The Seceders, 2 Vols by J.H. Philpot. 1931-1932

Strict Baptist Chapels of England Vol 5, R.W. Oliver. 1968

Wiltshire & Somerset Woollen Mills, K.Rogers. 1976
Warp & Weft, K. Rogers. 1986
The Book of Trowbridge, K. Rogers. 1984

Chartist Studies, Edited by Asa Briggs. 1962

Industrial & Commercial Revolutions, L.C.A. Knowles. 1947

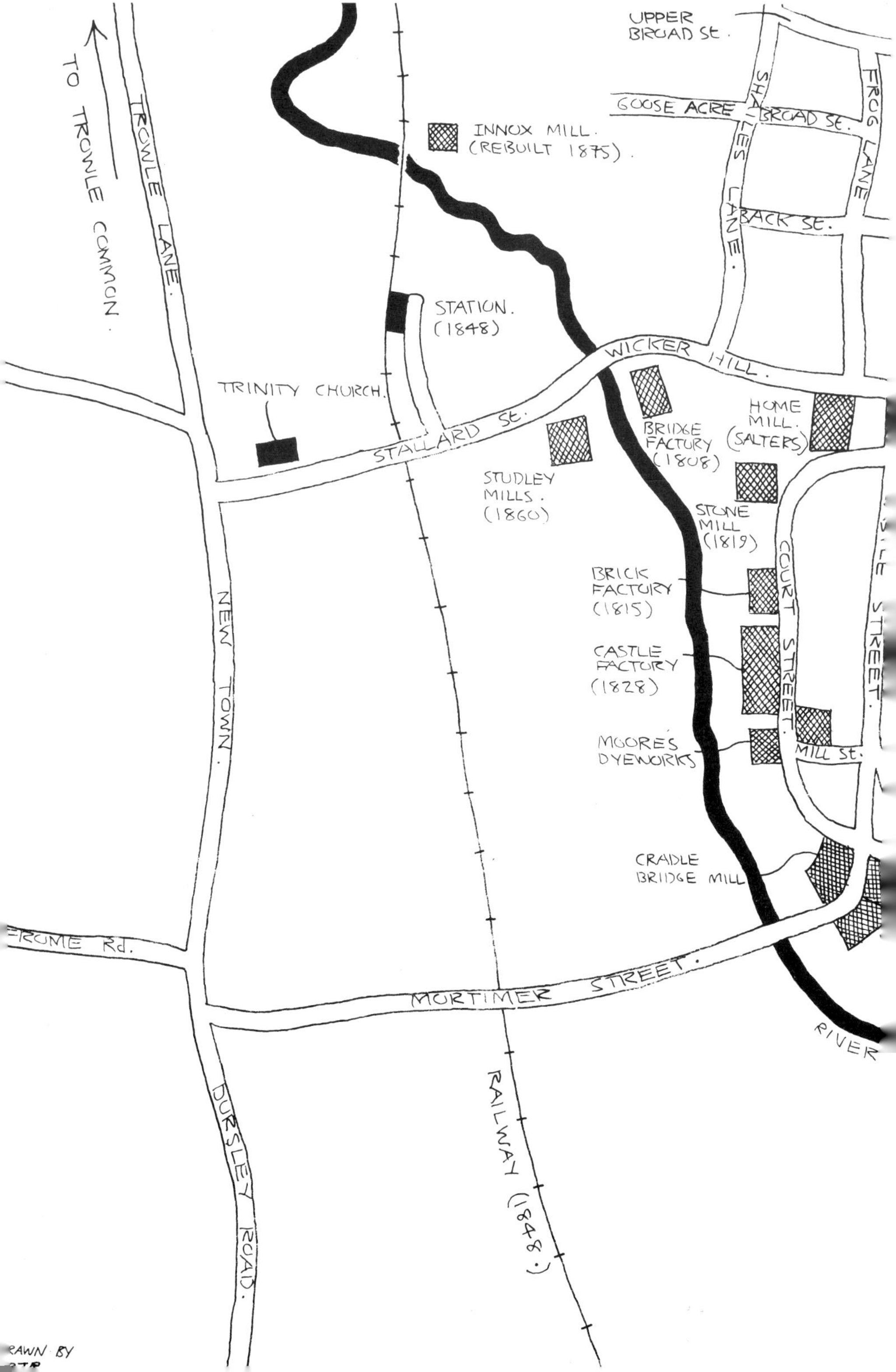

TO TROWLE COMMON.
TROWLE LANE.
UPPER BROAD St.
GOOSE ACRE
BROAD St.
FROG LANE
SHAPPLES LANE.
BACK St.
INNOX MILL. (REBUILT 1875).
STATION. (1848)
WICKER HILL.
TRINITY CHURCH.
STALLARD St.
HOME MILL. (SALTERS)
BRIDGE FACTORY (1808)
STUDLEY MILLS. (1860)
STONE MILL (1819)
COURT STREET.
CASTLE STREET.
BRICK FACTORY (1815)
NEW TOWN.
CASTLE FACTORY (1828)
MOORES DYEWORKS
MILL St.
CRADLE BRIDGE MILL
FROME Rd.
MORTIMER STREET.
RIVER
DURSLEY ROAD.
RAILWAY (1848.)
DRAWN BY